CREATIVE STARS

TRISH MACGREGOR

CREATIVE STARS

Using Astrology to Tap Your Muse

 ST. MARTIN'S GRIFFIN ✖ NEW YORK

www.stmartins.com

Design by Susan Walsh

ISBN 0-312-27505-6

First Edition: January 2002

10   9   8   7   6   5   4   3   2   1

For Megan and Rob,
the creative wizards in my life

Thanks, as always, to Al Zuckerman, for selling the idea,
and to Marian Lizzi, for giving it a home

CONTENTS

INTRODUCTION
Creativity Is

When I was a kid, I wanted more than anything else to be, well, *creative*. I took piano lessons, art lessons, ballet and tap-dancing lessons. But words were my passion. Language was my secret world, the place I retreated after my parents and my sister had gone to bed. I huddled in my closet or under my covers with a flashlight and I read, scribbled poetry and stories, and was transported.

At the time, I failed to realize that I was already creative. Each of us is. Creativity is our thrust, our passion, the thing inside of us that longs to get out. It's the deep itch that gets scratched only through the exploration of who we are and what we might become. It's the spark ignited when left and right brain find common ground. It's the dreams we seek to achieve, the fodder that our lives provide.

Creativity is expressed by the small child when she suddenly discovers that her legs actually have a function and eagerly crawls about exploring the boundaries of her world. It finds expression in the eighty-year-old grandmother who creates elaborate collages from photos in the family albums, or in the engineer who designs booster rockets. The teacher who triggers excitement and curiosity in his students is just as creative as the shaman who makes it rain or as the veterinarian who heals your cat or the author who wrote your favorite novel. The adventurer who breaks world records is just as creative as a movie director. Only the focus and expression of the creative thrust differs.

In Western society, we tend to believe that creativity is the exclusive domain of celebrities—the Lennons, the Spielbergs, the Rowlings, the Kings, the Picassos, the Streeps, the Oprahs, the Harrison Fords. We see these people as larger than life and don't realize that probably they, too, struggled with insecurities, inner censors, and the need for creative expression. We forget that we are born creative, that if not for creativity we would still be living in caves.

Each of us has a particular perception, a certain slant that is uniquely ours. It is the distillation of our experiences, thoughts, beliefs, observations, the sum total of who we are—our creative voice. Sometimes, in the process of living, the voice gets lost or squashed or goes into a kind of dormancy. You can live without it, but probably not for long. One way or another, that creative voice finds expression, and its expression may not be exactly what you'd hoped.

Zelda Fitzgerald, the wife of F. Scott, finally found a creative outlet in her madness. It may not have been what she'd planned, but it served a creative purpose. Even infamous people are inherently creative—Jim Jones, Ted Bundy, Lizzie Borden. The difference lies in the choices these people made.

In *The Muse,* a movie by Albert Brooks, a successful screenwriter tells his buddy, a fellow screenwriter whose career has stalled, the secret of his success. In Greek mythology, he explains, there were nine sister goddesses who presided over music and poetry, the arts and sciences. One of them (played by Sharon Stone) has taken human form, and she's available for consultation—for a price, of course.

The screenwriter calls her, but quickly discovers that Stone is a muse with specific needs—many of them quite expensive. Ultimately he discovers that she really isn't the source of his inspiration. *He is his own source.*

The screenwriter realizes what we must all realize if we are to fulfill our potential. We have to tap what author Julia Cameron calls our "vein of gold." We must do what Stephen King compares to an excavation.

We have to lure our own creative voice out of hiding, engage it, acknowledge it, embrace it, and then let it flow through us.

One of the most common misconceptions about creativity is that it has to entail suffering. *The artist must suffer for his art.* Who originally said that, anyway? How did that myth get started? We have visions of F. Scott and Zelda Fitzgerald, locked in their marital dysfunctions. Or we see a painting by Vincent van Gogh in a museum and think of how he cut off his ear and never made a penny on his art while he was alive. Or we read about Nikola Tesla, whose brilliance and creativity battled constantly against poverty and emotional pain.

Contrary to what we've been taught, creativity is meant to be joyful. We don't have to suffer to embrace and express it. But because it comes, in part, from emotion, from the depths of our feelings and desires, suffering and misery often intensify the thrust. And maybe that's why the myth took root. On the other hand, a walk in your neighborhood, a hike through the woods, a swim in the ocean, or having a cat curled in your lap can also intensify the emotional thrust of creativity. The choice is entirely ours.

How to Use This Book

When our creative voice is quiet, when the muse is dormant, certain tools can be helpful in luring her out—therapy, dream analysis, keeping a journal, joining groups that share our creative interests, hypnosis. One of the simplest tools, however, is astrology.

Armed with nothing more than your date of birth, you have a wealth of information at your fingertips about your creativity—its voice, its themes, and its expression. Your Sun sign describes the broad creative themes in your life and the possible expressions those themes might take. Part 1 of this book deals with the Sun signs, and a chapter is devoted to each of the twelve signs. The sign Jupiter was in when you were born (which you will find in the appendix) describes the role that serendipitous factors—people, events, experiences, your spiritual beliefs, luck—play in your creative voice. Part 2 of the book deals with the effects of Jupiter.

There's also a chapter on how to estimate your rising sign. At best this is only a guess; the only way to know the sign that was rising when you were born is to have your natal chart erected. If you have access to the Internet, www.astronet.com provides a free natal chart. Many New Age bookstores also provide computerized natal charts for a small fee.

But the Sun, Jupiter, and your rising sign aren't the full picture. They are only pieces, dots that can be connected within a full natal horoscope based on the date, exact time, and place of your birth. Your birth chart is a holographic representation of your potential. In a very real sense it's interactive, because you have free will; you're capable of making choices. Those choices determine if and how you fulfill the potential in your birth chart.

In researching creativity and astrology, I've confined myself to writers, artists, musicians, actors, and scientists who are well known and to people I know personally who are driven in a particular direction. One young man who is part of my database, for instance, has a chart called a "bundle," where planets are clustered in three or four of the twelve houses in a horoscope. His Sun and Jupiter are both in Scorpio. In a nutshell, that immediately tells me he works creatively at very deep levels and that he has the stamina and ambition to do what it takes to express himself in a creative fashion.

The angles all these planets make to each other describe the ease or difficulty with which his creative process will unfold. The rising sign describes the way other people perceive his creativity. In short, everything in his chart tells me something.

But *everything* is beyond the scope of this book. What I've tried to do is to isolate several components that appear in the charts of creative people so that you have a better grasp of what your own creative quest might entail. And in the end, it really *is* a quest, the equivalent of the moment when Arthur pulls Excalibur from the stone or when Luke Skywalker learns the true meaning of The Force. In the end, the quest leads you to the grail—a creative life.

PART ONE

Sun Signs and Creative Themes

To believe your own thought,
to believe that what is true for
you in your private heart is true
for all men—that is genius.

—*Ralph Waldo Emerson*

Astrology and Your Artistic Blueprint

Art is an alchemical process.
—Julia Cameron

The Midas Touch

We all know at least one of them, individuals who have the creative equivalent of the Midas touch, a magical something that transforms the mundane, the utterly ordinary, into something unique. When we enter their home or workplace, that magic seems to be everywhere, an ineffable quality that's hard to pin down. We immediately sense they are connected to something larger than themselves, that they have tapped into a creative flow that spills over into every area of their lives.

We expect this kind of Midas touch from people in the arts, from entrepreneurs, celebrities—in other words, people who have the money, time, and resources to be, well, *creative*. But creativity isn't the exclusive domain of any profession or type of individual, and it doesn't require a particular level of income. It cuts across all the usual boundaries of race and religion, culture and creeds. Creativity is about finding what you love and committing to it. It's an approach to living that is in line with your deepest beliefs and passions. It's about becoming who you are so that you can realize your greatest potential. To a large extent, that potential is described by your Sun sign, that archetypal bundle of talents, passions, and traits that characterize you as surely as the family into which you were born.

The Blueprint and Your Potential

A blueprint is a kind of map, a schematic that illustrates the size and shape of something—a house, a mall, a spaceship. It shows how the pieces fit together, where the connections occur, and what routes will take you from point A to point Z. But until the house or mall or spaceship is built, until the blueprint is *actualized*, it's only two-dimensional, a description of *potential*. Your astrological horoscope is a lot like that blueprint.

At the instant you drew your first breath, the Sun, Moon, and planets occupied certain positions in the sky and formed particular angles to each other. This configuration is a blueprint of your potential, your unique talents, passions, and proclivities, a description of your innate creativity, of the heart and soul of your inner artist. What you do with all that potential, however, is entirely up to you.

Take identical twins, born two minutes apart. Their natal horoscopes are virtually identical. Their potential is equal. Yet one becomes a renowned musician; the other spends most of his life in prison. What makes the difference? Free will.

As an astrologer, I often try to guess people's Sun signs just by listening to the way they talk. One night at a dinner party in Kansas City, for instance, I listened to an articulate young woman, an attorney, talking about her experiences as a foster mother to troubled teenagers, about the poetry she wrote, about shopping at a local co-op, and about the various humanitarian causes in which she was involved.

"Are you an Aquarian?" I asked.

She looked astonished, then laughed nervously. "How'd you know that?"

I knew because everything she said smacked of paradigm-busting, of nonconformity and a vision of the way things *should* be, hallmarks of the Aquarian muse.

Your muse is the voice of the artistic blueprint with which you were born. Her voice is the one that wakes you from a sound sleep and sends you running to your computer or prompts you to reach for your notepad to jot down the solution to the problem that has plagued you for weeks. Her presence is the light that goes off in your head when you're least expecting it, that flash of inspiration or insight that nudges your life in a new direction. She's the source of an urge to try something new or an impulse to try your hand at writing, sketching, or starting your own business. She expresses herself in ways that are unique to *you* and your goals and needs.

The challenge for you—for each of us—is to cultivate the art of listening to that muse and then entering into a partnership with her. This isn't as strange as it sounds and doesn't require that you sit in silence, waiting for something to happen. Creative people have numerous ways of getting in touch with their muses.

Novelist Isabel Allende, for instance, always starts her novels on the same day—January 8—and goes through a complicated ceremony. Writer Julia Cameron takes walks. For you, it may be something entirely different. The point is to use what works—a ritual of some kind that signals your muse that it's time for her to start talking and that you're open, eager, and receptive. In chapter 3, as well as in the chapter on your specific Sun sign, you'll find guidelines on how to meet and communicate with your muse.

Your Sun Sign and the Blueprint

Imagine that you can drink a particular elixir or nibble at a certain mushroom or wire yourself to a special machine that will tap your creativity and cause it to flourish. You are cautioned, however, that there are certain risks involved with the elixir or mushroom or machine. Would you take the risk?

Self-knowledge always involves risk. It entails a confrontation with who you are and who you hope to become, and at some point it requires commitment to a particular path. Some of us would rather stick to the status quo, to the known and the familiar, and as long as you can fulfill your potential that way, there's nothing wrong with it. But when habitual thinking begins to feel like a prison, when you feel that your creativity is being choked or suffocated, when you find that you can't climb out of the little box you've created, then the risk becomes secondary to the urge to *act*, to plumb the depths of who you are. In short, the act of self-discovery becomes what Carlos Castaneda called "the leap into the void."

Astrology is a tool that enables you to take the leap in a focused manner, according to the talents and creative impulses with which you were born. So pick a Sun sign, any Sun sign—Aries, Taurus, Gemini, Cancer. . . . Each sign is an archetype that describes your overall personality, your vitality, your life force. Your Sun sign also symbolizes the *creative theme* that is likely to become manifest at some point in your life.

For a Gemini, this theme or thrust is likely to involve communication of some kind; for a Leo, the creative hallmark involves drama; for a Pisces, it may involve healing others. Not all Geminis are writers or speakers, of course, all Leos aren't actors, and all Pisces aren't healers. These creative themes are only the broad strokes, the *archetypal potentials* for the particular signs. And yet most Geminis have the gift of gab, most Leos have a dramatic flair, and most Pisceans possess an abundance of compassion. The ways in which these themes are expressed in your life depend on how you choose to use what you have.

Most of us tend to think of choice as something that comes in pairs. *Should I buy the Pontiac or the Jeep Cherokee? Should I dress casual or dress up?* Yet in a given day, we make hundreds of choices without thinking about it. We have coffee and cereal for breakfast, take the freeway to work, drive our kids to soccer games after school. Our external lives are built on such choices. If we're not careful, those choices become habit, and eventually the habit takes over and we forget about living *consciously*. We learn to ignore impulses that might jerk us off the safe and familiar path we have so carefully established. We inadvertently stifle our creativity because we ignore what is going on deep inside us.

Creative choices deserve no less than what we allow ourselves in the rest of our lives. I have a Sagittarian friend whom I've known all my life. Our mothers were pregnant together; we refer to each other as prenatal friends. For years she lived a life that I envied: she was a flight attendant for Pan American and saw just about every country there is to see. Then she and her husband adopted a son and she quit flying. But she didn't quit traveling. She was always planning a trip or taking one.

When we were in our early forties, she confessed that she wished she led a more creative life. "Like you," she said. "You're living a creative life. You're doing what you love best."

I pointed out that she was also doing what she loved—still traveling and defining herself through her exploration of foreign countries. Part of the creative archetype for Sagittarians lies in foreign travel—it's their hunger, their need for foreign places and cultures, an impulse so strong that to ignore it is to deny their potential. This travel itch doesn't have to manifest itself through physical travel; for some Sagittarians, mental or spiritual odysseys fulfill the same need. But travel of one sort or another is the bottom line. Folded into the Sagittarian archetype is a need to embrace a spiritual worldview or set of beliefs that explains . . . well, *life*. If a Sagittarian's worldview can't explain life, then he'll settle for answers to some of the *big* questions.

Choices and their possible creative expressions: that's what our Sun sign theme is all about.

Luck and Your Creativity

"If only I could get the break I need."
"He has all the luck."
"She's always in the right place at the right time."
"He meets all the right people."

For many of us, luck seems to be what other people have. *Other* people win the lottery, get their books published, have their art exhibited. *Other* people get a callback on their first audition, land the dream job, find their artistic niche. Yet all of us are born with some element of luck in our horoscopes; it's called Jupiter.

It seems appropriate that Jupiter, as the largest planet in the solar system, symbolizes not only our luck but our spiritual beliefs. It allows us to see the larger picture even when circumstances would have us believe there isn't any larger picture. It also symbolizes how our sense of prosperity and faith in ourselves shapes our artistic expressions.

Jupiter stays in one sign for roughly a year, which means that everyone born in your birth year probably has Jupiter in the sign that you do. But that doesn't mean that two people with Jupiter in the same sign will experience luck and serendipity in exactly the same way. Again, free will enters the picture.

Take someone with Jupiter in Scorpio. This individual's creativity is developed and expressed through experiences and encounters that deal with the Scorpio archetypes—transformation at the deepest levels, life-and-death issues, other people's resources and money, or sexual and occult areas. Stephen King is a prime example. In his case, luck came through writing about the occult and transformation at the deepest levels.

Quite a bit has been written about creative expression as a spiritual path. When Natalie Goldberg, author of *Writing Down the Bones,* was studying Zen, her teacher asked why she didn't make writing her spiritual practice. "If you go all the way with the writing, it'll take you everyplace that Zen does. Anything you commit yourself to completely you'll have to face."

Ultimately that's what your natal Jupiter does for you. It gently nudges you onto a creative path where your life becomes a seamless whole rather than a fragmented prism. Yes, there are valid arguments that Jupiter also shows the ways in which we're lazy or excessive, but when its energy is working the way it should, it opens up universes.

Alchemy and Creativity

In the literal sense, alchemy is the process by which metal is transmuted into gold. But Carl Jung considered this process a metaphor for the psychological transformation we each undergo in becoming whole. In the artistic sense, alchemy is what happens when you observe, say, a tree and then express that observation and what it makes you feel in some way. It's the transmutation of the ordinary into the sublime.

The signs of your natal Sun and Jupiter are integral to the alchemical process in your creative life. Part of that process entails silencing your inner censor or critic so that you can hear your muse. That critic is the voice that stirs up our fears about living a creative life, cautions us against giving up our day job, and brings all our negative beliefs to bear against fulfilling our potential. Some of the more common laments of the inner critic are:

"You won't get a regular paycheck."

"You won't have benefits."

"You won't make it."

"The odds are against you."

"No one makes a living doing *that*."

You get the picture. Even though the critic isn't entirely without merit—it does, after all, help to keep us grounded and practical—it's often what holds us back from reaching for and attaining our dreams. It nudges us into a little box of habitual thinking and slams the lid shut. It prevents us from taking that leap into the void.

The first step in silencing the critic is to identify your negative beliefs. The second step is to replace those beliefs with their positive counterparts: the odds are in your favor, you'll do just great making a living at *that*. If you dislike your job or your relationships or your home life, there's a reason for it. Maybe it's your muse trying to seize your attention; to hear her, you need to turn down the noise in your head and listen to the whispers of your heart.

"Creativity, like breathing," writes Julia Cameron, "always comes down to the question, 'Are you doing it now?'"

Take a look at the list of Sun signs and their respective creative themes; then let's get started.

CHART 1 • Sun Signs and Their Creative Themes

SIGN	DATE	CREATIVE THEME
Aries ♈	March 21–April 19	The Pioneer
Taurus ♉	April 20–May 20	The Pragmatist
Gemini ♊	May 21–June 21	The Communicator
Cancer ♋	June 22–July 22	The Nurturer
Leo ♌	July 23–August 22	The Actor

SIGN	DATE	CREATIVE THEME
Virgo ♍	August 23–September 22	The Perfectionist
Libra ♎	September 23–October 22	The Harmonizer
Scorpio ♏	October 23–November 21	The Transformer
Sagittarius ♐	November 22–December 21	The Traveler
Capricorn ♑	December 22–January 19	The Achiever
Aquarius ♒	January 20–February 18	The Paradigm-Buster
Pisces ♓	February 19–March 20	The Healer

2

The Muse and the Critic

There is a muse, but he's not going to come
fluttering down into your writing room and
scatter creative fairy dust all over your typewriter
or computer station. He lives in the basement.
—*Stephen King*

Think of the muse and the critic as two sides of the same coin, the yin and yang of your creative life. One whispers, *Go for it*. The other snickers, *C'mon, are you for real?* The critic embodies linear thinking; the muse embodies holistic thinking.

Both serve a purpose in our lives. The muse shows us what might be, while the critic cautions us to be careful. One evokes freedom, the other restriction. They are polar opposites, these two, and they're never going to see eye to eye. However, they can be coaxed into a position of cooperation, of delicate balance, and that's really what you're striving for at first, a fulcrum between the two. The balance lies in understanding the differences between the muse and the critic and how these differences can be used to your advantage.

Every Sun sign encompasses traits that are uplifting and those that aren't, the light and the dark, the active and the passive, the visible and the invisible. Take Virgo. Her greatest creative strength lies in her attention to detail. While the rest of us are trying to figure out how to connect the dots, Virgo is born knowing how to do it and does it better than any other sign. Her muse seizes these details and rearranges them in new and novel ways.

Max Perkins, editor for some of the literary greats, was a Virgo. When he edited Thomas Wolfe, he whittled thousands of manuscript pages into a story line. Virgos are natural editors. Because they're so good at connecting the dots, they can see where these connections are lacking in a manuscript.

Their facility with details also makes them terrific writers because they create such convincing worlds. In *The Shining,* Virgo Stephen King creates such a convincing world of ghosts and things that go bump in the night in the Overlook Hotel that we are *there.*

On the shadow side, however, Virgo is an utter perfectionist. Virgo's inner critic constantly peers over the muse's shoulder, shaking its finger, scolding Virgo because what she produces or does *isn't good enough.* The challenge for Virgo is to take a creative risk even when the critic is breathing down her neck.

Despite appearances to the contrary, the critic isn't really *opposed* to creative risk. It just wants us to proceed according to what it deems an appropriate pace, in the appropriate way. But what the critic deems to be appropriate often runs against the intensity and flow of the creative process.

Your Inner Critic

The next time your inner critic is chastising you for one thing or another, try to identify the voice. Chances are it sounds a lot like a parent or other authority figure from your childhood, the person who was always telling you *no.*

There's a story about a young boy who was asked what his name was. "Michael," he said.

"But what's your last name?" the person asked.

"Michael No," he replied.

It's funny until you realize the boy was serious. He'd been told *no* so many times he believed it was his last name.

The voice of the inner critic often begins when we're toddlers, learning the boundaries of our world—what's allowed, what's forbidden, what's safe, and what isn't. It's a necessary step in the learning process, but the problem is that all too often that voice becomes the dominant voice in our lives.

"Creativity and perfection, like oil and water, don't mix," writes C. Diane Ealy, author of *The Woman's Book of Creativity.* "The creative spirit needs to be nurtured and encouraged. Perfectionistic behavior does the opposite."

In the movie *The Sixth Sense,* a young boy sees dead people. He knows that other people don't see them, and his inner critic tells him something is wrong with him, that he isn't *normal.* If he wants to be like other people, he must ignore what he sees; he must deny what he sees. This makes him a shy, introverted kid who walks with his eyes either cast down or darting anxiously about.

Enter Bruce Willis, shrink.

At first, Willis believes the boy has serious mental problems. But as their relationship develops, Willis realizes the kid actually does see dead people and his belief in the boy turns things around and ultimately heals both of them. Sometimes it takes someone else's strong belief in our experiences to silence the inner critic so that the muse can shine.

Before Stephen King was published, he tossed a manuscript in the garbage, convinced that it was worthless. His wife, Tabitha, salvaged the manuscript, *Carrie,* which became a best-selling book and a Brian dePalma movie and launched King's successful career.

Although the critic and the muse are highly individualistic, certain Sun signs tend to have a more difficult time with the critic. Virgo, because of her proclivity for perfection, is known to be deeply self-critical. Gemini, the sign of the twins, can be equally self-critical, depending on which twin dominates on a given day. Both signs are ruled by Mercury, the planet of communication, so it's not surprising that self-criticism for Virgo and Gemini often revolves around how they express themselves.

Cancer, the most emotional of the twelve signs, can be especially prone to self-criticism when it comes to his feelings. He can torture himself endlessly by scrutinizing why he feels as he does about certain people or situations. Of the fire signs—Aries, Leo, Sagittarius—Leo is probably the most prone to self-criticism. Despite his bravado and his apparent self-confidence, Leo doubts whether he's really up to snuff in whatever he tackles. And when he's deeply into the self-criticism mode, he picks relentlessly at himself. *I'm not as good as so-and-so,* or *I'm not smart enough—or handsome enough—or talented enough.*

In the chart in chapter 1, each Sun sign was assigned a creative theme. In the next chart, each Sun sign is associated with a "shadow motif," the means through which the inner critic is most likely to manifest itself.

CHART 2 • Sun Signs and Their Shadow Motifs

SIGN	CREATIVE THEME	SHADOW MOTIF
Aries	The Pioneer	I can do it myself.
Taurus	The Pragmatist	Prove it to me.
Gemini	The Communicator	I can't get centered.
Cancer	The Nurturer	Don't mess with my space.
Leo	The Actor	They don't like me.
Virgo	The Perfectionist	I'm very picky.
Libra	The Harmonizer	Peace at any cost.
Scorpio	The Transformer	I'm in control.
Sagittarius	The Traveler	I'm right, you're wrong.
Capricorn	The Achiever	The end justifies the means.
Aquarius	The Paradigm-Buster	My mind is everything.
Pisces	The Healer	Let me escape.

These motifs are only broad generalities. If you're a Cancer and aren't the least bit possessive about your space, then perhaps your shadow side is most apparent when it comes to the people and things you nurture. I've met Geminis who don't seem to have a moody, pouting side, but they may be so left-brained that their creative right brains have to struggle to be heard. In other words, if you feel you don't fit the shadow motif for your Sun sign, then take an honest look at your life and figure out how your shadow is manifested. Or ask your family and friends. Sometimes other people can spot our strengths and weaknesses more easily than we can. But if you ask, be prepared to hear the truth!

Creativity needs structure, which the critic can provide. But too much structure is just as counterproductive as too little. Pioneering Aries, for instance, may follow her creative impulses into new terrain, but if she insists on doing everything herself, she may be cutting herself off from other people's valuable creative input. When Sagittarius insists he's right and everyone else is wrong, he becomes myopic. He's like the horse wearing blinders, unable to see anything except what's right in front of him.

We all have a shadow side. But once we come to understand it and work with it, it loses much of its power over us.

Your Muse

She's the inspiration that comes to you in a flash in the middle of the night or en route to your kid's soccer game. She's the person in a dream who whispers what you need or takes you to some secret place where you find what you've been looking for. She's the force behind that book that falls at your feet in a bookstore or library, which just happens to contain a vital piece of some creative puzzle. She's the source and the vehicle of your creativity.

But *who* or *what* is she? Does she have a face? A shape? We typically refer to the muse as female, but it can just as easily be male. "Traditionally, the muses were women, but mine's a guy; I'm afraid we'll just have to live with that," writes Stephen King in *On Writing: A Memoir of the Craft*. And King's muse lives in the basement. "You have to descend to his level, and once you get down there you have to furnish an apartment for him to live in."

Your muse doesn't have to be male or female. It doesn't even have to be human. The symbol for your muse can be an animal—wolf, dolphin, eagle, cat or dog, frog or snake. Sometimes animal muses are closely aligned with the element of the Sun sign. A water sign—Cancer, Scorpio, Pisces—may perceive his muse as a dolphin or whale. An air sign—Gemini, Libra, Aquarius—may see his muse as a bird.

If you feel an affinity for a particular kind of animal, you might use that animal as a symbol for your muse. Cats have long been associated with writers, and many writers I know have at least one. The writer may not consciously associate the cat with her muse, but the sinuous movement of the cat around the writer's legs, the cat settling in her lap, or the cat's purrs become part and parcel of the writer's creative process.

During a shamanic vision quest, part of what happens is the discovery of your power animal. In a sense, the animal's power becomes your power, and you can summon it when you need it. This transfer of power also occurs between you and your muse. If you feel that a certain animal symbolizes your muse, then keep a figure of that animal in sight when you're doing your creative work.

"Animals serve a great purpose in our spiritual development," writes Ted Andrews in *Animal-Wise*. "In many myths and tales, animals speak, deliver messages, and call the individual to the hero's path of awareness. Animals are a part of the initiation process, leading individuals in and out of the wilderness of life."

My friend Vivian identifies strongly with dolphins. She swims with them, her home is filled with dolphin images, and when she needs creative guidance, it usually comes to her through something related to dolphins. Hardly surprising that she is a Cancer, a water sign.

At one time my husband and I led tours for travel writers to the upper Amazon. In Leticia, Colombia, we would board a former rubber-hauling boat and head 350 miles upriver to Iquitos, Peru. The area teemed with wildlife, but only the pink river dolphins brought everyone to the railings of the ship. They were the color of bubble gum, somewhat smaller than ocean dolphins, and remarkably friendly.

One of our bilingual guides, Hugo, was the son of a *rivereño,* a name given to the native fishermen, and had a special affinity for the pink dolphins. He could tell when they were going to appear, where they would surface, and seemed to understand the sounds they made. I finally asked him about his uncanny ability. When he was thirteen, his father had taken him into the jungle for his vision quest, which entailed drinking a preparation made from a hallucinogenic vine called ayahuasca.

"Many young boys in my village have experiences with jaguars during their vision quests," he told me. "But the jaguar I saw was going to attack me and I got away from it by becoming a pink dolphin."

The symbol for your muse might be something out of mythology, perhaps one of the goddess archetypes. It depends on the focus of your creativity. A marriage counselor might pick Hera, goddess of marriage, or Aphrodite, goddess of love, as a symbol for his or her muse. Both goddesses concern relationships and our abilities to nurture them. For someone who does creative work at home, Hestia—the Romans called her Vesta—might be an appropriate symbol for a muse. She's the goddess of home and hearth. In mythology, Athena was the goddess of arts and crafts and of wisdom. Creative yet pragmatic, she certainly would make an appropriate symbol for someone involved in the arts and sciences. Merlin, Arthur, Guinevere, Lancelot: do any of the characters from Camelot fit your idea of a muse?

Summoning the Muse

At times you work and work and work on something—a project, an idea, a novel or a painting, an invention, whatever it might be—and it still doesn't come together in the right way. It's as if your muse is out to lunch. How can you summon her when you need her?

People have different techniques—music, meditation, dancing, physical exercise, sleeping on it, requesting a dream, gardening. Some people get in their car, hit the highway, and drive. Other people take a bath or a shower or get out and walk their dog. The idea is to divert your attention. This silences the noise in your head and allows your unconscious to percolate along without your conscious interference. Creativity can't be forced. It must be lured. It must be summoned.

One effective technique is to find an object that holds personal significance—a stone, a figurine, a piece of jewelry, a special coin, anything that's small enough to carry on you. If the object is something you can immerse in water without damaging it, you should cleanse it first in a mixture of sea salt and water or just a dip in the ocean. Or you can smudge it with smoke from burning sage. This cleanses the energy of the object.

Afterward, take a few minutes to acquaint yourself with how this object feels in your hand when your eyes are closed. Let your fingers explore it. Memorize its shape. Feel its weight in the palm of your hand. As you continue to touch it, imagine that the object is connected to your muse. Visualize the connection any way you like. The more vivid and detailed you can make the visualization, the greater the object's power.

The next time you feel as if your muse is out to lunch, try summoning it by holding the object. Fold your fingers over it, rub your thumb over its surface, remember the connection that you visualized. The first couple of times you try this, your muse may remain elusive. But with practice, this is an excellent way to bring your muse out of hiding.

Vicki, a Leo and a feng shui practitioner, was in a store one afternoon and came across a small carved figure of a buffalo. She knew that she had to have it and bought it even though it was more than she could afford at the time. She put the buffalo on a chain, named it, and now uses it as both a pendulum and a way to summon her muse.

Maya, also a Leo, is a talented gardener. Her yard is an advertisement for living in the tropics and has an almost Amazonian lushness that seems impervious to Florida droughts. She even grows pineapples, the first I have ever seen in south Florida in the more than thirty years I've lived here. She doesn't need an object to summon her muse when she gardens; her creative energy flows every time she touches a plant. And the plants respond.

Ideally, that's how our creativity should always flow. We shouldn't need objects to connect us to our muse. We shouldn't have to give our muse a shape. We should be able to just step into the flow and *do it*.

Mihaly Csikszentmihalyi, a professor of psychology at the University of Chicago, spent five years interviewing a hundred creative individuals to learn something about the creative process and is the author of several books on the subject. He splits creativity into two distinct camps: Creativity with a big C and creativity with a small c. The first, he says, alters the culture in some way—the discovery of the light bulb, of penicillin and the polio vaccine, the internal combustion engine, the first airplane. Creativity with a small c is what he calls "a more personal experience that a person has in the way they approach life, in the way that you experience life, with originality, openness, freshness . . . the personal creativity that makes life enjoyable. . . ."

And isn't that the point?

Conversing with Your Muse

So how do we talk to something that has no shape, no voice as we understand it, and no discernible reality other than our subjective perceptions? Obviously this sort of activity entails an awareness that our inner reality is just as real as our external reality.

One method comes from dream researchers, who suggest entering into a dialogue with a dream to interpret its meaning. In other words, you play the various roles that appear in your dream. One moment you're the beggar on the street who is being interviewed by the reporter; the next moment you're the reporter interviewing the beggar. In terms of creativity, this would mean that you alternate your roles as muse and yourself in search of the muse. Confusing, isn't it? It can also be time-consuming. But if you have the time and the patience, it can be immensely rewarding.

For people who are pressed for time, a simpler method is to give yourself a suggestion as you're falling asleep that your muse will solve a creative dilemma or problem by the time you wake in the morning and that you'll remember whatever it is. In some cases the result will be a dream that is heavily steeped in symbolism. In other instances the dream's meaning will be obvious. Elias Howe, inventor of the sewing machine, had been working long and hard to solve the essential puzzle of what he had envisioned. He finally gave up and that night he dreamed that he was surrounded by natives who carried spears with holes at the end of them. When he woke, he realized that his sewing machine needle needed a hole at the end through which the thread could be inserted. In his conscious mind, he'd given up, but his unconscious mind—his muse—solved the problem.

Jane Roberts, who channeled more than twenty books by an "energy personality" who called himself Seth, used to go to a "psychic library" in her dreams, where she would find the completed book she was working on. She would take it off the shelf and read the section she needed.

When she woke the next day, she didn't always consciously remember what she'd read, but she was usually able to overcome what had been an obstacle the day before.

"Part of my function as a writer is to dream awake," writes Stephen King in Naomi Epel's *Writers Dreaming* (based on interviews with writers talking about the connection between their dreams and their creativity). "If I sit down to write in the morning, in the beginning of that writing session and the ending of that session, I'm aware that I'm writing. I'm aware of my surroundings. . . . But in the middle, the world is gone and I'm able to see better. Creative imaging and dreaming are just so similar that they've got to be related."

Writer Julia Cameron contends that the most powerful creative tool at our disposal is walking. "If I am snagged on a story line, I walk it out. If I am stymied about what to work on next, I walk until it comes to me," she says in *The Vein of Gold*. This kind of walking is a lot like the "dreaming awake" that King mentions, a shift in consciousness in which thinking no longer follows a linear path. We go within to find our way out.

One of the facts that emerged in Csikszentmihalyi's research was the importance of developing a "rhythm of work and rest." To do this, a routine is important. If you have a set schedule each day for your work, this makes it clear to your muse that she should be in attendance. Your down time is just as important; it's when ideas percolate.

Part of the rhythm of creative work is related to your particular body rhythms. If you're the type who absolutely loves getting up before the sun and watching it rise on your corner of the world, then this may be your most creative time of the day. If you love being awake late at night, then it's probably the time of day when your creative juices are flowing.

Science fiction writer Joe Haldeman rises around 4:30 A.M. and works till noon; then he is finished for the day. His brother, Jay, also a science fiction writer, does his best work at night. Larks and owls: which one are you?

When my husband and I quit our day jobs to become full-time writers, we experimented with our sleep patterns, hoping to find the pattern most conducive to creativity. We would sleep for stretches of four or five hours—eleven to four, for instance—then go to work, nap in the afternoons, and maybe work some more after dinner. The problem with this schedule was that if we didn't nap, we were wasted by evening. After a week we had remembered numerous dreams but hadn't noticed any great surge in creativity or productivity. We went back to our regular schedules, which included eight hours of sleep a night.

In an interview in *Writers Dreaming*, Sue Grafton says that she gets up at six every morning, goes for a three-mile run, and is at her desk by nine. She then works until three-thirty or four-thirty in the afternoon and later takes a walk to wind up her day. In other words, she has a set schedule—and she has down time. One is as important as the other.

As writer James W. Hall put it, "It's important, to be healthy psychologically, to know that the world out there is just as good and at least as important as the world in here, the interior world."

Balance is the key to all creative endeavors.

3

The Little Box

We are what we think.

—*Buddha*

In preschool and kindergarten, our teachers urge us to keep within the lines when we color. The better we do that, the prettier our drawing is and the better the grade we get.

In elementary school, this same theme is repeated in many different ways. We are encouraged to be like other kids—smart, cute, polite, do your homework on time, cross your t's, dot your i's. We quickly get the message: although it may be okay to be a *little* bit different from other people, it's not a good idea to be *too* different. If you're too different, you become suspect.

In high school, many of us begin to rebel against these artificial strictures. We break rules, dress weirdly, dye our hair pink, wear unmatched shoes. We may experiment with booze, drugs, sex. We intend to discover who we are outside the box of what we've been taught. *We color outside the lines*.

By the time we hit college, we may or may not have a clearer sense of who we are. We may have periods when we feel pretty good about ourselves and other times when we feel absolutely miserable about who we are. We're rebels, but we're also living within the little box and trying to figure out where we fit in.

Some of us never figure it out, never grow into who we are. We stay in jobs or careers that we detest, in relationships that don't work, in lives that feel borrowed from our parents or our professors or other authority figures in our lives. "We think that the little cubicle in which we live and the little routine that we learn is life," says Csikszentmihalyi in *Writers Dreaming*. "Then that's it. There's nothing interesting outside of that."

This cubicle is the little box of habitual thinking. We are herded into it when we're young and some of us become trapped inside it. How do we get out?

In astrological terms, the escape from that little box hinges on the polarity of your sign—that is, the sign that is directly opposite yours, in a different but compatible element. Your Sun sign and its opposite form an astrological seesaw. The elements of the opposing signs are always compatible: fire and air, water and earth. The opposing signs also have the same modality—they use energy in the same way. Charts 3 and 4 summarize the elements and modalities for easy reference. Chart 5 lists the polarities of the signs.

CHART 3 • Sun Sign Elements

SIGN	ELEMENT	MEANING
Aries, Leo, Sagittarius	Fire	Active, aggressive, action-oriented
Taurus, Virgo, Capricorn	Earth	Practical, efficient, ambitious
Gemini, Libra, Aquarius	Air	Mental, communicative, idea-loving
Cancer, Scorpio, Pisces	Water	Emotional, intuitive, psychic

CHART 4 • Sun Sign Modalities

SIGN	MODALITY	MEANING
Aries, Cancer, Libra, Capricorn	Cardinal	Focused energy, moves primarily in one direction, initiates new ideas

SIGN	MODALITY	MEANING
Taurus, Leo, Scorpio, Aquarius	Fixed	Set in opinions, persistent
Gemini, Virgo, Sagittarius, Pisces	Mutable	Adaptable, flexible, can be too malleable

CHART 5 · Sun Sign Polarities

SIGN	OPPOSITE
Aries	Libra
Taurus	Scorpio
Gemini	Sagittarius
Cancer	Capricorn
Leo	Aquarius
Virgo	Pisces

The activity that follows is to help you identify limiting beliefs and attitudes that may be holding you within the little box of habitual thinking.

ACTIVITY ✸ Your Beliefs

Check the statements that apply to you.

_____ 1. I'm not ready yet.

_____ 2. It's who you know, not what you produce.

_____ 3. I don't know enough.

_____ 4. I'm not good enough.

_____ 5. It has to be perfect.

_____ 6. Other people are at fault when things don't work out.

_____ 7. I'm too old (or too young) to be creative.

_____ 8. Artists have to struggle to make ends meet.

_____ 9. I can't afford to do what I love.

_____10. Creativity is hard work.

_____11. I'm not the least bit creative.

_____12. I don't know where to start with my creativity.

_____13. I'm not deserving.

_____14. I can't find the time.

_____15. No one makes a living as a writer (artist, photographer, etc.).

These statements are some of the most commonly held beliefs about creativity. But beliefs can be changed—and once your belief changes, so does your reality. Next to any of the statements you checked, write an affirmation that is the opposite. For example, if you checked number 10, _Creativity is hard work_, a positive affirmation to counter that belief might be _My creativity flows through me effortlessly_. Or take a look at number 13, _I'm not deserving_. Why aren't you deserving? Who says you aren't? A positive affirmation to counter this belief might be _I desire creative abundance_.

Affirmations work. But they have to be repeated frequently, with intent and emotion. If you back each affirmation with a vivid visualization, it increases your chances of changing the belief.

Escaping the Box

ARIES/LIBRA

Cardinal Fire/Cardinal Air

Aries is volatile, independent, passionate, and totally fearless. He's the pioneer of the zodiac, the lone wolf—and hey, he's proud of it. His box is about doing things himself because no one else can do it better or faster or more efficiently. He's so busy doing, in fact, that he often leaves himself no time for creative thought and cuts himself off from creative input that other people might provide.

To get out of this box, Aries needs Libran energy. Libra strives for a spirit of cooperation and balance within relationships and when working with groups of people. Libra usually thinks before he speaks or acts, thus avoiding confrontation with others that may drain his creative energy.

ARIES ACTIVITY

Join a group that shares one of your interests or take a course on something about which you would like to learn more. It should be an in-person group rather than something you do online. Experiment for a stipulated length of time—a month, six weeks, whatever feels right for you. Try not to initiate your own group, because you probably would end up being in charge. The point here is to surrender your take-charge attitude and learn how to function within a group.

Note any changes that occur in your thoughts, beliefs, and creativity during the course of your experiment.

Another experiment you may want to try involves working on a creative project with one other person. The project can be anything on which you mutually agree, but should be something that sustains your interest, that doesn't entail critiquing or criticizing, and in which you both have equal say and control. For an Aries, this can be more challenging than a group activity.

TAURUS/SCORPIO

Fixed Earth/Fixed Water

Taurus is stable, patient, and persevering. She endures long after everyone else has given up and gone home. She's the most stubborn of the twelve signs, slow to change her mind and opinions unless you can prove to her why she *should*. This attitude often creates her box of habitual thinking; she may pursue a creative idea or project the way she has in the past, even when that way doesn't work anymore.

Scorpio, her polar opposite, is an intense, intuitive sign suspicious of easy answers. If she sees that something isn't working, she keeps probing into the matter, going deeper and deeper, stripping away layer after layer, until she finds what she needs. Even more importantly, she trusts absolutely that she will succeed.

TAURUS ACTIVITY

For two weeks keep a dream journal. Each night before you fall asleep, give yourself a suggestion that you will have a dream that provides a new idea, the solution to a problem, or any other thing that you need for a creative project. In general Taurus has good dream recall, and the mystery of dreams appeals to the mystical side of her nature. But to get the most out of this activity, she must go deep, as deep as Scorpio would.

If this doesn't produce the results you want, forget about it for a week. Quite often you get the answer you've hoped for when you release the desire.

GEMINI/SAGITTARIUS

Mutable Air/Mutable Fire

Gemini is full of ideas, a master of trivia, a perennial student. He can work on two or more creative projects simultaneously, but needs to be organized to do so. His little box is that he becomes lost in trivia and is often so willing to change to accommodate other people's needs that he tailors his creativity to someone else's parameters.

The remedy lies in Sagittarius. This sign always has his sights on the bigger picture. He knows his goal, and even though he's adaptable, like Gemini, he rarely creates to someone else's specifications. He follows his finely honed instincts.

GEMINI ACTIVITY

Set a creative goal to attain by the end of one week. Then each morning during that week, set a creative goal for the day that will bring you closer to the week's goal. Write down the weekly and daily goals.

Your weekly goal doesn't have to be anything huge; you don't have to write the great American novel in seven days. Pick something you know you can attain if you work toward it each day. Set aside a certain period of time each day when you will work on your daily goal. Again, this doesn't have to be a big time commitment. The point is to work toward the completion of the larger goal at the end of the week.

If this activity works for you, then extend your larger goal to a month and set weekly goals that will help you meet the monthly goal.

CANCER/CAPRICORN

Cardinal Water/Cardinal Earth

Cancer has a rich, creative imagination and can be quite focused when she sets her mind to it. Her personal space is important to her sense of well-being and she's happiest when she's creating within that space. Her little box has to do with her emotions. She sometimes feels so much that her feelings distract her from her creative goals.

Enter Capricorn. She's focused, all right. She sets her sights and goes for it, come hell or high water or the end of the civilized world. She seeks to make her creativity practical, and nothing gets in her way. From her, Cancer can learn to use her emotions to create rather than procrastinate.

CANCER ACTIVITY

For one week, keep a journal about the thoughts that run through your head. It's likely that many of your thoughts concern how you feel about certain people, situations, and events. Each time you find yourself getting caught up in your feelings about your life, divert those feelings toward your creative endeavors, whatever they are. At the beginning of your journal, set a weekly goal. Then, each day, do what Capricorn would do: decide what your creative goal is and lay a strategy to attain it.

LEO/AQUARIUS

Fixed Fire/Fixed Air

Leo has the drive and stamina to seize his creativity and run with it. He is dramatic and bold in everything he does, in large part because he enjoys being the center of attention. His little box grows from the focus on *me me,* so that when he's really living inside it, that box *is* the world. That box is everything.

The focus of Aquarius isn't emotional or egocentric; he's an intellectual humanitarian and his creative ideals usually reflect this. From him Leo can learn how to turn the *me me* of his creative focus into something that will touch everyone.

LEO ACTIVITY

For one day—no more, no less—notice how often you think about yourself and note what you're thinking. Every time you do, think immediately of the larger world of which you are an integral part. For example, if you're thinking about how you look as you enter a room, think immediately about how other people look. Notice how they are dressed, their expressions, how they speak. Divert your attention away from yourself. On day 2, practice detachment from thoughts of yourself while focusing on a creative goal that you have. Do one thing that furthers that goal.

If you are working on writing a book, for instance, spend thirty minutes on day 2 working on your idea. If you want to paint, go out and buy the tools you'll need. The point is to remain detached from thoughts of yourself throughout the exercise. Focus on your creative goal.

Try this for one week. On the eighth day evaluate what you've done, how far you've come. Then unleash the full power of your emotions in a visualization. See and feel yourself fully engaged in your creative project. Make it so vivid that you smell the paint or hear the printer spewing out sheets of your novel. Establish your rhythm; believe that you'll attain your goal.

— VIRGO/PISCES

Mutable Earth/Mutable Water

Virgo excels at details. Her creative mind buzzes with practical, creative ideas, and she has no problem implementing them. But when she becomes inundated with details, she loses her way, unable to think her way clear to the resolution. Then the boundaries of her little box get smaller and smaller until she feels that she's suffocating.

This is where Pisces can rescue her. Pisces explores the world through her emotions and lives in a sea of psychic impressions and dream images. To get past the details, Virgo must sink into herself, past her restless intellect, down into the watery depths of her own soul, and let her creative process unfold.

VIRGO ACTIVITY

Whether you're actively engaged in a creative project or about to begin one, set aside five minutes a day for one week. During this five minutes, quiet your mind, forget about details, and give yourself the suggestion that an image will come to you that will help with the project.

If your mind starts to buzz with thoughts during this five-minute period, ignore it, breathe more deeply, and allow yourself to surrender to the primordial sea of your own being. With practice, you'll be able to call up this deeply relaxed state of mind just by shutting your eyes. The purpose of this activity is to allow unconscious images to surface that are directly related to your creativity.

LIBRA/ARIES

Cardinal Air/Cardinal Fire

Libra is such a social, relationship-oriented sign that his little box fills quickly with other people. He spins his wheels trying to balance all these relationships, often putting other people's creative needs before his own.

His means of counteracting this is to strike out on his own creatively—Aries traits. He must find a rhythm and pace separate from that of other people. In doing so, he finds or refines his unique creative voice.

LIBRA ACTIVITY

Regardless of how busy your schedule is, find thirty minutes a day, for at least a week, when you can devote yourself entirely to your own creativity. This adds up to three and a half hours a week, not much in the bigger scheme of things, but enough to get you started.

During the second week, set aside forty-five minutes or an hour a day for your creative projects. Each week afterward for a total of six weeks, add another fifteen minutes or half hour a day to your schedule. In this way you establish a pace or rhythm for your creative schedule.

SCORPIO/TAURUS

Fixed Water/Fixed Earth

Scorpio is so immersed in her own investigation of what is hidden, of what lies beneath her or other people's notice, that she loses sight of finer beauties in life and forgets to enjoy the moment. Her deep passions and commitments consume her.

To break free of this little box, she should do something that keeps her fully in the moment. She must draw on Taurus's ability to focus on the here and now. Remember the story about Ferdinand the Bull? All he wanted to do was laze in his field and smell the flowers. If Scorpio can cultivate this type of moment-to-moment awareness, his creativity flows unimpeded.

SCORPIO ACTIVITY

Some of the best solutions are also the simplest. So take a walk, Scorpio. The purpose of this walk is to fully immerse yourself in the moment. Notice your surroundings—the colors, the smell of the air, the firmness of the ground beneath your feet.

You're not investigating right now. You're not probing to find what is hidden. You're simply walking through a series of consecutive moments, walking out of your little box and into the full power and scope of your creativity.

SAGITTARIUS/GEMINI

Mutable Fire/Mutable Air

Sagittarius knows where she wants to go creatively. She has the big picture. She can see the forest in all its magnificence. Her problem is that she can't see the trees; she can't figure out how to get where she wants to be.

This is where Gemini comes in. Sagittarius needs to do what Gemini does, collect the facts and information, all the connect-the-dots material that applies to her creative idea or project. This data provides her with the means to bring her creative project to fruition.

SAGITTARIUS ACTIVITY

Take one of your creative ideas or projects and dig up as many facts about it as you can find. Scour the Internet and the library; network with people you know. When you've got your facts, use them to implement your creative concept. Remember, you're drawing on the strength of your opposite sign for this activity.

Maybe your creative project involves photography, specifically photos of people involved in pursuits that make them joyful. Part of your fact-finding might involve talking to other people about what makes them happy.

CAPRICORN/CANCER

Cardinal Earth/Cardinal Water

In his relentless climb to success, Capricorn's emotions can get shoved aside. In a sense, he forgets the importance of emotions in the creative process. Without emotion, without passion for creative thoughts and projects, he is merely going through the motions.

He needs to rekindle his awareness of how he *feels* about what he's doing, Cancer's domain. Is he gratified by his work? Are his creative goals in alignment with his spiritual beliefs? Is he climbing the mountain toward success just because some authority figure in his life told him he should, or is he doing it because he wants to?

CAPRICORN ACTIVITY

Yes, you're busy, but this won't take long. Jot down ten creative goals that you have. Don't give it too much thought—just write what comes to mind.

Once you have your list, explore your feelings about each item. Okay, this may be tough to do at first. But with a little practice, exploring your feelings about what you're doing will come more easily. Write a succinct sentence about what you feel concerning each goal. If you find that you don't feel anything one way or another about an item, delete it. If you end up deleting all the creative goals on your list, start over again. Keep at it until you have the ten goals.

In this way, you discover what is really important to your personal creativity.

AQUARIUS/LEO

Fixed Air/Fixed Fire

Whereas Capricorn's emotions often get lost in relentless ambition, Aquarius's emotions simply aren't as important, because she lives so much of her life in her mind. At times she may lack the emotional commitment and drive to bring her creativity to life.

This is where Leo's dramatic boldness comes into play. As Aquarius brainstorms for ideas and tackles creative projects, she needs to do it with the *me first* enthusiasm of Leo. *Do I absolutely love this project? Am I absolutely crazy about this idea? Does this speak to* me, *as opposed to humanity at large?*

AQUARIUS ACTIVITY

List five ideas or projects in your creative life about which you feel passionate. Explain why you feel passionate about them. Now, for any creative endeavor you undertake, "test" yourself about how you feel. Are you passionate? If you don't feel the passion, think twice about tackling the endeavor.

Keep in mind that you are drawing on the strength of your opposite sign for this activity. Leos are passionate and dramatic people.

PISCES/VIRGO

Mutable Water/Mutable Earth

Dreamy Pisces thrives in the realm of imagination. He enjoys himself so thoroughly in that special place that it can easily become his little box of habitual thinking—his private prison. He doesn't know how to bring his imagination into the practical world.

But Virgo does. He plucks details from this fantasy, details from that fantasy, then mixes them in a way that makes them concrete, real, tangible. This is the energy Pisces needs to bring his rich creative potential to fruition.

PISCES ACTIVITY

Choose one idea from the vast array of ideas that you carry around in your head. Make a list of what you think this project or idea will require in terms of time, people, money—whatever is involved. Decide how you can make this idea tangible and practical.

Yes, this activity will initially go against your grain. You'll balk, you'll resist. But do it anyway. Then let your imagination go wild.

Cultural Creatives

Are you a cultural creative? This group is what Csikszentmihalyi would call creative with a big C. It is composed of roughly fifty million adults in the United States—26 percent of the population—and is gradually changing our worldview.

"While Cultural Creatives are a subculture, they lack one critical ingredient in their lives: awareness of themselves as a whole people," write authors and researchers Paul H. Ray and Sherry Ruth Anderson. "We call them Cultural Creatives precisely because they are already creating a new culture." In an interview in *Magical Blend Magazine*, Ray and Anderson note that fifty million is probably a conservative estimate. They feel the movement is going to accelerate as soon as its members realize they aren't alone.

So who are these people, fifty million strong and still growing? Ray and Anderson say the constituency grew out of various new social movements beginning in the sixties and continuing right up to the present day. The women's movement, civil rights, the environment, new kinds of spirituality and personal growth psychology—all have converged in a new worldview.

In their book *The Cultural Creatives: How 50 Million People Are Changing the World* and on their Web site (www.culturalcreatives.org), Ray and Anderson have isolated a number of factors that unite this group:

* Reading books and listening to radio outrank watching TV.

* Big on arts and culture, they are more likely than other groups to be involved in the arts as amateurs or pros.

✳ Spirituality/religion is important to them. Most are concerned about the role of the religious right in politics.

✳ They desire authenticity. Forget plastic, throwaway, poorly made. Forget clichés. These people want the real thing.

✳ They're careful consumers. They do their research, then buy.

✳ They're health conscious. They fuel the alternative health industry.

✳ Exotic vacations and travel attract them. No cruises for these folks. Eco-tourism, photo safaris, and spiritually oriented vacations are their thing.

✳ They're experiential consumers. They want experiences that are uplifting: workshops, personal growth seminars, spiritual gatherings.

If you are seeking to expand, explore, or express your creativity in new and original ways, you may be part of this movement—and not even know it!

Creativity and Money: Another Box

If your creative endeavors are what you would like to be paid for, then sooner or later you'll face the creativity and money question. What is your creativity worth? Can you attach a price tag to it?

The answer depends less on what you're producing than it does on your beliefs about your creativity and about money in general. Glance through the following list of limiting beliefs about creativity and money. Do any of them apply to you?

✳ Creative people don't make much money.

✳ Creative people are poor.

✳ No one gets paid fairly for doing what they love.

✳ Money doesn't grow on trees.

✳ I can't subject my creative products to public scrutiny.

✳ I can't handle criticism.

✳ I create only for myself.

✳ Creativity can't be equated with a financial value.

The statements in this list are similar to the ones at the beginning of the chapter. If any of these beliefs are yours, then your first task should be to use your creativity to change them.

4

Creative Energy and Your Sun Sign

All creativity and consciousness is born
in the quality of play. . . .
—Jane Roberts

Birth Chart Basics

At Disney World, the haunted house is filled with images of ghosts and monsters that leap and float and fade into the darkness. In *Star Wars,* the robot R2D2 projects a beam of light that becomes a three-dimensional image of Princess Leia. In *Total Recall* Arnold Schwarzenegger uses a gadget that projects an image of himself to escape his pursuers. These are all examples of holograms, three-dimensional images made with a laser.

In much the same way, when an astrologer erects your birth chart, he or she sees a holographic depiction of who you are and might become, a three-dimensional reprint of your soul's unfoldment. One of the first things an astrologer looks for is the sign and horoscope placement of your natal Sun, as well as any aspects or angles formed with it by other planets. This alone yields vast amounts of information about your self-image, the types of people and experiences that are likely to interest you, your creative talents, your strengths and weaknesses, the areas of your life in which you shine, even some of the themes you have brought with you from previous lives.

A birth horoscope looks like a pie with twelve unequal pieces. These pieces, called houses, represent twelve different areas of your life and provide other layers of information. The size of a house depends on the number of degrees it contains. Even though the blank horoscope in the following example has equal houses, the houses aren't equal in the actual birth chart. The placement of your Sun sign in a particular house is especially revealing about the expression of your creativity.

In the blank chart that follows, the horizontal line that cuts the circle in half is called the rising, or Ascendant, axis. It's the local horizon for the time you were born. Any planets above that horizon when you were born were in the visible part of the sky. Any planets under that horizon were invisible at the time of your birth.

East is found to the left of the horizon, west to the right, the exact opposite of a map. So if you were born in the evening, the Sun had recently set, which means it would be found just under the horizon on the right-hand side of the chart, in the sixth house. Planets rise on the left side of the chart (Ascendant) and set on the right side of the chart (Descendant).

The line that cuts the chart in half vertically is known as the MC/IC axis. The top is called the Midheaven (MC or medium coeli), and the direction is south, the exact opposite, once again, of a map. If you were born around noon, your Sun is located right around here. The bottom of the vertical line is called the IC (imum coeli), or Nadir. If you were born around midnight, your Sun is located in this area.

In essence, a birth chart is constructed upside down because here in the northern hemisphere, we're essentially on top of the planet, whereas people in Australia, for instance, are on the bottom of the planet. So when the Sun in our hemisphere reaches its peak—around noon—it's actually due south of where we are. To avoid confusion, just think of the birth chart directions as the opposite of a map's.

The numbers on the inner circle of the blank chart pertain to the houses. Planets move through them daily in a clockwise direction unless the planets are in retrograde motion, when they appear to move counterclockwise.

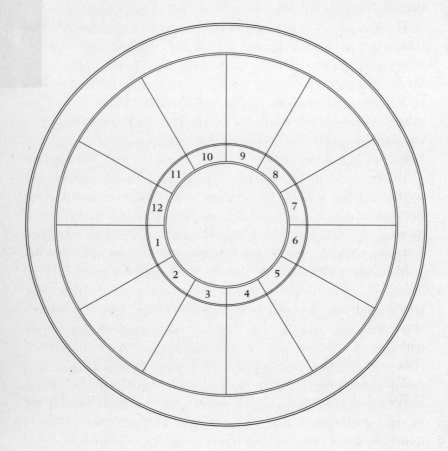

The meanings of the houses encompass not only areas of life but our experiences within these areas. Take the seventh house, which encompasses marriage, intimate relationships, and one-to-one business partnerships. To understand a person's seventh house, I would look at which planets, if any, were in that house, the sign on the Descendant (cusp of the seventh), and the aspects or angles formed with planets in that house by other planets in the horoscope.

This wouldn't give me the name of the person's significant others, business partners, or marriage partners, but it would give me a pretty good idea of the person's experiences, hopes, and expectations within the arena of intimate relationships. If the person's Sun were in the seventh house, then one thing I would be fairly certain of is that the individual's intimate relationships had the potential for success and shared creative goals. It might even be important to the individual to work creatively with a partner.

The four most important points in a chart are the Ascendant and Descendant and the MC and IC. The most important houses are the first, fourth, seventh, and tenth. These are called angular houses and are associated with action, motivation, and inspiration. Any planets in these houses or near these angles are considered to be especially powerful.

Michel Gauquelin, a French statistician, undertook a study of astrology in an attempt to disprove it. By comparing charts of many prominent people in various types of professions, he found an above average chance of Mars being placed close to an angle for people renowned in sports, Jupiter close to an angle for actors, and Saturn close to an angle for scientists.

Astrologer Robert Hand, in *Horoscope Symbols,* notes that the effects of angular planets "color the people's entire personality and may be in just about every form of behavior or choice of profession, but only insofar as people are adjusted to their world and are able to be themselves. Maladjusted people and those who feel compelled by early childhood training or experience to hide much of their true personalities from the world usually will not follow a profession appropriate to an angular planet but will instead try to manifest its function in other ways."

Based on Gauquelin's studies, Hand considers the cusp of a house (the point of transition between two houses) to be the peak of that house's energy. That would mean that planets on either side of a cusp influence and color both houses. But to keep things simple, just think of the cusp as the beginning of a house.

The houses following the angular houses are called the succedent houses—the second, fifth, eighth, and eleventh. These houses *sustain and stabilize* the actions initiated in the angular houses. The cadent houses—third, sixth, ninth, and twelfth—tend to rearrange, streamline, and dissolve what has been sustained and stabilized in the succedent houses.

Confused yet? Don't fret. Here's a rundown of what the houses mean. Take a look at the chapter on rising signs, too.

Ascendant or Rising Sign

* ✳ How other people see you

* ✳ How you present yourself to the world

* ✳ Your physical appearance

First House: Personality

* ✳ Your early childhood

* ✳ Your ego

* ✳ Your body type and how you feel about your body

* ✳ Your general physical health

* ✳ Your defense mechanisms

* ✳ Your creative thrust

Second House: Personal Values

* ✳ How you earn and spend your money

* ✳ Your personal values

* Your material resources and assets

* Your attitudes toward money

* Your possessions and your attitude toward those possessions

* Your feelings of self-worth

* Your attitudes toward creativity

Third House: Communication and Learning

* Your personal expressive style

* Your intellect, mental attitudes, and perceptions

* Your siblings, neighbors, and relatives

* How you learn

* Schooling until college

* Reading, writing, and teaching

* Short trips (to the grocery store versus Europe in seven days)

* Earthbound transportation

* Creativity as a communication device

IC, or Fourth House Cusp

* Sign on IC describes the qualities and traits of your home during early childhood

* Describes the roots of your creative abilities and talents

Fourth House: Your Roots

* Your personal environment

* Your home

* Your attitudes toward family

✳ Your early childhood conditioning

✳ Your real estate

✳ Your nurturing parent. Some astrologers say this house belongs to Mom or her equivalent in your life; others say it belongs to Dad or his equivalent. It makes sense to me that it's Mom because the fourth house is ruled by the Moon, which rules mothers. But in this day and age, when parental roles are in flux, the only hard-and-fast rule is that the fourth house belongs to the parent who nurtures you most of the time.

✳ Conditions at the end of your life

✳ Early childhood support of your creativity

Fifth House: Children and Creativity

✳ Your kids, your first-born in particular

✳ Your love affairs

✳ What you enjoy

✳ Your creative talents

✳ Gambling and speculation

✳ Your pets. Traditionally, pets belong in the sixth house. But that definition stems from the days when pets were chattel. These days we don't even refer to them as pets. They are animal companions who bring us pleasure.

Sixth House: Work and Responsibility

✳ Your day-to-day working conditions and environment

✳ Your competence and skills

✳ Your approach to creativity in daily work

✳ Your experience of employees and employers

* Your duty—to work, to employees

* Your health. Noted astrologer Robert Hand believes that illness associated with the sixth house usually occurs because the person's work "does not serve the individual's interests or . . . demands too much of the individual's energies for the benefit obtained. When one understands the reasons for illness, it is often possible to improve one's life tremendously."

Descendant, or Seventh House Cusp

* Qualities sought in your intimate or business relationships

* Qualities of your creative partnerships

Seventh House: Partnerships and Marriage

* Your marriage

* Your marriage partner

* Your significant others

* Your business partnerships

* Your close friends

* Your open enemies

* Your contracts

* Your art

* Your creative partnerships

Eighth House: Transformation

* Sexuality as transformation

* Your secrets

* Death, taxes, inheritances

* Resources shared with others

✳ Your partner's finances

✳ The occult (read: astrology, reincarnation, UFOs—everything weird and strange)

✳ Your hidden talents

✳ Psychology

✳ Life-threatening illnesses

✳ Your creative depths

Ninth House: Worldview

✳ Philosophy and religion

✳ The law, courts, judicial system

✳ Publishing

✳ Foreign travel and cultures

✳ College, graduate school

✳ Your spiritual beliefs

✳ Your creative faith

MC, or Tenth House Cusp

✳ Qualities you seek in a profession

✳ Your public image

✳ Your creative and professional achievements

Tenth House: Profession and Career

✳ Your public image, as opposed to the job that pays the bills (sixth house)

✳ Your status and position in the world

✳ Your authoritarian parent and authority in general

✳ People who hold power over you

✳ Your public life

✳ Your career/profession

✳ Your creative goals and achievements

Eleventh House: Ideals and Dreams

✳ Your peer groups

✳ Your social circles (your writers' group, your bridge club)

✳ Your dreams and aspirations

✳ How you can realize your creative dreams

Astrologer Steven Forrest has a great definition for this house. When talking about the people associated with the eleventh, he writes: "By embodying the future we want for ourselves, those people help stabilize our own intentions. For us, they symbolize the future. And by interacting with them, our own aim is made more real to us."

Twelfth House: Personal Unconscious

✳ Power you have disowned that must be claimed again

✳ Institutions—hospitals, prisons, nursing homes

✳ What you must confront this time around, your karma, issues brought in from other lives

✳ Your psychic gifts and abilities

✳ Your healing talents

✳ What you give unconditionally

Every house is packed with meaning, and not all the meanings of a given house will be expressed in your life. Some issues will never come up—or will come up in unexpected ways. To give you an example, I have Neptune in the twelfth house. Years ago during my first astrology reading, the astrologer saw that Neptune and clicked her tongue against her teeth. "Oh, my. Confinement may be part of your life pattern."

"Confinement?" I didn't like the sound of that one at all. "What kind of confinement?"

"Hospital. Mental institution. Prison."

Hardly the stuff you want to write home about. However, I worked as a librarian and Spanish teacher for three years in a medium-security prison for youthful offenders, and my mother spent two years in an Alzheimer's unit, which necessitated my close participation. Neptune in the twelfth did find expression, but not exactly in the way the astrologer said it would.

Signs and Symbols

Astrologers use symbols to represent the planets and signs. It's a kind of shorthand that prevents a chart from looking cluttered. To understand what you're looking at in the horoscope that follows, glance through these symbols.

CHART 6 · Symbols for Sun Signs and Planets

SUN SIGN	SYMBOL	PLANET	SYMBOL
Aries	♈	Sun	☉
Taurus	♉	Moon	☽
Gemini	♊	Mercury	☿
Cancer	♋	Venus	♀
Leo	♌	Mars	♂
Virgo	♍	Jupiter	♃
Libra	♎	Saturn	♄
Scorpio	♏	Uranus	♅
Sagittarius	♐	Neptune	♆
Capricorn	♑	Pluto	♇
Aquarius	♒	North Node	☊
Pisces	♓	South Node	☋

Rulership

Centuries ago it was believed there were only seven planets, and they were assigned rulership of the signs. Some of the rulerships didn't fit very well, but there weren't enough planets to go around, so the rulerships remained in effect.

Everything got shuffled around, though, with the discovery of the outer planets: Uranus (1781), Neptune (1846), and Pluto (1930). Astrologer Steven Forrest puts forth an intriguing theory about the discovery of these "transpersonal" planets. How, he asks, could the Chaldeans and the ancient Egyptians, living in a time before electric lights and atmospheric pollution, have missed these three planets? "[W]e discover them astronomically about the same time that we discover them psychologically," he writes in *The Inner Sky*.

It's likely that he's onto something with this theory. The discovery of Uranus coincided with the beginning of the scientific era; the American Revolution had just taken place, and the French Revolution was around the bend. In other words, the individual suddenly realized he had rights, and one of those rights involved questioning authority. As you'll see in the next chart, these traits are in line with what Uranus represents.

The discovery of Neptune coincided with the rise of the spiritualist movement, Romantic literature, the beginning of occult organizations like the Theosophical Society, and the inception of the Salvation Army and the Red Cross. Again, when you glance at the next chart, you'll see that compassion is one of Neptune's traits.

The discovery of Pluto coincided with the Atomic Age, the rise of existentialism, and the Great Depression. Coincidence? "In the astrologers' universe," writes Forrest, ". . . no perception is unrelated to deeper events in the consciousness experiencing it."

Chart 7 provides a handy reference for current rulerships of signs. The signs formerly ruled are in parenthesis.

CHART 7 · Rulerships

PLANET	RULES	SYMBOLIZES
Sun	Leo	The essence and energy of life, where you shine
		Thematic creative ability
		Ego, individuality, yang energy
		Father or husband
		Children in general
		Power and authority
		Rules heart, back, spine, spinal cord
Moon	Cancer	Creative inspiration
		Intuition, feminine or yin energy
		Mother or wife
		Emotions and emotional reactions
		Childbirth, pregnancy, relationship between mother and child
		The holistic mind, the right brain
		Rules mammary glands, womb, conception, bodily fluids
Mercury	Gemini, Virgo	Intellect, mental quickness, acuity, communication
		Logic and reasoning, the left brain
		Routine travel
		Contracts, writing, teaching, speaking, books
		Rules arms, hands, shoulders, lungs, nervous system
Venus	Taurus, Libra	Love life, romance
		Beauty, artistic instinct, sociability
		Wife, women, maternal love (no strings attached)
		Ability to attract people

PLANET	RULES	SYMBOLIZES
		Ability to create close personal relationships
		The arts
		Has some bearing on material resources, earning capacity, and spending habits
		Rules neck, throat, thyroid gland, ovaries, kidneys, veins
Mars	Aries (Scorpio)	Energy, aggression, sexual drive, action
		Individualization process in romantic relationships
		Athletes and competition
		The military, war
		Rules the head, general musculature of body, male sex organs, red corpuscles, anus, hemoglobin
Jupiter	Sagittarius (Pisces)	Luck, serendipitous experiences, success, prosperity
		Expansion and integration, growth, achievement
		Abstract mind, spiritual interests, creativity
		Rules blood in general, arteries, hips, thighs, feet
Saturn	Capricorn (Aquarius)	Responsibility, discipline, limitations and restrictions
		Obedience, authority, structure, foundation
		Rules bones and joints, skin, teeth
Uranus	Aquarius	Individuality, genius, eccentricity, originality

PLANET	RULES	SYMBOLIZES
		Breaks with tradition and old patterns, revolution
		Sudden, unexpected disruptions
		Questioning of authority
		Astrology, electricity, lightning, inventions, computers
		Rules involuntary nervous system
Neptune	Pisces	Visionary self, illusions, what is hidden
		Psychic ability and experiences, spiritual insights, dreams, compassion
		Mystical tendencies, escapism, delusions
		Dissolution of boundaries, idolization
		Rules the feet, poisons, viruses, the immune system
		Co-rules bodily fluids
Pluto	Scorpio	The darker side: Darth Vader instead of Luke Skywalker
		Death, sex, regeneration, reincarnation
		The power we have over others
		The power others have over us
		Deep transformation

A Writer's Chart

On pages 54 and 55 is the chart of a well-known writer. For the time being ignore the aspectarian—the graph that accompanies the chart; we haven't covered aspects yet. Focus on the horoscope.

At the time this writer was born, Cancer (♋) was rising at 29 degrees and 52 minutes (left-hand side of chart). His Virgo sun (☉) was at 27 degrees, 24 minutes in the third house. Immediately this says that communication (third house) is important to him and that he's apt to be a perfectionist (Virgo, ♍) about it. Virgo is also on the cusp (the border between houses) of his third house (communication), so the perfectionist theme is amplified.

Neptune (Ψ), which shares the third house with the writer's Sun, is one of the slower moving outer planets. Since it stays in one sign for so long, its collective impact is generational. Neptune entered Libra in August 1943 and left it in late December 1955, so everyone born during those years has Neptune in Libra.

On a personal basis, Neptune is our connection with dreams, illusions, mysticism. It is the part of us that exists separately from the ego. It rules works of the imagination, certainly a domain this writer has mastered. Neptune in the third house with the Sun indicates that this writer plunges into his own imagination when he writes. Neptune also rules escapism, usually through drugs and alcohol. This also fits the writer. In a nonfiction book, he writes about his past alcoholism and cocaine use. With Venus (♀) sitting between the Sun and Neptune, his intellectual interests center around literature, music, and the arts. He takes great pleasure in his siblings, neighbors, and relatives. It's interesting that the writer plays in a band, which goes right along with the Venus and Neptune placements in the third house.

Notice Mercury (☿) just inside the fourth house, almost on the cusp of the Nadir, or IC. Mercury, as ruler of Gemini, also rules communication, writing, books. It's likely this writer's personal environment entails writing, books, a lot of communication. Even if I didn't know this man was a writer, the cluster of these four planets in the third and fourth houses indicate writing talent. With Neptune tossed in, the talent focuses on storytelling that could take a variety of forms.

Jupiter (♃) in Scorpio also falls in the fourth house, indicating that the writer works in the privacy of his own mind and that his imagination is vast and incomprehensible to other people. His luck and serendipitous experiences revolve around his home and that "muse who lives in the basement." He also owns a lot of real estate and lives in a large home, other attributes of Jupiter in the fourth. With Scorpio (♏) intercepted—or contained—within the fourth house, he has the

Stephen King

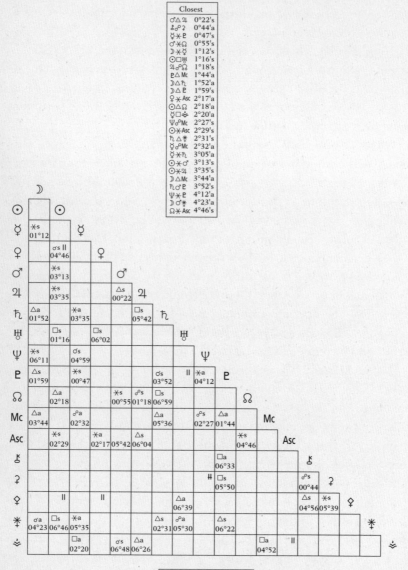

Closest	
♂△♃	0°22's
⚷☌♄	0°44'a
☿✶♇	0°47's
♂✶☊	0°55's
☽✶☿	1°12's
☉□♅	1°16's
♃☌☊	1°18's
♇△Mc	1°44'a
☽△♄	1°52'a
☽△♇	1°59's
♀✶Asc	2°17'a
☉△☊	2°18'a
☿□⚷	2°20'a
♆☌Mc	2°27's
☉✶Asc	2°29's
♄△⚸	2°31's
☿☌Mc	2°32'a
☿✶♄	3°05'a
☉✶♂	3°13's
☉✶♃	3°35's
☽△Mc	3°44'a
♄☌♇	3°52's
♆✶♇	4°12'a
☽♂⚸	4°23'a
☊✶Asc	4°46's

Adjusted Calculation Dates
0h= Jun 29   12h= Dec 29

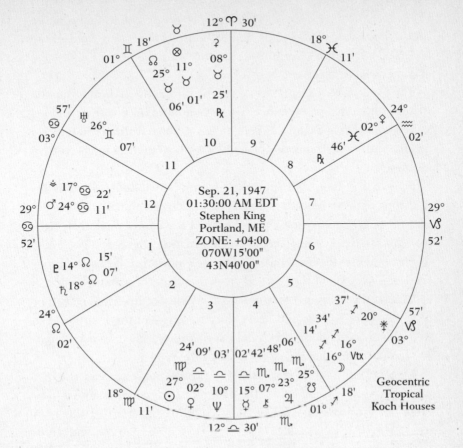

Sep. 21, 1947
01:30:00 AM EDT
Stephen King
Portland, ME
ZONE: +04:00
070W15'00"
43N40'00"

Geocentric
Tropical
Koch Houses

Sunday Sep 21, 1947
The 264th day of the year
01:30:00 AM EDT +04:00
LMT: 00:49:00
UT: 05:30:00
UT-LMT: 04:41:00
ST: 00h46m01s
RAMC: 011°30'
Local Apparent Time: 00:55:33
Equation of Time: 06m33s
Planetary Hour: Venus (♀)
7th Hour of Saturn-Night
Sunrise (approx.): 06:30EDT
Sunset (approx.): 18:38 EDT
Moon in 1st Quarter
☉/☽ Angle: 078°51'
☽'s Motion: +12°07'54"

Pl	Geo Lon	Rx
☽	16° ♐ 14' 24"	
☉	27° ♍ 23' 30"	
☿	15° ♎ 02' 11"	
♀	02° ♎ 09' 08"	
♂	24° ♋ 10' 38"	
♃	23° ♏ 48' 22"	
♄	18° ♌ 06' 51"	
♅	26° ♊ 07' 02"	
♆	10° ♎ 03' 06"	
♇	14° ♌ 14' 57"	
☊	25° ♉ 05' 56"	
Mc	12° ♈ 30' 28"	
Asc	29° ♋ 52' 08"	
Vtx	16° ♐ 34' 27"	
Eq	10° ♋ 34' 34"	
⊗	11° ♉ 01' 15"	
⚷	07° ♏ 41' 35"	
⚴	08° ♉ 25' 07"	Rx
⚵	02° ♐ 45' 41"	Rx
⚶	20° ♐ 37' 23"	
⚷	17° ♋ 22' 22"	

ability to penetrate to the deepest levels of his psyche to find what he needs. The other symbol in the fourth house is the South Node of the Moon (☋). It and the North Node are important points in a horoscope and are covered at the end of this section.

The Moon (☽) in Sagittarius (♐) in the fifth house indicates that the writer's serendipitous experiences revolve around his creativity and his kids. The Moon in Sagittarius demands emotional truth in whatever he creates and suggests that this man's mother is supportive of his creative aspirations.

Now look at Pluto and Saturn (♇, ♄) in the first house. Pluto is another one of those generational planets, the slowest moving of them all. Pluto entered Leo in June 1939 and didn't leave until more than eighteen years later. As the planet of transformation at the deepest levels, its placement in the first house is extremely powerful. It demands constant regeneration of the self and gives this writer the ability to drastically alter his personal environment. With Saturn—the planet of restrictions, discipline, and heavy duty lessons—in the first house as well, this man's childhood was not easy. Poverty may have been a factor, and there may have been issues with the father.

Mars (♂) in Cancer (♋) shares the twelfth house with an asteroid. This isn't a good placement for the planet of aggression because it indicates deep, unconscious anger. In Cancer, it suggests that this man takes everything personally. However, if that aggression can find a creative outlet, it can be an immensely powerful placement. Also, Mars rules his Aries Midheaven, indicating his ability to plunder his unconscious for ideas and inspiration and apply it to his profession. That Aries Midheaven also suggests that the writer is something of a pioneer, that his professional endeavors may be like the *Star Trek* motto, "boldly going where no man has gone before." Other writers have probably "gone there," but not in the way this writer has.

Now look at the eleventh house, which holds Uranus (♅) in Gemini (♊). Uranus is another of the slow-moving planets. It entered Gemini in May 1942 and left that sign about seven years later. On a personal level, Uranus represents our genius, the development of our individuality, our ability to question authority and consensus reality, the sudden and the unexpected. In the eleventh house of aspirations and social circles, it indicates varied and eccentric friends through which there are unexpected gains. It can also indicate a sudden and unexpected beginning—or ending—to an aspiration.

The writer to whom this chart belongs is Stephen King. What I found particularly interesting about his chart is how closely he seems to be living out and realizing his potential. In his book *On Writing, A Memoir of the Craft,* he talks about his father's desertion of the family when King was two and the financial deprivation that followed (Pluto, Saturn). Books, movies, and writing were apparently his passions even when he was young (Mercury, Neptune), and his past alcoholism and cocaine use also fit with Neptune.

The potential of Uranus in Gemini in the eleventh house was vividly realized the day he learned that the paperback rights to *Carrie* had sold for $400,000, of which he was entitled to half. The suddenness is right in line with Uranus. This also ties in with Pluto in the first—the ability to drastically alter his personal environment.

Cancer rising suggests that King is deeply intuitive and that his approach to life is very subjective, with a drive to establish some sort of foundation or home base that grounds him. Since the Moon rules Cancer, the Moon rules the chart. With his Moon in the fifth, people perceive him as a creative person. The Moon also represents the mother, so King's mother apparently supported his creativity and so does his wife (Venus in Libra in the third).

What about the Moon's nodes? What do they tell us? The two form an axis, a delicate fulcrum of energy because they are always opposite each other. King's South Node (☋) in Scorpio (♏) in the fourth house symbolizes *Been there, done that.* It represents the attitudes, traits, and talents with which he's most familiar, his deeply ingrained habits, the issues he has dealt with in past lives. The North Node (☊) in Taurus (♉) in the tenth house symbolizes the future toward which he must evolve this time around.

For King, this combination suggests that he needs to empower himself this time around by building dreams that are for himself first. Money isn't really what he's looking for, but security might be big on his list of priorities—security for himself and the people he loves. The North Node in the tenth house suggests that part of what he is here to learn is how to deal with fame and his public self.

That Taurus North Node combined with the discipline of the Virgo Sun and the relentless pressure of Mercury (communication) opposed to his Midheaven forces King to persevere even when he'd rather kick back and do something else. His Scorpio South Node indicates that the themes of the books he has written are themes he has used before, in other lives. Dark stuff, some of it, and completely fascinating to the rest of us because it brings our deepest fears up close and personal. His reading public is represented by the eleventh house, and Uranus there symbolizes his sudden realization of a dream, his sudden rise to fame and wealth.

With only two planets above the horizon—Mars ($\male$) and Uranus ($\uranus$)—he really does like his privacy. With eight out of the ten planets under the horizon, the lens through which he views the world is heavily subjective. The shape of his chart is called a bucket, with the planets lying in only half the chart. Houses six through ten are vacant of planets—only points and asteroids show up there. No major issues in those areas this time around. However, the daily movement of the planets through these houses triggers his experience of events and situations, which in turn impact the birth planets.

When an astrologer erects a horoscope, he or she has dozens of house types to choose from. The most common are Placidus and Koch. I've experimented with a number of them and now use the Koch system, which is the house system I used for King's chart.

When I did King's chart using the Placidus house method, his Jupiter and South Node fell into the fifth house, and the North Node, into the eleventh. Jupiter's placement would explain his prodigious output of work. The South Node would suggest that in previous lives he was also very creative, but lacked the ambition or the drive or the need for public recognition. Only King would know which placement feels right.

Even though the differences between the house systems are often small, they can be significant.

If someone had told me this was the chart of a novelist who has had at least one best-seller a year for the last twenty-six years, I wouldn't see it. Maybe another astrologer would, but I don't. I would expect a Moon at the MC, like George Lucas, or even at the Ascendant, like ex-Beatle George Harrison, or a Sun at the MC, like Einstein. I would expect a rock concert in the tenth house of profession and career, the place so jammed that not another planet could squeeze in. Aspects haven't been covered yet, so perhaps we'll find something there.

What is abundantly clear, however, is the breadth of King's creative drive, his ability to delve into his own unconscious (straight down to the basement, where the muse lives, as he says) and to bring his stories together in such a way that they appeal to a vast cross section of the population. In other words, his creativity is the point.

5

The Sun Through the Houses

When it is your time to write, write.
—*Natalie Goldberg*

Ascendant, or Rising
FIRST HOUSE: PERSONALITY

Born between 5 and 7 A.M.

On a spring day, throw open a window on the world. Let the sun shine in. Inhale the fragrance of earth and sky. You've got plenty to celebrate. With the Sun in the first house, the deck is definitely stacked in your favor.

Your creative potential is enormous, and you have the strength of will to bring that potential to fruition. Your creativity can find expression in virtually any endeavor about which you feel passionate. The real question, the good ole bottom line, is simple: How hard are you willing to work to fulfill that potential?

Physically, your health is generally good and you're proud of your body and strive to keep in shape. In fact, depending on the Sun sign, your body may be a vehicle for some aspect of your creativity—you may be an athlete, a yoga instructor, a professional trainer, a massage therapist.

The first house is under the horizon, and it's considered to be a more subjective, internal house than those above the horizon. But *internal* doesn't mean isolated. The subjective lens through which you view the world is colored by your relationships with other people. This can be said of most of us, but with a Sun in the first, other people recognize your magnetism—often before you even realize it's there. When Barbra Streisand (Taurus Sun first house) first sang "People" on the Johnny Carson show, she was just a girl from Brooklyn who had big dreams and a voice to match. But people *recognized* her talent, felt it viscerally, and that momentum propelled her into the stratosphere.

The closer the Sun is to the Ascendant, the stronger the magnetism, the more powerful the creative voice. And it's the voice that other people react to: *Star Wars; Indiana Jones* (George Lucas, Taurus Sun in the first house); *Roots* (Alex Haley, Leo Sun); *Imagine* (John Lennon, Libra Sun). The Sun in the first house often shows up in the charts of writers and musicians, perhaps because it's a house of self-expression.

True to the nature of the Sun beneath the horizon, we don't hear much about Lucas the man. We don't know anything about how Streisand lives her daily life. Does she grocery shop? Go to the beach? What matters with a Sun in the first is the expression of your creativity, its form and content, its mythology.

When author and reincarnational researcher Carol Bowman (Libra Sun in the first house, *Return from Heaven* and *Children's Past Lives*) first appeared on *Oprah,* she was simply a housewife who had discovered her son's past life as a Civil War soldier and started to gather information from other mothers who had similar experiences with their children. But even then, her creative voice came through loud and clear. She had stumbled upon her mission, and it became her life.

Mystery writer Agatha Christie (Virgo Sun in the first house) created one of the most beloved characters in fiction. But we really don't know much about Christie's life. In her way, she was just as private an individual as Streisand.

The first house Sun is born with a creative voice. The trick is finding it and releasing it.

SECOND HOUSE: PERSONAL VALUES

Born between 3 and 5 A.M.

Ralph Nader has his Sun in the second house. So did Charles Darwin. Neither man is known for wealth, but both are famous for the expression of their personal values—Nader for his consumer advocacy and Darwin for his theories on evolution. They embody one of the themes of the second house—*personal values.*

If your Sun falls into the second house, then a lot of your creative energy goes into defining your personal values and attitudes toward possessions and into making money. The Sun here augurs well for all financial matters.

Self-worth is also one of the themes of the second house. The Sun here usually means you don't question what your time and creative talents are worth; you already know. But at some point you may run the risk of identifying too closely with your possessions or may see your possessions and finances as status symbols. This is a sure route for sending the creative muse into hiding.

With the Sun in the second, you've got everything going for you in your *potential* for making money. An Aries Sun has an idea every minute for how to get rich quick. A Taurus might collect original art. A Gemini might collect rare books or write a best-seller. The way you express your creativity in this area is heavily influenced by the sign of your sun.

The second house is also about what we value, what is personally important to us. To a Leo Sun in the second house, children, drama, and animals are significant, and creativity may revolve around one of these themes. To a Gemini Sun in this house, communication of some kind is important and plays a part not only in *how* you earn a living but in *why* you do what you do to earn that living.

Ask yourself this: If you knew that a natural disaster was going to hit your block and you had to evacuate, what would you take with you? Limit yourself to five items. This list should give you a pretty concise idea about what you value.

Writer Margaret Mitchell had her Scorpio Sun in the second, writer/translator Richard Wilhelm (the *I Ching*) had his Taurus Sun here, and aviator Charles Lindbergh had his Aquarian Sun here. All three were most famous for a single work or act. Wilhelm's Sun in Taurus gave him the relentless persistence to spend most of his adult life interpreting the *I Ching* for lay readers, thus bringing to life a vast panoply of Chinese thought and one of the most intriguing and complex divination systems ever devised. Mitchell, in *Gone With the Wind,* brought the South's perspective of the Civil War to life in a way few writers before or since have done. And Lindbergh, of course, became a national hero after making the first solo flight across the Atlantic. In all three instances, what the individuals *valued* provided the impetus.

THIRD HOUSE: COMMUNICATION AND LEARNING

Born between 1 and 3 A.M.

You're a gossip or a networker or an information addict. You have a vision or a belief system that you feel compelled to communicate. You have wisdom to impart, skills to teach. Your Sun is in the third house, and oh baby, you're in for a wild and often unpredictable ride.

Just what is it you want to communicate, anyway? Carlos Santana (Cancer Sun in the third) nurtures his vision of the strange and the mysterious through his music. Paul McCartney (Gemini Sun) seems to have been born to music and songwriting; he simply had to make it happen. Writer Jack London (Capricorn Sun) discovered his voice through nature and the wilderness and a facility with language. Painter Paul Cézanne (Capricorn Sun) followed his creative voice straight into the Impressionist movement. Then there's Edgar Allan Poe (Capricorn Sun), whose stories and poetry have endured for a century and a half.

But communication isn't just words, art, or music. It can be teaching and speaking or sitting in your neighbor's kitchen sharing ideas, information, and common interests with friends. It can mean networking.

This is the house where we often act out of habit, coasting along on cruise control through our daily lives. Part of your creative task with a Sun in this house is to identify those habits, then redirect or break them, thus forcing yourself to find new ways of doing things. This may be one of the reasons why people with third house Suns often have various jobs or careers before they're able to bring their passion to fruition.

Stephen King (Virgo Sun in the third house) was a teacher before he started to write. Carole Nelson Douglas (Scorpio Sun), author of the *Midnight Louie* mysteries, was a newspaper reporter. Mystery writer Susan Dunlap (Gemini Sun) was a social worker.

So even if you're working at a job you don't particularly like at this point in your life, don't lose sight of the dream that will fulfill you creatively. Work toward it. Define and refine your vision. Trust that you're on the right path.

IC, FOURTH HOUSE: YOUR ROOTS

Born between 11 P.M. and 1 A.M.

If you were born right around midnight, then your Sun is very close to the Nadir, or IC, the cusp between the third and fourth houses. The fourth is the most subjective of the houses under the horizon. So much that goes on here happens under the surface, out of sight, in utter privacy and secrecy. It's a place of mystery, this house, the basement where the muse often hangs out.

Your home and personal space are important to you, and you enjoy doing your creative work at home or wherever you call home. You're able to draw on your family roots and, even more deeply, able to tap the collective unconscious in finding and expressing your creative voice. The Sun typically isn't what allows us to do it—that's the Moon's domain—but the closer the Sun is to the IC, the clearer the conduit.

With a Sun in the fourth, whatever you produce creatively may speak collectively to a great many people. That's certainly what happened with author Jane Roberts (Taurus Sun) when she began channeling the Seth material. Then there's author Michael Crichton (Scorpio Sun), who wrote *Jurassic Park*. Shortly after the movie's release I recall reading that the book was flying out of his publisher's office at the rate of 60,000 *copies a day. The Aquarian Conspiracy* by Marilyn Ferguson (Aries Sun) tapped into the same collective energy. Pablo Picasso (Scorpio Sun) made the Cubist movement a household word.

If your creativity isn't geared toward writing best-selling novels or starting art movements, you nonetheless have the ability to delve into this collective sea that connects all of us. You also can draw extensively on your background and heritage in expressing your creativity. It's likely that you feel a deep affinity for the place and community into which you were born, even to the slice of earth where you lived as a child.

This affinity, this sense of belonging to a particular place, community, and family, plays a vital role in your creativity. If, for instance, one or both of your parents are especially talented in a particular area, then this talent influences you. With a Sun in the fourth, however, one of their talents may hold special significance for you.

Seventeen-year-old Chase (Scorpio Sun) grew up in a musical household. Both his parents play the piano, and there's always music playing somewhere in the house. Chase has been playing drums for years, now plays with two other teens who are equally talented, and their group is about to cut their first CD. Even if he doesn't end up as a professional musician, environmental influence and the support of his parents surely played a part in his abilities. This is the special significance of his Sun in the fourth.

The closer the Sun is to the IC, the actual cusp of the fourth house, the stronger the influence.

FIFTH HOUSE: CHILDREN AND CREATIVITY

Born between 9 and 11 P.M.

You're a kid of maybe five or six, old enough to hold a pencil and draw. You spot a mouse scampering across the floor with a bit of food and sketch it fast. You're alone, playing by yourself, having fun. Sketching is what you do for the sheer pleasure of it.

Little do you know that your name will one day become synonymous with theme parks, TV channels, movies, and books. Little do you know that the publishing house named after you will have a logo on its doors in the shape of a mouse's ears. You're Walt Disney, and today you're only five or six years old and sketching a mouse for the fun of it.

Sagittarius Sun, fifth house. It has the blessing of Jupiter (ruler of Sagittarius), and that's big. Very big.

This is where creativity really begins. The fifth house is about pleasure—what brings us pleasure, how we seek pleasure, our attitudes and concepts of fun, how we seek fun and pleasure. First and foremost, creativity is fun and pleasurable for you. It makes you feel good. With a Gemini Sun here, communication in one or several of its various forms brings you pleasure. With a Capricorn Sun here, you're disciplined enough to structure your pleasure into something concrete. An Aquarius Sun is visionary. *When you do what you love, prosperity follows.*

Diarist Anais Nin (Pisces Sun in the fifth house) chronicled her inner life with such exquisite pleasure that it eventually brought her fame. Diana Ross (Aries Sun) probably sings in the shower and thrives on competition. The name Gloria Steinem (Aries Sun) is synonymous with the feminist movement, so we have to assume this woman was having the time of her life as she fought for women's rights. Then there's Mozart (Aquarius Sun), who certainly composed music for the love of doing it, and J. R. R. Tolkien, whose *Lord of the Rings* trilogy remains a paragon of imaginative writing.

If you can somehow spend most of your waking life doing what you love, what brings you enormous pleasure, then you and your creativity are one, inseparable.

SIXTH HOUSE: WORK AND RESPONSIBILITY

Born between 7 and 9 P.M.

While the fifth is what we do for pleasure, the sixth is where we earn our daily bread. It represents the tasks we perform on the job, our relationship with work in general and with our employers and employees. With the Sun here, you have the opportunity to express your creativity in your day-to-day work, to get fully involved in what you do, and to offer your unique perceptions.

One facet of this house is service—things we do for other people without expecting compensation. Service requires competence and creative skills, and with the Sun here, you have a burning need to be recognized for your skills. Steven Spielberg (Sagittarius Sun in the sixth), Robert Redford (Leo Sun), and Bob Dylan (Gemini Sun) are all good examples of how the Sun functions creatively in this house. Spielberg is probably the best-known director in the world. Redford is known not only for his skills as an actor and director but also for his environmental work. And Dylan, of course, has been at the top of his profession for decades.

The older definition of the sixth as the house of servants and slavery seems rather absurd in the twenty-first century. But as astrologer Robert Hand points out, it captures the idea of the sixth. If your work is merely what you do to earn a living and has no purpose, then you are not free, and illness may be the result.

Since the sixth represents small animals (as opposed to pets, which I place in the fifth), part of your creativity may involve working with animals. My daughter, for instance, has her Virgo Sun here. Early on she showed a definite love of animals and is now an avid horseback rider. But what she loves just as much as riding is the grunt work: cleaning stalls, saddling the horses, taking the horses out to the paddocks, all the small details (Virgo's specialty) that go into maintaining a stable. She's a relentless worker who does it for the love of it, is performing a service (Virgo in the sixth), and is recognized by other people at the stables for her skills and competence (sixth house).

DESCENDANT, SEVENTH HOUSE: PARTNERSHIPS AND MARRIAGE

Born between 5 and 7 P.M.

When Dustin Hoffman played an autistic savant in *Rain Man,* he became that character. He spoke and acted and perceived like an autistic person. He shed his own personality so completely that at certain points in the movie I forgot he was Hoffman. Not surprisingly, Hoffman's Sun in Leo lies in the seventh house.

This is how creativity functions with a seventh house Sun. You identify with another person so completely that you feel what that person feels. This is an enormous asset in any creative endeavor. The success of Herman Hesse's books—*Magister Ludi, Steppenwolf, Siddhartha, Demian, The Journey to the East*—was due to his ability to identify so completely with his characters that Hesse himself disappears. Hesse's Cancer Sun gave him the ability to button himself into the skins of his characters. Similarly, the creative genius of Carl Jung (Leo Sun) was being able to set aside his own point of view, which was heavily influenced by the conventional psychological beliefs at the time, and allow his patients' dreams and symptoms to speak to him at an intuitive level.

A Sun in the seventh can also indicate working successfully with a partner in creative endeavors. The partnership must be equal, however, for things to work, and there must be rapport between you and the other person, a magic that happens when the parts are greater than the whole. The partnership, whether it's romantic or professional, is pivotal to your creative expression.

The closer the Sun is to the cusp of the house, the more powerful its influence.

EIGHTH HOUSE: TRANSFORMATION

Born between 3 and 5 P.M.

Death and resurrection, highly charged emotional issues, a sense of fated or destined encounters, other people's resources and money: this is all stuff of the eighth house. The Sun's placement here makes for complex creative expression.

Take F. Scott Fitzgerald's Libra Sun in this house. Much of the material he used in his novels came straight out of his relationship with his wife, Zelda. She represented the "shared resources" on which he drew creatively. His novel *Tender Is the Night* is a thinly disguised portrayal of her breakdown, institutionalization, and eventual madness—the kind of transformation that fits right into the eighth house. Or how about Sylvia Plath (Scorpio Sun), who used her own breakdown as creative fodder?

Your creativity can find expression through any of the eighth house themes or ideas: sexual transformation, murder, reincarnation, any perception that lies beyond consensus reality. It doesn't mean you are or will be a murderer, but your creative voice may gravitate toward the dark, the strange, the mysterious, the deeply transformative.

During her impressive career, Susan Sarandon (Libra Sun) has played many roles that deal with eighth house issues. Three that leap to mind are *The Rocky Horror Picture Show,* in which she made a journey to "transsexual Transylvania"; *The Hunger,* in which she played a vampire's lover; and *Dead Man Walking,* in which she played a nun who was the confidante of a man on death row (she won the Oscar for that one). But her creativity is also expressed through another eighth house theme—sharing of resources. She is involved in raising money for and consciousness about AIDS.

The sharing of resources can mean many things, but in terms of the eighth house Sun, it nearly always revolves around *transformative* issues. So if your Sun is here, ask yourself: How can I make the best use of these energies?

NINTH HOUSE: WORLDVIEW

Born between 1 and 3 P.M.

In Frank Herbert's classic science fiction tale *Dune,* we are transported to an arid world where only one thing is valued more highly than water—*spice.* It gives powers to those who take it—the ability to see the future, to hear other people's thoughts. Those who control the spice in this world control everything.

When you read *Dune,* you are fully there. You can taste the sand on your tongue, feel its grit in your eyes. And when you put the book down, you are suddenly conscious of how much water flows freely from the tap in your kitchen sink. You think about the giant serpents who produce the spice. You run back to finish reading the book.

Herbert's classic is a prime example of one way creativity can manifest itself with a Sun in the ninth house—through a worldview and belief system completely different from our own. The ninth is about our personal worldview, our particular model of the universe and the nature of reality. This is why areas like philosophy, religion, law, higher education, and publishing fall into the domain of the ninth. Each of these expands our worldview.

With the Sun here, your muse urges you to travel—not down the street to the next town, although that will do if a longer trip isn't possible, but across the ocean, past the international dateline, to someplace utterly foreign to you. Here, in this place that might be Singapore or the Australian outback, you are confronted with the differences between you and *them.* It shocks you. Excites you. *It changes your worldview.* And somehow, in some way, your muse finds a way to express it.

Cultures that are alien to our own are also represented by the ninth house. Picture this. A young graduate student meets a Native American man who seems to know a lot about personal power and other realities. He enters into an apprenticeship with the old man. And in the early sixties, *Conversations with Don Juan: A Yaqui Way of Knowledge* becomes the first of many best-sellers by the enigmatic Carlos Castaneda (Capricorn Sun in the ninth). Castaneda was so mysterious and private that his real name, actual birthplace, and time of birth are open to question. Even his death was shrouded in mystery. Perhaps that, too, is part of the creativity of the ninth house Sun: the message, not the messenger, is the point.

Perhaps your creative voice lies in some facet of publishing. In this case you may influence the worldview through the types of books you acquire, edit, or publish.

The closer the Sun is to the Midheaven, the stronger its influence on the outer world and the more powerful its creative voice in changing the worldview.

If your Sun is here, be grateful for it and get moving.

MC, TENTH HOUSE: PROFESSION AND CAREER

Born between 11 A.M. and 1 P.M.

This is it. The zenith. High noon. The planet or planets that congregate in this house have reached the top. This is as public as it's going to get, right out there in front of the crowd.

The Sun in the tenth involves your public identity in some way, how others tag you. *He's a lawyer, she's a doctor.* In terms of creative expression, the Sun here helps you discover a public identity that's compatible with your inner needs. When the Sun here functions as it should, your public identity accurately reflects who you are. Your creativity flourishes.

When supported by other facets of your chart, the Sun here holds the potential for fame. Albert Einstein (Pisces Sun) and author Toni Morrison (Aquarius Sun) won Nobel Prizes. Harrison Ford (Cancer Sun) has been on everyone's favorite list since he first appeared as Hans Solo. Jim Morrison (Sagittarius Sun), leader of The Doors, found his calling early—and left early, at the age of twenty-eight. Van Gogh (Aries Sun), Natalie Wood (Cancer Sun), and the astrologer Charles Jayne (Libra Sun) made their marks early, left early, and their legacies live on.

Just because you have the Sun in the tenth house doesn't mean you'll be famous—although that's one possibility, if fame is supported by other facets of the chart. What it does mean, however, is that you are called to find a high-profile creative direction. My sister (Capricorn Sun) started her professional life as a shift nurse in a hospital—certainly a public sort of job—then took time off to raise her kids. When she returned to nursing, she became the wellness director at an assisted living facility. This suits the creative calling of her Capricorn Sun (Saturn, as the ruler of Capricorn, suggests—among other things—an ease in and talent for working with the elderly).

When the potential of the tenth house Sun is tapped to its fullest, you find *your* creative path rather than the path your parents or society think you should follow. And that path may take you right before the public, in a high-profile, creative direction.

ELEVENTH HOUSE: IDEALS AND DREAMS

Born between 9 and 11 A.M.

For years the meaning of this house eluded me. Then I found my mother's birth chart, which listed her time of birth, and discovered she had three planets in the eleventh—the Sun, Mars, and Mercury—and the North Node. And suddenly certain facets of her life snapped into clarity.

She had numerous friends whom she met through her group affiliations—bridge buddies, charity buddies, animal rescue buddies. She sent her friends cards for their birthdays, visited them when they were ill, and always gave generously of her time. She lived fully in the moment, but with an acute awareness of the future. "Set goals," she would say. "Know where you are and where you are going." And that's a big part of the meaning of this house.

The Sun in the eleventh asks that you set a goal. If you want to act, to write, to be a professional photographer, then it's natural for you to gravitate toward groups that have those same goals. Through the friends you make in these groups, you find support for your goals—and provide support for other people's goals. Once you commit yourself to the pursuit of your goal, whatever it is, it becomes your aspiration, your dream. The Sun in the eleventh also indicates goals that may be unusual in some way, even eccentric, and that your social and group affiliations may also be somewhat eccentric.

Enter Cher, Taurus Sun in the eleventh. An image comes immediately to mind of a skinny young woman wearing beads and flashy clothes, with hair like a black waterfall, playing Sonny Bono's sidekick in one of the most eccentric partnerships on TV. Skip ahead a number of years to Cher in *Silkwood,* playing supposedly second fiddle to Meryl Streep as the gay friend of Karen Silkwood. From one-half of an eccentric singing duo to Oscar-winning actress for *Moonstruck,* Cher's Taurus Sun has maintained a steady path into stardom and always found an audience.

Without aspirations and dreams, we are merely filling time. The Sun in the eleventh stacks the deck in your favor for fulfilling and attaining goals, for eventually living your dream, but no matter how stacked the deck is, dreams don't reach fruition unless you do your part, too.

TWELFTH HOUSE: PERSONAL UNCONSCIOUS

Born between 7 and 9 A.M.

The twelfth is also referred to as the house of troubles, the house of institutions, the house of confinement. While all these tags are certainly part and parcel of the twelfth house, they all boil down to one thing: the personal unconscious. In a sense the twelfth is the psychic garbage heap where we bury the experiences, emotions, and power we have disowned.

The creative expression of the Sun in the twelfth uses the stuff you have disowned and strives to externalize it. The shape it takes depends on what you've buried. Zelda Fitzgerald's Leo Sun in the twelfth brought her all the attention she craved, but probably not in the way she'd hoped. She lived out the confinement and institutional energy of the twelfth, yet in retrospect she became just as intriguing a character as her husband.

Mick Jagger, another Leo Sun in the twelfth, found creative expression in music and as a flamboyant performer. Even though Jagger had problems with drugs and alcohol (the "escape" part of the twelfth house) and with women, his creative use of that Leo Sun is certainly preferable to Zelda's.

To make maximum use of the Sun in the twelfth, it helps to have some idea of what you've buried here. Meditation, yoga, tai chi, prayer, and visualization are all excellent tools for discovering the content of your twelfth house. Nancy Pickard (Virgo Sun), author of *The Whole Truth, Ring of Truth,* and numerous other novels, meditates regularly, has practiced tai chi and yoga, and is also an avid student of the *I Ching.*

This placement of the Sun also responds well to dream work and dream recall, where you're involved in a creative partnership with your own unconscious. Any fan of Kurt Vonnegut's is struck by the crazy, dreamlike quality of his writing, the absurdities that he makes so plausible. It makes perfect sense with his Scorpio Sun in the twelfth.

Your creative expression may be a bit like that, rising out of the psychic abyss into the light of the day where you can make sense of it and use it.

Parting Thoughts on Houses

No single house or planet makes or breaks a birth chart or ensures or denies success and creative expression. But certain planets, houses, and aspects make the process more fluid and accessible to our conscious minds. Regardless of whether a chart indicates difficulty or ease, all of us have the capacity for creative expression. Which house the Sun was in at the time of your birth is one piece of the puzzle. Which *sign* the Sun was in is also a big piece, as we'll see in the next chapters.

6

Aries, the Pioneer ♈

There is nothing in your exterior experience
that did not originate within you.
—*Jane Roberts*

MARCH 21–APRIL 19

CARDINAL FIRE

SHADOW: I CAN DO IT MYSELF

Creative Theme

Pioneers are the ones who head out to discover new worlds while the rest of us stay at home and cheer them on. They're a fearless group, but it isn't just courage that propels them forward. They have a burning desire to know what lies just beyond their village, right over that hill and the next hill and the next one. It's a need so deep they can't ignore it, and pity the poor soul who tries to hold them back.

This pioneering spirit is so essential to the creative theme for this sign that it's almost impossible for an Aries to ignore it. To pioneer doesn't necessarily entail heading out in a covered wagon to find the America that once was or being the first person to spend a year on the space station. Aries Marilyn Ferguson didn't cross America in a covered wagon, but she pioneered a study about an emerging phenomenon and then wrote about it in *The Aquarian Conspiracy*. Aries actor Billy Dee Williams didn't go into space in real life, but in the second *Star Wars* movie, he lived in an alien city in the clouds.

The pioneering spirit of Aries manifests itself according to the individual's interests and passions. It's unlikely, for instance, that an Aries actor will tackle a sociological phenomenon and write a best-seller about it. However, the actor may recognize a role that taps into the collective spirit of that phenomenon.

When the creative theme is functioning the way it should for Aries, he naturally seeks out new terrain, new ideas, and quicker, more efficient ways of doing things. He's an innovator, and once he has an idea, he's quick to act. He's often described as impulsive and rash, qualities that can grate on other people. But these are the very traits that fuel creativity for Aries. In fact, when Aries is impulsive and rash, it usually means he's forging through what other people see as obstacles, that he's moving ahead at full steam, that he's on a creative roll.

Picture the space shuttle, a habitat surrounded by solid booster rockets filled with oxygen and hydrogen. It blasts away from the launchpad with bone-shattering force and moments later hurtles free of the Earth's atmosphere, sheds its rockets, and blazes a trail into the blackness of space. This is Aries in high gear, the most volatile energy imaginable—the element of fire, the cardinal thrust, and a masculine (yang) style that mows down everything in its path. This is fearlessness in action.

Now go back to the point where the shuttle sheds its booster rockets. It's the point of no return, right? With the booster rockets gone, the shuttle maintains its trajectory into space. But when the fire fizzles out for an Aries, when his passion falls away, that's it. His creativity is burned out, and he simply walks away without regret, leaving the loose ends for other people to tie up.

Remember: Aries is a trailblazer. Once he has initiated something, he's on to the next adventure.

Marilyn Ferguson wrote her best-seller and then proceeded to establish the *Brain/Mind Bulletin,* a research newsletter that explores the nature of consciousness. Billy Dee Williams is still acting but is also an accomplished artist. Aries Warren Beatty had a full acting career, then went on to direct. It's not uncommon for an Aries to wear several hats, but their versatility is due to their innate restlessness rather than to the adaptability found with the mutable signs.

Aries Vincent van Gogh held several jobs during his life—as an assistant in a bookstore, as a lay pastor, in an art gallery, as a teacher. But these were merely jobs that he took to earn money. His lifelong passion lay in art, and after five dark years in The Hague, where he was plagued by poverty and illness, his brother Theo invited him to stay with him in Paris. There Vincent attended classes at the Academie Cormon and met some of the Impressionist artists about whom his brother had raved: Toulouse-Lautrec, Pissaro, Cézanne, and Gauguin.

During his two years in Paris, Vincent produced two hundred paintings and sketches, then moved on to Arles, where he produced another two hundred in less than fifteen months. This focused, intense creativity is what can result when the Aries passion for what he's doing is sustained and deepened by the sheer fever of creation.

This same fever, however, is what put van Gogh in an asylum just outside of Arles fifteen months after his arrival. He remained there for a year, alternating between violent episodes and periods of productivity that resulted in a hundred and fifty more paintings. He left the asylum in the spring of 1890 to live with a physician in Auvers, who had recognized his genius and was also supposed to be an expert in nervous diseases. During this period his creative frenzy reached another fever pitch—in just two months, he painted more than seventy canvases. Once again that Aries creative fever did him in, and this time it was permanent. On July 27, 1890, van Gogh shot himself in the chest and died two days later. In his thirty-seven years, he had sold only one painting, for about thirty bucks. On what would have been van Gogh's 134th birthday, one of the sunflower paintings that he produced during his fifteen months in Arles sold at auction for nearly forty million dollars, the highest amount ever paid for a single painting at that time.

Van Gogh's life is a prime example of what can happen when the creative energy of Aries consumes everything else. While there are certainly other facets of van Gogh's chart that reinforce his acute focus on painting, the creative theme of his Sun sign dominated his life—and ultimately destroyed it. But he is also an example of what Aries does best: scaling mountains. Van Gogh persisted in his passion despite poverty, illness, despair, and loneliness. He kept moving ever forward in the grasp and expression of his own talent.

Aries Creativity in Ordinary Life

So how does all of this translate into the ordinary world of jobs, romance, kids, families, obligations, finances, and all the rest of it?

Aries comes into the world armed for survival. It's his keenest instinct and lies at the heart of his battle cry: *This is my life and I'll live it the way I want.* Since the sign is ruled by Mars, the god of war, this is hardly surprising. Aries fights for the right to *be* however he wants to be. He fights for his freedom. This instinct can find expression as combativeness, an outright chip on the shoulder, like the kid who stands in the middle of the road egging the bullies on, just daring them to come after him. It can find expression in arguments, anger, a constant contentiousness.

The survival instinct can manifest itself in other ways, too. Sharon, a customs broker and mother of two kids, was widowed before she was thirty-five, shortly after she and her husband had bought a home. Initially her reaction was grief and anger at the hand that had been dealt her and her kids. Then she began to draw on her innate Arian courage and creativity.

When there were electrical or plumbing problems in her house, she tackled them herself and learned how to fix them. Instead of hiring a pool service to take care of the swimming pool, she learned how to clean the pool, regulate the chlorine, change the filter for the pump, replace parts—you name it, she learned how to do it. This is an instance where the shadow motif, *I can do it myself,* may actually have been Sharon's salvation.

The sign's creative theme thrives on tension. The use of personal will is vital in using that tension as a springboard to initiate *something.* When that something isn't clear, Aries feels miserable and makes everyone around him feel that way, too. If he can't find a conscious outlet for this creative itch, then one way or another he stirs up circumstances to result in a crisis of some sort.

At a much deeper level, it may be that the confrontation or crisis is a product of Aries creativity. Any Aries reading this would balk. *What? That's nuts. I didn't create getting fired. It happened to me.* Or *I didn't leave him. He left me.* When something unpleasant like this happens to Aries, a bit of honest introspection goes a long way toward understanding the cause. Maybe deep down he longed to leave his job but couldn't quite bring himself to surrender the regular paycheck. So the universe did it for him. Deep down perhaps she had known the relationship was over but couldn't walk out because she would construe it as failure. So he walked out.

Creativity, after all, isn't just about art and music, poetry and acting. It's about how we create our lives from moment to moment. So look around, Aries. What do you see? Happiness? Health? A life filled with wonderful experiences? Or do you see the opposite, or something in between? Whatever it is, you've created it with your beliefs and emotions. Whatever it is, it reflects what began inside of you.

"It might help if you imagine an inner living dimension within yourself in which you create, in miniature psychic form, all the exterior conditions that you know," writes Jane Roberts in *The Nature of Personal Reality.* As she says in the quote at the beginning of this chapter—and it bears repeating—*"There is nothing in your exterior experience that did not originate within you."*

Read that quote again, Aries. Post it where you will see it frequently. Let it sink in. Once it does, it becomes heady stuff. It means—and this is the strange part—that everything you experience—every event, situation, and relationship—is what you have created through your deepest beliefs or drawn to you because of those beliefs.

> *Things happen to me.*
>
> *All my relationships eventually fall apart.*
>
> *Nothing good happens to me.*
>
> *I can't get out of debt.*
>
> *I don't have good ideas.*

Again, these are merely beliefs about reality, and beliefs can be changed. *Your point of power always lies in the present.* More so than any other sign, Aries possesses the innate capacity to live in the moment and to use the moment as a creative springboard.

Even the core of his shadow motif—*I can do it myself*—can be turned around to his advantage. A matter of need can turn things around, as it did with Sharon. Despair or joy can do it. Years ago I knew an Aries man who awed me. No one could hold a candle to this guy for raw creative talent. He could do virtually anything. What I saw as an obstacle was merely a challenge to him. Given a task that interested him, he tackled it with all that Aries energy and enthusiasm and found solutions that eluded lesser beings. But his personal life was a mess. He claimed he wanted to write, yet couldn't sit still long enough to type the first word. There were too many distractions: beautiful women and esoteric workshops, life in all its varied richness.

At some point he realized that he was here to taste a little of this, a little of that, that he was a kind of experience gourmet. I have no doubt that he'll leave his mark, but only when he has uncovered the passion that, like van Gogh's, leads him into the heart of his personal darkness and, hopefully, through it to the other side.

Aries Traits That Enhance Creativity

PATIENCE. Okay, this is tough because it's an inner thing. Aries is happiest when the challenges are external—a mountain to conquer, a deadline to meet. Aries is a master at translating an inner need into an external action without thinking about it too much. But patience requires, well, *finesse, forethought, an inner grasp of the other person.* Patience requires allowing the creative process to *unfold* rather than trying to force it into being. This is where Aries may fall short.

To remedy it, think before you speak, Aries. Don't blurt it out; mull it over first. Nurture patience. Nurture it until you can find the calm, deep center of yourself. Then pull the plugs and let your creative fever do the rest.

A SPIRIT OF COOPERATIVE ADVENTURE. Oops. That doesn't compute, says Aries. He doesn't want to be part of the office clique; he wants to be the boss, the director, the CEO, the head ho᷄ doesn't want to consult the underlings about what *they* think ᴄ wisdom is enough, thank you very much. But without the cᵢ put of other people or, at the very least, assistance of some kind, Aries invariably reaches a point beyond which he just can't move alone.

This is where Aries can draw on the traits of his polar opposite, Libra, and attempt to work in partnership with someone he trusts: a spouse, a friend, a neighbor, even a son or a daughter. The partnership might involve something as simple and fun as a biking excursion through a park. Or a camping trip. Or it could be something as involved as co-authoring a book. Whatever the project, Aries should enter it with a willingness to embrace cooperation.

ACKNOWLEDGING THE UNIQUENESS OF OTHERS. Aries can be so wrapped up in himself that he forgets to appreciate other people's uniqueness, except when the other person's abilities help him in some way. In a nutshell, his selfishness and egocentrism can blind him. Once he begins to nurture an awareness of other people's uniqueness, however, he also develops a deeper appreciation for his own creativity identity. One brings about the other.

Start close to home. Appreciate the people who love you.

COUNTING TO TEN. This is along the same lines as bite your tongue. The Aries temper is often legendary and nowhere is it more apparent than in the creative process. When things aren't going well creatively, Aries can be sharp-tongued, blunt, and unpleasant to be around. Instead of saying the first thing that comes to mind, which is usually something you can't take back, it would be beneficial to count to ten first.

The good news about the Aries temper is that once he blows, that's it. The tantrum is over, and he rarely holds grudges.

Aries Traits That Deplete Creative Energy

VICTIM THINKING. The surest way for Aries to discover whether he thinks like a victim is to listen to himself speak. *Nothing good ever happens to me. People take advantage of me. I can't do it.* Many of us aren't aware of the habitual things we say, which are often aphorisms we've picked up in childhood from our parents and other authority figures. Sometimes it takes another person to point out repetitive patterns in our speech, so if Aries has a trusted friend or significant other who is willing to do this for a couple of days, it can be immensely helpful, but only if it doesn't put Aries on the defensive.

POINTLESS CONFRONTATION. It may begin with something small—the way his significant other leaves the cap off the toothpaste, a driver who cuts him off in traffic—and suddenly the warrior side of Aries goes on red alert and what started as a minor thing becomes major: an argument with his significant other; a pursuit on the interstate to cut off the driver who cut him off. You get the picture here. Pointless confrontation is what can result when Aries can't find a creative outlet. It invariably drives other people away by putting them on the defensive.

Aries must learn to channel his energy into something constructive. One Aries man finally got the hint when his wife bought him a pair of boxing gloves and hung a punching bag in the garage. Every time he felt uselessly aggressive, he went out to the garage for a few rounds with the bag. It not only helped his disposition, but it helped him physically as well.

How Aries Can Avoid Creative Burnout

"My addiction is hiking and walking in the mountains," says Aries Pamela Cooper, a personal manager and producer. "Without walking I would be a lost soul. Every weekend I'm out there doing about ten miles, and almost every morning I walk two miles. Just being outdoors, in all that quiet, keeps me sane."

Spoken like a true Aries. With Mars ruling this sign, Aries individuals tend to enjoy athletic pursuits. It doesn't mean they all look like muscle babes or compete in the Olympics. But it does mean that physical activity is generally important to them and it's one of the best ways for an Aries to rejuvenate himself and avoid creative burnout.

The less strenuous types of activities—meditation, for instance—aren't especially appealing to restless Aries, unless these activities are part of a spiritual practice.

Sleep is also important. When Aries is burning the candles at both ends, sleep is the first thing to go. He can actually function for quite a while without sleep, but eventually his nerves begin to fray, his fuse shortens, something snaps. To replenish himself, he needs sufficient sleep. If he doesn't get it at night, a short nap during the day will help. What it all comes down to, of course, is balance, the domain of Libra, his polar opposite. Even if his creative life isn't balanced, he can make sure that the rest of his life is.

Summoning the Aries Muse

If Aries figures the muse will be there when she's needed, he'd better think again. The muse has to be summoned. This can be difficult when you're speeding through life at 75 mph and climbing mountains in your spare time. The best bet for Aries lies in the power of suggestion, and the tricky part is timing.

For the physically active Aries, the suggestion will work best when given right before he sets out for his hike, his swim, his mountain climbing. Possible wording for the suggestion might be "During my hike [swim, whatever], the ideas I need come to me. I am open to universal abundance." This should be repeated several times, with emotional power and conviction.

For the Aries who is proficient at recalling his dreams, a similar suggestion should be given as he's falling asleep at night or before he is fully awake in the morning. If he uses the suggestion as he's waking, he might add that throughout the day he will be alert for signs and symbols in his waking life that will provide the idea or solution he needs.

Some Aries individuals will see results with this almost immediately. For others it may take practice. If results aren't forthcoming within three days, then Aries should stop giving himself the suggestion. Quite often the act of releasing it will bring about what he desires.

Another technique that seems to work for Aries is to follow his impulses, the most visceral and immediate experience of his muse's voice. Perhaps on his way home from work one afternoon he suddenly has an impulse to stop by the local Friendly's for an ice cream cone (even though he doesn't even like ice cream). He follows the impulse and runs into Fred, whom he hasn't seen in a decade. Fred just happens to be looking for a Web expert to build his business online, and Aries just happens to do this in his spare time. Fred is willing to pay big bucks for the expertise and wants to know when Aries can start.

Yesterday, Aries replies.

The Aries Muse Speaks

An impulse is the most direct communication from the Aries muse and the easiest to act on. *Do I stop at Friendly's or keep heading for home?* But suppose the message is couched in a dream image or some waking symbol? Given the action-oriented nature of the sign, Aries isn't likely to spend a whole lot of time in self-reflection. But once he's aware of how his muse works, he won't have to meditate for meaning. The meaning will be obvious.

Lauren, an amateur photographer and an Aries, was offered her first professional job—to photograph a family reunion. On her way home from her regular job that afternoon, she was mulling over the offer and her inner resistance to taking the assignment. The man who had hired her—the patriarch of the family—had told her he wanted posed family portraits, like wedding photographs. This wasn't the sort of photography she had in mind; her interests were more artistic. However, the pay was good and she didn't think she should pass up the job.

She suddenly noticed a sign along the highway that read, THINK TWICE, THINK BIG, and right then she understood that what she really objected to about the assignment was the type of photos the man wanted. To her, nothing was more boring or less creative than posed pictures. When she "thought twice" about it, she decided to propose that she wander around the reunion for the entire weekend—instead of just one evening—and try to capture the emotions of the family, how they felt toward one another, scenes that depicted who and what they all were.

The man's first reaction to her suggestion was that he didn't intend to pay her any more than what they'd discussed. That was fine with Lauren; all she wanted was creative freedom. So she got her creative freedom, it didn't cost the man any more than it would have if she had taken posed photos, and he liked the results so much that he recommended her to other people.

Think twice, think big. Lauren had passed this sign before, but it hadn't meant anything special to her until she needed it. Signs and symbols often work like that. She might have interpreted it to mean that she should think twice about the offer—and turn it down. But being an Aries with a financial incentive, she turned the situation to her advantage.

Signs and symbols can appear virtually anywhere—on billboards, the sides of trucks, through a voice on the radio or TV, in something we overhear or read. They seem to occur when we're seeking answers, solutions, and guidance and when we're open to the possibility that such answers may come from any source. For the Aries who has begun to search, accepting the possibility that answers can come from anywhere usually isn't difficult to do. If the message isn't immediately apparent, it helps to interpret the signs and symbols in much the same way that a dream might be interpreted.

If Aries finds that his muse speaks to him frequently through dreams, then it's to his advantage to keep a journal of his dreams and, over time, to note the most common symbols and what they mean. In this way he compiles a personalized dream dictionary that relates directly to his creativity. Once a week or once a month he can page through the journal, looking for symbols that are repeated. This shouldn't take more than five or ten minutes of his time and should prove vital to his creative process.

When Aries needs ideas immediately and signs and symbols haven't been forthcoming in dreams or in the external world, the brainstorming technique below can be an invaluable tool.

ARIES ACTIVITY ✳ Brainstorming with the Muse

THE WHEEL

This tool is great to use when you're under the gun and need ideas fast. In the center of a blank piece of paper, write a word or phrase that describes what you need or what you're working on. Then, without giving it much thought, move clockwise around that word, jotting down whatever comes to mind, so that the phrases form a kind of wheel around the central word or phrase. Keep writing until you run out of things to write.

By doing this activity rapidly, your right brain is freed from the censorship of the left brain. It shouldn't take more than a few minutes and you can do it anywhere, at any time. If you don't want to write it down, use a recorder. This speeds up the process even more.

When one Aries man was fired from his job as a computer programmer, his focus phrase was: *Need employment*. Around this, he wrote: *new job or consulting? need to network, opportunity not disaster, didn't like old job, need freedom not confinement, feel good about this, $ OK for now, work from home, all things possible now.*

From this simple brainstorming activity, he realized that getting fired was an opportunity for him to strike out on his own, possibly as a consultant. He could work out of his home, be his own boss, and have the freedom to come and go as he pleased—all the things that appeal to an Aries. Even though he'd disliked his job, he hadn't quit because he was reluctant to relinquish a regular paycheck. The last phrase he wrote is certainly telling: All things were possible now.

In typical Aries fashion, he never regretted what had happened, and he forged ahead to establish a successful computer consulting business.

Aries and Goals

Setting goals may seem incompatible with creativity, but they can actually provide the backbone for any creative work that you do. If you're a truly impatient Aries, then set goals that you can attain quickly—within a week or two. Or set "bite-size" goals for specific creative projects. *Today I'll write a thousand words.* Or *Today I'll take a dozen photos for my portfolio.*

These bite-size goals should be easy to accomplish in a day or two. They'll provide you with a sense of accomplishment and continuity in the unfolding of your creativity. Once you become comfortable setting bite-size goals, expand them in terms of content and time—fifty pages a week, two hundred pages a month, a polished portfolio in six weeks, four completed canvases by Thanksgiving.

If you keep this up, a regular schedule for your creative work eventually emerges, and your muse becomes accustomed to showing up when you're ready to work.

If your creative work isn't how you earn your living and you would like to earn a buck by doing what you love, then setting goals becomes even more important. If you believe that in a year you can be working for yourself, then make that your goal and work toward it. Do whatever it takes to achieve that goal—save your money, sacrifice immediate gratification for the long term, set aside time each day for your creative work. If you approach your creative life as something that is both sacred and necessary, the universe responds.

Affirmation for Aries

Post the following where you will see it frequently:

My creative life flourishes.
Everything I need creatively comes to me easily.

7

Taurus, the Pragmatist ♉

In the realm of possibility, we gain our
knowledge by invention.
—*Rosamund Stone Zander*
and Benjamin Zander

APRIL 20—MAY 20

FIXED EARTH

SHADOW: PROVE IT TO ME

Creative Theme

She hears music in her body, feels color in her bones, sees language as a flowing tide. She has the soul of a poet, she's a mystic in disguise. She is Taurus, the most enduring, taciturn, and physical of the twelve signs.

With Taurus, what you see is not all there is. Like an iceberg, two thirds of what goes on with her occurs beneath the surface, out of sight, within the still, silent waters of her inner being. Somehow she must bring shape and form to what lies beneath, she must *create* something from what she cannot articulate. And ultimately she must make it practical.

Creativity and pragmatism: it sounds like a contradiction. Yet without pragmatism, things we take for granted—electricity, automobiles, jets, refrigeration, and a host of other modern conveniences—might have remained nothing more than interesting ideas. What Aries pioneers, Taurus cultivates.

One of the ways Taurus's creativity manifests itself is through her personal surroundings. Her aesthetic sense is evident where she lives and works. Her office, for instance, may have unusual art on the walls or eye-catching colors. There may be a lot of greenery—plants flourishing in windows, on her desk, flowers brightening shadowed corners. At home she may have a garden as well, her little Walden in the midst of urban life. My husband, a double Taurus (Sun and rising), is able to walk into an utterly barren yard and see how it *might be,* and then he slowly and meticulously transforms the landscape into a tropical lushness that is also infinitely practical. Paths through the lushness, fountains, sitting areas.

Taurus's traditional ruler is Venus, which gives the sign its aesthetic appreciation. But given Taurus's sheer physicality, an Earth rulership seems just as likely. This would explain Taurus's physical strength, her need for solitude and nature, and her talent for physical activities like yoga, sports, gardening.

George Lucas isn't just the creator and director of one of the most successful movie trilogies ever. He also created *his* private Walden at Skywalker Ranch. It sits on 2,000 acres in northern California, surrounded by redwood forests and rolling fields. Four or five buildings that resemble Victorian homes dot the landscape, each one a world unto itself. In the building that houses his library are display cases that hold paraphernalia from the *Star Wars* and *Indiana Jones* movies: Indy's hat and whip, Darth Vader's helmet, the stuff of movie legends.

When my husband was working on one of the prequel novels for *Indiana Jones,* which he wrote for LucasFilms, he had the opportunity to use the library at Skywalker Ranch, where Bill Moyers later filmed his interviews with mythologist Joseph Campbell. While Rob was doing his research, I had a chance to wander around the grounds. I was struck not only by the utter beauty of the place but by how perfectly Lucas had played out the aesthetic sense of the Taurus archetype. By following his own vision to create a kind of mythology in his films, he was able to indulge the Taurean need for nature and beauty in his personal surroundings.

As a fixed earth sign, Taurus is a relentless worker. Give her a task and she completes it. She may not be the fastest worker in the zodiac, but she is one of the most thorough. This kind of endurance is an obvious plus in creative work. Regardless of how Taurus expresses her creativity, she is dependable in its execution. If she says that a project will be done by a certain time or date, it is. Her word is her bond.

Taurus doesn't burn with creative passion the way Aries does. But when she's in the act of creating, she works from the deepest levels of her creative reservoirs. She is *plugged in* to her muse. Taurean Barbra Streisand shot to stardom as a singer, then expanded her creative canvas to movies and directing and is still a star decades after she first sang "People" on the *Tonight Show*. She is in for the long haul, just like Lucas. And throughout these decades, she—like Lucas—has managed to preserve her Taurean penchant for privacy.

Where Aries has an itch that has to be scratched, Taurus has a calling that beckons from way down deep in those still waters of her soul. She may be able to ignore it longer than Aries can ignore his pioneering spirit because her nature is more patient, more dilatory. But even Taurus can't ignore the muse's call forever. And once she answers that call, her real journey begins.

Taurus Creativity in Ordinary Life

Where Aries feels he must fight for the right to live his life the way he wants, Taurus is born knowing she has the right. She won't defend it the way Aries does. Taurus simply digs in her heels and refuses to budge. Her stubbornness can be infuriating. It's a wall that other people come up against and nothing can break through it. But this very stubbornness is intrinsic to Taurus's creative thrust.

When Shirley MacLaine wrote *Out on a Limb,* about her metaphysical search, she risked ridicule from her peers and the general public. But she stubbornly refused to repress what she had to say, and as a result, publishers and bookstores discovered that the New Age was a viable commercial topic.

Imagine a European who spent the bulk of his adult life in China, interpreting ancient Chinese texts so that their wisdom could be brought to a world audience. That was his mission, his passion, the creative expression of his deepest self. Richard Wilhelm, whom Carl Jung once referred to as "the messenger from China," undertook the interpretation of a Chinese divination system that is more than five thousand years old and made it comprehensible to the Western mind.

Anyone who has used the *I Ching* realizes immediately that this is no small task. "Wilhelm fulfilled his mission in the highest sense of the word," wrote Jung. "Not only did he make accessible to us the past treasures of the Chinese mind, but . . . he brought with him its spiritual root, the root that has remained alive all these thousands of years, and planted it in the soil of Europe."

Wilhelm personifies the creative power of Taurus, the inner drive and infinite patience to make the esoteric practical, the stubborn core that insists on the expression of its own vision. In true Taurus fashion, he devoted his life to that vision.

This doesn't mean that every Taurus has a singular vision or a particular mission. But every Taurus has the capacity to dive into the still waters of her own being to find her passion and coax it to the surface. Every Taurus can use her stubbornness and endurance to nurture her creativity and fulfill her potential.

We can't all be a Wilhelm, a Streisand, or a Lucas. The world is also made up of plumbers, cops, and teachers, and some of them are born under the sign of the bull. In fact, when Taurus's creativity doesn't find expression in her profession or career, it invariably shows up elsewhere. This can be said of any sign, of course, but it's especially true of Taurus. She's an extraordinary gourmet cook, a magnificent gardener. She collects the finest art or wines or rare books. Or she works magic with money.

Money is one of the areas where the creativity of Taurus excels. When she's motivated, Taurus can figure ways to make a buck go a mile. She can also cruise through a store and, within minutes, spend her next three paychecks on things she simply *must have*. But whether she's saving money or spending it as if there's no tomorrow, she does it better and with more finesse than other signs. Most of what she does is like that.

In romance, her creativity comes through loud and clear. The fresh flowers on her table, the candlelight, the wine, the erotic fragrances: her personal touch is everywhere. And because she is so physical, because touch is one way she explores creatively, she is a fine and accomplished lover, her body an instrument of her will.

So how can this kind of energy go wrong?

The same traits that make Taurus a creative genius can also make her maddeningly bullheaded. As a fixed sign, she'll see whatever it is through to the end, even when she knows better. If she has started a creative project that she senses won't work, she often plows ahead anyway simply because she *has to finish it*. In part it's a matter of pride. But more deeply, it's Taurus's inflexibility in action.

The same will of iron that allows her to pursue her creative goals long after everyone else has fallen out of the race can make her as inflexible as iron. *This is how it is, and that's how it's going to stay, now and forever, amen.* In short, her inflexibility can result in total stagnation creatively, personally, professionally, straight across the board. Then her inner stillness becomes a kind of prison, a place from which she desperately seeks to escape.

There are various forms of escape for Taurus, but they all have one thing in common: a kind of gross materialism that feeds Taurus's basic need for security. She becomes a creature who craves comfort the way a mole craves darkness. She is defined by her possessions, her investments, her art collection, her Keogh plan. If she sticks to this path, her creative urge is repressed in favor of what is known, what is safe. She no longer takes risks. Her creativity shrivels. She becomes unchangeable and her experience ultimately reflects this sameness, this utter boredom.

Taurus Traits That Enhance Creativity

FAITH. This type of faith has very little to do with religion. It's a spiritual faith, a deep conviction that life is an unfolding process that we set in motion through our beliefs, intents, and emotions. Change the beliefs, the thoughts, the emotions, and the outer experience also changes to reflect the inner shift.

This is something that Taurus understands. Down in those very still inner waters, there's a mystic in the making, an essential energy with which Taurus connects when she goes off into nature. When she reaches deeply enough, she can find it, articulate it, bring it to the surface, and use it consciously to alter her life. This is the faith that is called for when she takes a risk and leaps into the void, secure in the knowledge that she will land on her feet, in precisely the spot where she is supposed to be.

COMMUNICATION. Taurus isn't much of a talker, not unless other elements are strong in her chart. In a crowd, she is the one who says the least. Her opinions and thoughts belong just to her. If asked, she'll say what she thinks; otherwise she isn't likely to volunteer information. But when she communicates more readily about her own feelings and beliefs, she opens the door to creative brainstorming with other people. This doesn't mean she has to do it *all* the time or all at once. She simply has to try it.

FLEXIBILITY. This can be a tough area for Taurus to tackle. Her very nature rebels against it. However, by becoming aware of inflexibility related to her creativity, she'll learn not to waste time pursuing an idea or project that she senses is futile. She'll learn to rely on her intuition in these matters and take another approach.

RELEASING ANGER. It takes a lot to anger a Taurus, but when she blows, it's big time. Although the "bull's rush" clears the air, it's often counterproductive because it disrupts Taurus's need for quiet and harmony. If she can learn to express her anger when it occurs rather than repressing it, she will find that her creative energy is more plentiful and more focused.

Taurus Traits That Deplete Creative Energy

MYOPIA. Most of us are selfish in one way or another. We have to be to survive. With Taurus, however, selfishness is a kind of myopia that prevents her from seeing how her words and actions affect others. If she gets it into her head to do something, then she'll do it regardless of who objects.

When she brings this trait to her creative projects, she unnecessarily narrows her options, opportunities, and ideas. Her insistence on doing things the way they have worked in the past can squash originality. When she falls into this rut, it may take someone else to point it out to her. She may balk initially, but once she sees it for herself she can usually find a way out.

BLAMING OTHERS. When a project turns sour or doesn't work out as hoped, Taurus sometimes reacts by blaming others. It isn't that she sees herself as a victim, which is how Aries may react in a similar situation, but that it's simply easier to place the blame elsewhere than to scrutinize her own beliefs, attitudes, and ideas about what went wrong.

If she recognizes this tendency in herself, she's usually eager to take steps to correct it. The challenge, though, is the recognition itself. When placing blame elsewhere is a lifelong habit, recognition can be difficult and sometimes painful. But Taurus can rise to any challenge, and ultimately she benefits enormously by owning up to her mistakes.

How Taurus Can Avoid Creative Burnout

Even when Taurus is intensely involved in a creative project, she seems to have an innate understanding of the importance of balance and, because of it, rarely suffers from creative burnout. But when she does, regular physical exercise is vital to her creative health.

Some of the favored types of exercise for Taurus are gym workouts, yoga, running, swimming, and biking. In each instance, she competes against herself. She increases the weights on the machines she uses, perfects her yoga postures, her running time, the laps she swims, the distance she bikes. Her physical outlets often provide the time she needs to work out a creative twist or path or a solution to a creative project. In this sense, the means she uses to avoid creative burnout are often as productive as the work itself.

Music serves the same purpose as physical exercise for a Taurus, except that it nurtures her soul. It stirs the artist who sings in her blood. Even when music isn't her primary creative focus, she benefits from playing an instrument or singing in a choir (or even in the shower!). Her need for music is something she shares with Libra, which is also ruled by Venus.

Gardening is another way for Taurus to avoid creative burnout or to bypass an apparent creative block. When my husband the double Taurus gets stuck in something he's writing, he heads outside to dig and plant, water and fertilize, and transform the yard. More often than not, he returns to his computer refreshed and invigorated, with the block gone and new ideas flowing. It's as if the act of rooting around in the earth allows him to do the same thing internally, thus freeing up energy he can use creatively.

Another technique that seems to work well for Taurus is taking a nap. Even though this seems contrary to the physicality of the sign, napping enables Taurus to swim through those still inner waters to come up with what she needs. Lynn, a graphic artist, finds that even when she isn't burned out, just shutting her eyes for a few minutes can bring up vivid mental images that often relate to something she's working on.

Meditation is also an excellent way for Taurus to avoid creative burnout. While Aries is usually too restless and action-oriented to meditate, Taurus generally takes to it like the proverbial duck to water. This also happens to be one of the best ways for Taurus to summon her muse.

Summoning the Taurus Muse

Thanks to Taurus's need for quiet and solitude, meditation comes easily to her. In fact, music and meditation work together in summoning the muse. She pops in a CD of Celtic love tunes, shuts her eyes, and in comes the muse: it can be that simple.

The meditation technique she uses can be something as formal and ritualistic as a mat on the floor of an empty room, with a single candle burning nearby, and Taurus whispering her mantra. But she can meditate just as easily on a square of grass in the shade in her backyard. Or she can sit at the beach and shut her eyes.

The Taurus muse can also be summoned through physical disciplines that bring on altered states of consciousness, like tai chi and yoga. Regardless of the technique Taurus uses to summon her muse, however, she has to be able to recognize her when she appears. This can be tricky, because the muse can appear in virtually any form, or she may not have a shape at all. She may be a soft whispering in Taurus's head or merely a presence that she senses.

Sometimes the Taurus muse must be summoned in a more active, yang way—not through physical activity but by taking a risk, by thinking outside her box. Taurus might ask herself: *What am I afraid of? What makes me uneasy? What am I reluctant to do?* Maybe she's afraid of riding roller coasters or swimming in the ocean at night. Maybe she's reluctant to have Sunday dinner at her mother's house. Whatever it is, she should do it.

By confronting whatever it is that frightens her or makes her uneasy, she suddenly finds herself outside her box, her habitual mode of thinking. Her perceptions shift, her reactions change, and the muse rises to the challenge.

The Taurus Muse Speaks

The Taurus muse may also speak through synchronicities. It goes something like this. For days now Taurus has been thinking of her old friend Anita, with whom she went to grade school. They haven't seen each other in fifteen years. One night while she's searching for Anita on the Internet, the phone rings—and it's Anita!

According to Carl Jung, who coined the phrase, what we think of as coincidence isn't random at all and actually holds special significance because it hints at an underlying order in the universe. "Synchronicity takes the coincidence of events in space and time as meaning something more than mere chance, namely a peculiar interdependence of objective events among themselves as well as with the subjective (psychic) states of the observer or observers," Jung wrote.

When the Taurus muse speaks through synchronicities, she offers hints about following a particular path, pursuing a particular project, or running with a particular idea. Sometimes a word or phrase may show up repeatedly. Other times the synchronicity involves repetitive references to a person, place, or thing. *Pay attention,* the synchronicity seems to be saying. *Listen up.* And when Taurus listens, when she follows these hints wherever they might lead, she hears the muse loud and clear.

Recently my Taurus husband was casting around for an idea for a new novel. He'd just finished a novel (*PSI/NET*) that involved remote viewing, a technique for gleaning information through psychic means, and a remote viewer whom he'd met through the Internet directed Rob to his site on the topic. One of the pieces that caught his attention was about Edgar Allan Poe, who apparently had some involvement with remote viewing. Rob started doing some research, and suddenly references to Poe cropped up everywhere—in the newspaper, in bookstores, in casual conversation with friends.

Rob knew he was on the right track because the synchronicities kept multiplying, creating a trail that led deeper into the labyrinth of Poe's life and the mysterious circumstances surrounding his death. He's now writing *Romancing the Raven,* a novel in which Poe plays a most unusual role.

Anyone can be alert for and use synchronicities in creative work. But Taurus, perhaps because of her deeply mystical qualities, seems especially equipped for recognizing them.

Taurean Jane Roberts, author of nearly two dozen books on the nature of reality as well as several works of fiction, spent the last twenty years of her life channeling an "energy personality essence" who called himself Seth. Her husband, Robert Butts, used to transcribe the sessions in a kind of shorthand and also annotated the books with information about what was going on in their daily lives, thus providing considerable insight into how the creative process unfolds in ordinary life.

"Consciousness is, among other things, a spontaneous exercise in creativity," Seth said in *Seth Speaks*. "The physical senses force you to translate experience into physical perceptions. The inner senses open your range of perception, allow you to interpret experience in a far freer manner and to create new forms and new channels through which you, or any consciousness, can know itself."

Through the understanding and manipulation of her own consciousness, Taurus doesn't just hear her muse speak but enters into a partnership with her.

TAURUS ACTIVITY ✸ Brainstorming with the Muse

THE POEM

Aries was invited to draw a wheel. You, Taurus, are asked to write a poem. It can be about anything, but whatever it is should stir your emotions. It can be any length, any form or style; it simply has to be written from the heart. Don't fuss over it too much. Don't get trapped in the belief that every word has to be absolutely perfect. Just write a poem. It will help to put on your favorite music or, if you can, to wander out beneath a wide slope of sky and jot your poem surrounded by trees and the scent of the outdoors.

_____

(Title of Poem)

_____

_____

_____

_____

_____

_____

_____

_____

Now answer these questions:

1. What is the underlying emotional theme of the poem?

_____

_____

2. What does the poem tell you about the nature of your creativity?

_____

_____

3. Would you show this poem to a friend? If so, why? If not, why not?

_____

_____

4. What does the poem tell you about yourself and your concerns?

_____

_____

Whenever you get into a creative bind, write a poem. Your muse loves gestures, Taurus, and this one is sure to seize her attention.

Taurus and Goals

Fixed earth, remember? That means you understand what is concrete, tangible, and practical. You don't have any trouble setting goals—even if you've never consciously set a goal before. Where to start?

Well, that's the easiest part. What creative dream do you hold closest to your heart? If you were at the end of your life looking back, would you feel regret for the path not taken? Regret for a dream you didn't pursue? Then that's the place to start.

Today, right this second, jot down a phrase that defines your creative dream. Maybe you've always had a secret desire to act or to dance but figure you're too old for those dreams or have convinced yourself you don't have the time. Forget age, forget time. For this moment, pretend you have no limitations, no restrictions. How would you proceed to work toward the achievement of your dream? What concrete steps would you take?

Under the phrase that defines your creative dream, jot down steps in a strategy that brings you closer to attaining it. Then go for it, Taurus.

Affirmation for Taurus

Post this where you'll see it frequently:

I have everything I need to live creatively.
Now I make it so.

Gemini, the Communicator ♊

What we focus on expands.
—*Lynda Madden Dahl*

MAY 21–JUNE 21

MUTABLE AIR

SHADOW: I CAN'T GET CENTERED

Creative Theme

There's no busier mind in the zodiac. His head buzzes constantly with information, bits of conversations, what he said, what they said, what all of them might say in the future. He's the consummate communicator, eager to share what he knows, to hear what other people know, curious about virtually everything.

Yet beneath this gift of gab and this insatiable curiosity lies a perception that is odd by most standards because it doesn't insist on linear answers. It doesn't even care if the answers make sense. Gemini himself will make sense of the answers by finding the common thread, the connective tissue that unites answer A with answer Z or this bit of information with that.

For Gemini, life begins with a single burning question: Why? Why is the sky blue? Why does he have to share his things with his sister? Why does his math teacher think he's trouble? From here the questions grow more numerous and complex. Why does his significant other get angry so often? Why is the space station going to be only as large as a football field? Why is his deadline for the project so short?

He starts out looking for facts to support and answer his questions. But for some Geminis, this quest becomes an ever deepening labyrinth that leads into places even Gemini never imagined going. As he uncovers answers throughout his quest, information gets filed away in mental compartments. If this filing system were an actual system that other people could see, it probably would look entirely chaotic and without any organization at all. But that's fine with Gemini. He knows how to call up what he needs when he needs it.

Gemini is here to sample a vast smorgasbord of experiences and then to communicate what he discovers. His peculiar perceptions and curiosity are exceptionally well suited for the task. In the course of his life, he's likely to find creative expression in any number of fields and professions—writing, music, films, teaching, public relations, and research are some of the most common for this sign.

S. Lee Gifford, a movie agent and producer and a Gemini, has a funny story about a job interview he had some years ago. When his prospective employer glanced through his résumé, he remarked that Gifford had had thirty jobs in the last ten or fifteen years. Gifford thought about this for a moment, then shrugged. "Who could stand keeping the same job for ten or fifteen years?" he countered.

Gifford didn't get *that* job. Good thing, too. He went on to establish his own niche.

But regardless of how many jobs Gemini has or how many creative projects he takes on, the bottom line is always about *why*.

Gemini Whitley Streiber started out as a writer of horror fiction. His vampire novel, *The Hunger,* became a film in which Susan Sarandon played one of her first roles, and it's now considered something of an underground classic. In the eighties, with five novels to his credit, Streiber turned to nonfiction. *Communion,* a personal story about his alleged abduction by aliens, was rejected by twelve publishers, and Streiber was advised to publish the book as fiction. Eventually, however, he was paid a million dollars for the book.

It became a best-seller and was followed by *Transformation, Break-*

through, and *The Secret School. Communion,* which grew out of Streiber's Gemini questions—*Why is this happening? Why is it happening to me? And what's it really about?*—launched what can only be described as a movement to investigate the UFO and abduction phenomena and explain them once and for all.

Suddenly UFOs had their own sections in bookstores, and the number of titles proliferated at an astonishing rate. Streiber puts forth various theories about UFOs and the abduction phenomenon and expertly weaves his questions through his personal experiences. In true Gemini fashion, his questions about UFOs and abductions by aliens became much larger questions about the nature of reality and truth and about access to information in a free society. As the Internet took off, Streiber reacted in a very Gemini-like fashion. He put up a Web site (www.unknowncountry.com) and a message board so that information could be freely shared.

In the nineties, Streiber ran into financial problems, was forced to sell the home where many of his abduction experiences took place, and subsequently moved to Texas. His career also went through a dramatic shift. He and radio talk show host Art Bell (also a Gemini) teamed up to write *The Coming Global Superstorm,* and Streiber acted as a guest host on Bell's *Dreamland.* When Bell left the show for personal reasons, Streiber took over. It's an ideal platform for a Gemini's creative talents. He continues to investigate UFOs, the abduction phenomenon, government cover-ups, and anomalous weather patterns through his radio show and Web site.

The Internet is the ideal vehicle for a Gemini like Streiber. It provides rapid access to information, allows him to communicate with people worldwide and to disseminate his viewpoint, and enables him to collect data rapidly from numerous sources. Unlike the publishing industry, where it may take a year or more for a manuscript to be published, there's very little lag time with the Internet. This certainly suits Gemini's impatient nature. It would seem that Streiber has found two perfect venues for his mission—the Net and live radio.

Streiber represents one kind of Gemini—the focused, creatively disciplined type with a particular vision that has grown from a personal question. But as the sign of the twins, the Gemini archetype is multi-

faceted. So let's take a look at the other type of Gemini. This type is often described as superficial, fickle, and with other unflattering adjec-
tives. What we're actually talking about here is the other twin, the
shadow side of Gemini.

This twin may talk incessantly and even when he appears to be listening, he's probably planning what he's going to say next. It isn't that
he's rude; he's only eager to pass on information, stories, gossip, whatever he has discovered. It's his method that others may find objection-
able, his utter lack of awareness that he isn't listening, that he hasn't
heard a thing the other person has said.

Gemini can be mean-spirited, moody, inconsiderate, and, yes, superficial—but not all at once, not all at the same time. Remember:
we're talking about *facets*. This side of Gemini may make a date for
lunch and call at the last minute to cancel because he doesn't feel like
going. He may start a creative project in one direction, get sidetracked
along the way, and end up doing something totally different. This isn't
necessarily bad, at least not from Gemini's point of view, but it can be
immensely aggravating to people with whom he might be working. The
good news, though, is that Gemini usually finishes what he starts.

Gemini, like Aries, tends to move and think quickly, close to the
speed of light. One of the things this means is that he can't fit everything
he wants to do into a normal time frame   i.e., sixty minutes to the hour,
twenty-four hours to the day. So when he's involved in something creative, certain things don't get done. He procrastinates about doing the
tasks he finds boring. Phone messages pile up on his desk, letters go
unanswered, bills aren't paid. Real life gets put on the back burner and
that's how things stay until he finishes whatever he's focused on.

When Gemini becomes impatient with a creative endeavor, the end
result can be far less than he'd hoped for. This is difficult for him to see
when he's in the thick of things; all he wants then is a light at the end
of the proverbial tunnel. At times like this, he figures that faster is better when, in fact, faster may cause him to trip over his own feet.

Gemini's shadow side rarely dominates for very long. It appears and
vanishes, here one moment, gone the next, like some mischievous
trickster who really means no harm. Perhaps its true function is to keep
the other twin on his toes, so that eventually the two merge.

Gemini Creativity in Ordinary Life

Gemini's daily life is usually busy, running here and there, on the phone with friends, reading books, surfing the Net, busy busy busy. But when he finally gets all that out of his system, he is still confronted with the same burning questions: *Why?* Or *How do all the pieces fit together?* In the course of his life, nothing will deter him from answering these questions. He may take detours, the questions may get lost in the labyrinth of his mind, but sooner or later he must find those answers.

One of the most creative Geminis I've ever known was a psychic named Richard Demian. From the time he was quite small, he'd had "feelings," visions, impressions, precognitive experiences. The question that dominated his life was simple: *What's the source of these things I feel and hear and see?*

Throughout most of his adult life, he sought to answer this question by doing readings for other people. Sometimes he used cards or astrology or psychometry (picking up information about people or events by holding an object that belongs to the individual in question). Sometimes he simply shut his eyes and tuned in. True to the Gemini nature, he knew something about many things. He was an avid reader and eagerly shared what he learned. Toward the end of his life, he had developed an intuitive system concerning dates that proved astonishingly accurate. As a Gemini myself, I was fascinated by this system and kept asking him to teach it to me, but he died before he shared it with anyone.

Even though Richard worked at other jobs to help pay the bills, he never stopped doing readings, because he knew the answer to his question lay in uncovering newer and deeper layers of his talent. His question became his life.

In much the same way, Gemini Jacques Cousteau's curiosity about the world beneath the sea became his life. It's difficult to imagine him anywhere except *in the water*. Similarly, in the minds of people who have grown up with his music, Gemini Bob Dylan is *always playing the guitar*. Whatever the question is that drives him, music is his life.

This isn't to say that if your creativity doesn't become your life's work, you've failed as a Gemini. You're here, after all, to sample experience and hone your perceptions. But there will always be a common thread that runs throughout your experiences, a single question or vision that guides you, and this question or vision will be intrinsic to your creative life.

Gemini Traits That Enhance Creativity

CURIOSITY. This is Gemini's most valuable resource. He's meant to poke around in everything and to connect things that make no sense to the rest of us. The more he nurtures his curiosity, the deeper his need to communicate what he discovers and the greater the benefit to himself, the people around him, and even the larger world.

Jacques Cousteau's love of and curiosity about the ocean began as a personal interest but ended up enriching humanity's knowledge about life beneath the sea. In his quest to understand, his name became synonymous with underwater exploration.

HUMOR. Gemini's humor is a definite asset in creative work, helping him to keep things in perspective when he's moving like the wind. As offbeat as this humor can be, it's one of the things that attracts other people to him. Comedian Bob Hope is a good example of Gemini humor at work.

A BIT OF PATIENCE. Notice that it says "a bit" of patience—not a lot, not patience across the board, just a little of it. The best way for a Gemini to cultivate a bit of patience in his creative work is to apply it to some other area of his life first. A challenge for Gemini is to take the thing he likes to do the least and attempt to do it with a little patience. Once he learns what this feels like, he might try it with something else he finds distasteful. By tackling distasteful things first, Gemini can adequately gauge whether a bit of patience is beneficial.

STORYTELLING. I've yet to meet a reticent Gemini, although I have known some shy ones. Even shy Geminis have stories to tell, however, and this talent should be nurtured and developed. Through the art of storytelling, Gemini becomes more aware of his own life as a story that can be changed and reinvented. He realizes that he writes the script of his own life from moment to moment and that, as the writer, he can change what he dislikes and add more of what he likes.

BELIEF. The single most important trait Gemini can bring to his creativity is a genuine belief in his own abilities and talents. This may be said of most of the Sun signs, but for Gemini the communicator it's especially important. Unless Gemini is born with this certainty, there's no fast and easy way to acquire it. It's something that happens over time, as he finds his own creative voice or as others recognize his talents.

The sign and house placement of Jupiter plays a vital role in this process. Jupiter on the cusps of the fourth or tenth houses, for instance, can indicate parental support and validation of one's talents, which gives Gemini a deep basis for believing in his own abilities. Refer to Part 2 of this book for more information.

Gemini Traits That Deplete Creative Energy

BEING TOO ADAPTABLE. As a mutable sign, Gemini is adaptable. Nothing is likely to change that. It's one of his survival mechanisms. However, Gemini can sometimes be *too* adaptable, *too* willing to change his agenda to fit someone else's agenda.

Anne, a Gemini writer, had a particular vision for a novel that she was working on. Her agent and her editor each had some ideas about how to improve the novel. Both sets of ideas sounded good, even though they were somewhat different. Anne wanted to please both people, so she tried to implement their ideas, and her novel quickly fell apart. She eventually had to toss out the whole thing and start over, using her own vision as the launching point.

Creativity is an inner process. Gemini feels his way through the process with his mind, and when he tries to impose other people's ideas on this process, he quickly finds himself in a quandary. It may sound corny, but the adage "Be true to yourself" fits Gemini's creativity.

NOT LISTENING. Listening is an art that can be cultivated, whether it's listening to the muse or to other people. Gemini is sometimes so caught up in his own thoughts that he doesn't really listen to what other people are saying. Valuable bits of information and stories are lost in this way. A level of enrichment is neglected.

COLLECTING TOO MANY FACTS. The quickest way for Gemini to get buried in the minutiae of life is to accrue so many facts that his creativity becomes buried beneath a pile of trivia. The point of culling facts, after all, is to build a catapult for his creativity.

An example is the Gemini who sits down with a stack of books on one subject and finds some obscure fact that sends him rushing off to the library or the bookstore or the Internet to find more information on this single fact. Pretty soon he is so far from where he started that he may not even remember what he was doing.

How Gemini Can Avoid Creative Burnout

Gemini has such abundant energy that burnout shouldn't be an issue. It often is, though, because Gemini believes he can do everything at once. While it's true that many Geminis can juggle several projects at a time, problems arise when they have too many balls in the air and are also attempting to meet the demands of everyday life.

Burnout usually shows up first in Gemini's nerves. He may have trouble sleeping, can't focus on anything for very long, tends to be irritable, and is generally miserable to be around. Sleep, the very thing he needs, is the first place where he cuts back, figuring that if he can get by on five hours instead of eight, he'll have more hours in the day to get things done. Even if he makes more hours, however, his head is so fuzzy from lack of sleep that very little gets done.

Some type of physical outlet helps mitigate the effects of burnout. Exercise burns off that excess nervous energy and also keeps him physically fit and grounded. Any kind of hobby or leisure activity provides much-needed distance from his creative endeavors and gives him a chance to mull over what he's doing.

Just as music is one of the remedies for Taurus burnout, books, bookstores, and reading can work miracles for the frazzled nerves of a Gemini. Movies, getting together with friends who share his interests, surfing the Web, and a spiritual practice of some sort can have a calming effect.

Marilee, a Gemini mother of five, pours a lot of creative energy into her family. When she needs downtime, she indulges herself by playing around with new computer software or spending time with the many animals who call her backyard home. In other words, Gemini needs an outlet that brings him pleasure. All too often in his frenzied life, he forgets how to have fun!

The other surefire way for a Gemini to avoid burnout is to travel. It doesn't have to be complicated—a weekend away does wonders for Gemini's nerves and energy and alters his perceptions enough so he returns renewed.

Summoning the Gemini Muse

As the most restless of the mental air signs, Gemini probably won't choose meditation for summoning the muse. But some small ritual might be just the ticket. The mere act of lighting a candle or a stick of incense can signal the muse that Gemini is ready and eager to get going.

As a Gemini, my rituals change from project to project. But I have one consistent ritual that I do regardless of what the project involves. When I'm ready to start a new book, I clean my desk. This usually entails wading through piles of papers which, during the course of the last book, got tossed into a pile until I could get to them—which was always tomorrow.

The desk cleaning invariably extends to the floor around my desk, where stacks of books have accumulated, and then to the entire office. Quite often I end up rearranging the furniture, bringing in new hanging plants, cleaning out files. All this cleaning and organizing is practical, certainly, but it's also symbolic: I'm cleaning out the old to make room for the new.

Interaction with other people can summon the Gemini muse quite easily and effortlessly. Parties, dinner and a movie or the theater with friends, even just sitting over coffee with people you enjoy, can coax the muse out of hiding. The Gemini muse is stimulated by conversation, particularly when the conversation turns to ideas and information.

When Gemini is casting about for new ideas, a surefire way for him to get the muse's attention is to take a course or workshop on something he knows nothing about but that interests him. Once Gemini's intellect and curiosity are engaged, his muse can't resist the challenge. She sweeps in with all the enthusiasm of a kid who has discovered a treasure and takes charge.

Another effective way to summon the Gemini muse is through travel. It can be any kind of travel—air, train, car, boat—but the destination should be an unfamiliar one. In fact, the more unfamiliar and strange the destination, the quicker the muse appears, absorbing cultural and topographical differences and creatively weaving these diverse threads into some new tapestry.

Books and the Internet—in fact, anything or anyone that conveys ideas and information—can also help Gemini tap into his muse.

The Aries (fire) muse thrives on action, the Taurus (earth) muse comes alive in physical activities, and the Gemini (air) muse is summoned through the intellect.

The Gemini Muse Speaks

Most of us have experienced one of those *Aha!* moments when something suddenly snaps into utter clarity. These peak moments are when the Gemini muse is shouting at the top of her lungs, dancing in wild circles, celebrating the marriage of left and right brain. These moments are when Gemini better grab his creative tools, whatever they are, and get down to the business of creating.

Marilee, the Gemini mother of five mentioned earlier, is married to a Gemini engineer, Don. While the rest of the world was signing up with service providers and discovering the convenience of E-mail, Don and Marilee didn't even have a computer. Then they finally broke down and bought one for the family. It quickly became apparent that seven people vying for time on a single computer wasn't going to work out for anyone. So Don, in one of those *Aha!* moments, decided to take apart the computer, figuring that if he understood how it worked, perhaps he could build another computer for the family.

Don not only figured out how the computer worked, he built one with spare parts bought at computer shows. Then he built another one. And another one. And now everyone in the family has a computer and Don just keeps right on building or improving them. While he is the hardware expert, Marilee has become a software expert. Spurred on by a need, Marilee and Don solved the problem. This is pure Gemini creativity in action.

Diversity is another way the Gemini muse speaks. Actor Liam Neeson has played a wide spectrum of roles in his thirty-one movies, from his Oscar-winning performance as the German who saved Jews in *Schindler's List* to a Scottish hero in *Rob Roy*. Diversity is the name of this muse's game. Give Gemini variety and the muse leaps out of hiding.

Solitude is something every Gemini needs, if only to process all the information he has taken in, to absorb all the new ideas that have flitted through his mind. And in solitude, the muse's voice can be heard in the wind, in the color of the sky, in the whisper of the grass as it grows. In solitude, he must open himself to that voice, then allow it to move through him.

Hilary Hemingway, a Gemini, niece of Ernest Hemingway, and the author of several books, including *Hunting with Hemingway*, has this to say about her muse: "The muse part seems to be that voice we all tap into, the inner voice that tells a narrative story. I go into each book knowing what my subject is, but haven't a clue what the book is really about until it's finished. The best part of writing—for me—is really rewriting. I think of this as carpenter work. In the first draft you have picked the kind of wood you want, in other words, the genre. . . . Cutting it into planks becomes the scenes and then building it into a chair is the story. Writers are the carpenters of language."

GEMINI ACTIVITY ✳ Brainstorming with the Muse

LEFT BRAIN, RIGHT BRAIN

Without giving it too much thought, list ten topics that fascinate you. Quick! Whatever comes to mind.

1. _____
2. _____
3. _____
4. _____
5. _____
6. _____
7. _____
8. _____
9. _____
10. _____

If you didn't give this much thought and just jotted down whatever was foremost in your mind, then your *right brain* made this list. Now look it over carefully. Check the items about which you know little or nothing but would like to know more. List the numbers below.

_____

_____

_____

Listing the numbers was your *left brain* speaking. With the second list, you had to think about your choices.

From this list, select the items that seem most viable to investigate or learn about at this point in your life. List them below.

_____

_____

_____

What you've done is allow your left and right brains to merge. The topics you selected in the last list deserve closer scrutiny. In fact, you may want to sign up for a course, workshop, seminar, online class, or group in which you can learn about the topic you selected. Embrace this new direction. File it away for future reference.

Gemini and Goals

Some years ago, my husband and I led trips for travel writers to the Amazon. To enter this region is the equivalent of plunging headfirst into the unconscious, and it doesn't matter if you're doing it in five-star comfort or in a canoe. The Amazon basin is so vast and untamed that you can't go into it without being changed at some fundamental level.

During those trips, I used to wonder how I would ever use any of it in a novel. How could I possibly describe the river dolphins, pink as bubble gum, in any fictional setting that made sense? These were the creatures, after all, that local mythology said were shape-shifters. On the night of the full moon, they were said to assume human shape and go into villages dressed entirely in white. There they would seduce the most beautiful woman in the village, whisk her away to the river, and impregnate her. We used to joke that the mythology had been created to explain pregnancy out of wedlock. *Oh, the dolphin did it.*

How could I ever hope to create a thriller out of that?

The closest I have come to that goal is a short story called "Rivereño," which was published in an anthology, *Stalkers,* and a novel called *Vanished.* The short story takes place entirely in the Amazon and uses all the mythology about dolphins and shape-shifters. The novel takes place in the United States. The point is that, as a Gemini, nothing you experience is ever lost. You may think you can't remember something clearly, but as soon as you begin to work creatively with the memory, it all comes back.

So today, right this second, take one memory that you have and work creatively with it. If your focus is writing, write something about that memory. If it's art, sketch or paint something that deals with that memory. Whatever means of expression you use, allow the memory to surface by actively engaging your senses. Are there scents or tastes associated with this memory? Are there certain sounds or sights that go along with it? Is touch involved? What emotions are associated with it? Reach back, Gemini. Then move forward.

Affirmation for Gemini

Post this where you'll see it often:

I'm on a creative roll.

Cancer, the Nurturer ♋

We will return to form, pure form. . . .
—*Herman Hesse*

JUNE 22–JULY 22

CARDINAL WATER

SHADOW: DON'T MESS WITH MY SPACE

Creative Theme

She is intimately attuned to emotions—her own and those of other people. No other sign is able to so precisely and effortlessly zip herself into another person's skin, feeling what they feel, hurting and yearning as they hurt and yearn. And when she feels what other people feel, she reaches out to nurture them. It is Cancer's gift and her curse.

Her inner world is often more interesting to her than anything in the outer world. Within, she can move through the labyrinth of her feelings, reliving how she felt about events and experiences in the past, how she feels right this second, and how she may feel tomorrow. She may be a collector of memorabilia, too. These items usually hold such a deep personal significance that she can instantly connect emotionally to the memory surrounding that object.

Cancer's extraordinary memory can be attributed to the Moon, which rules the sign. The Moon is connected to our deepest emotions and our intuitive selves, which is why astrologers say that the Moon never forgets. A familiar scent or taste can send Cancer back in time so completely that she's simply *there* again, wherever the memory was formed. It's as if time doesn't pass for her in the same way that it passes for the rest of us, perhaps because time, like everything else in Cancer's life, is perceived through a subjective lens.

Despite the depth of Cancer's emotions, she avoids emotional confrontations. She becomes evasive, coy, her movements like that of a crab, the animal that symbolizes the sign. She is most comfortable in her private world of symbolism and feeling. This is one of the best reasons for her to funnel her emotional sensitivity into her creativity.

In fact, when she's able to do this the results can be astonishing. Think of Cancerian Tom Hanks in *Philadelphia,* playing an AIDS victim, or in *Cast Away,* playing the FedEx employee stranded on an island. In both roles Hanks was able to disappear inside the character he played and to do it so convincingly that Hanks the actor vanished.

Writer Herman Hesse, a Cancer, is best known for novels that have Eastern themes (*Siddhartha, The Journey to the East*) and themes about the duality of man—*Demian, Steppenwolf, Narcissus and Goldmund,* and *The Glass Bead Game.* In *Siddhartha,* the duality is encompassed in two characters, Siddhartha and Govinda. One represents devotion; the other represents rebellion. In *Demian,* the duality also entails two characters, Demian and Sinclair. Even though Demian is the narrator, he isn't a physical person. He is Sinclair's deepest self, who helps him perceive the magical quality of life. In *Narcissus and Goldmund,* the characters are separate people but represent the opposing tendencies we all have, thought versus action.

The rich symbolism in Hesse's writing tapped into the collective unconscious, the realm of mythology and archetypes that links us all.

In *C. G. Jung and Herman Hesse: A Record of Two Friendships,* Chilean author Miguel Serrano describes his odd friendship with both men during the final years of their lives. Serrano, who traveled halfway around the world to meet them, movingly describes Hesse's penchant for privacy in his last years, certainly a Cancerian trait. Over Hesse's front door was an inscription in German that Serrano later learned was a translation from old Chinese. The gist of it is that when a man is elderly and has done what he came here to do, he's entitled to peace.

This penchant for privacy is endemic to Cancer, even among those

Cancerians who achieve some measure of renown during their lifetimes. Harrison Ford, Meryl Streep, Linda Ronstadt, Carlos Santana, Ringo Starr . . . How much do we really know about any of these people? Other than their press releases, official bios, and public appearances to promote their creative product, they aren't the types who actively seek the limelight. Their photos don't appear regularly in the tabloids. They aren't regular guests on TV talk shows.

When Cancer finds her creative niche, she usually digs in for keeps. The cardinal nature of the sign keeps her focused. When Meryl Streep's lover John Cazale (Fredo in the *Godfather* trilogy) died of bone cancer, she threw herself into her work. To date she has earned eleven Oscar nominations and won two Oscars. Singer Linda Ronstadt, the daughter of a professional musician, has been involved in music most of her life. Her musical styles have been diverse—country rock, country, rock and roll, Latino, soul—but at the heart of it all lies the music, that singular path.

The nurturing theme of the sign comes through most strongly when Cancer has found her path, when she is *in the groove* of her creative passion. Then she nurtures it as dearly as she would her child. She coddles it, listens raptly to her muse, does whatever is necessary to make sure it flourishes and grows.

The nurturing quality inherent in Cancer seems to speak to audiences. I did a very informal survey among friends about Tom Hanks. My question was simple: *What do you think of him?* Invariably people said, *He seems like a really nice guy.* On screen, that nurturing, compassionate energy of Cancer embraces audiences.

The shadow side of Cancer—*Don't mess with my space*—manifests itself as possessiveness about personal space and belongings, clingy behavior, and too much "mothering," which may make other people feel smothered. When Cancer is in her shadow mode, her own needs and desires too easily become subsumed by those of other people. Her imagination seizes on the smallest slights and hassles and blows them completely out of proportion. She scrutinizes her own behavior and feelings and weaves endless scenarios about how she *should have* behaved and felt or how she *will* behave and feel in the future. If she can recognize this process for what it is—a waste of time and energy—then she can usually break the pattern before it's too far along and get back to the business of living.

Cancer needs a creative outlet that satisfies her rich inner life and allows her to use her imagination and her compassion in a positive way. Once she finds her niche, she pursues it with focused diligence.

Cancer Creativity in Ordinary Life

The challenge for Cancer—for all the signs, really—is how to approach daily life in a creative, positive way.

When she first awakes, what thoughts are running through her mind? What's her general mood? Does she leap out of bed, eager to embrace the day, or does she groan and roll over? These first few moments after she awakens are the most revealing of how she approaches her daily life. The more genuinely positive she is when she wakes up, the more creative she will be, the more *in the flow* she will be. And when she's in the flow, she's hooked into the deepest parts of her creative self.

Lynn Grabhorn, in her book *Excuse Me, Your Life Is Waiting,* explores the power of emotion in creating the kind of life we want. "Didn't you ever feel like there's some secret part of you that knows everything there is to know but just doesn't stick its head out? There is. It's that broader, older, wiser part, that vastly expanded extension of each of us that communicates with us in the only way it knows . . . through feelings!" she writes.

In Grabhorn's scheme of things, this wiser self vibrates at a particular frequency. When we're feeling good about everything, "we're vibrating faster, the way we were designed to do. . . . We're in that space where we can get answers and Guidance. . . ." We're also in that space where creativity unfolds with utter ease.

"We get what we focus on," says Grabhorn. Or in Jungian terms, *Like attracts like.* If you awaken in the morning feeling discouraged and focusing on what you *don't* have, on *lack,* then you attract more of the same. If, however, you awaken feeling grateful for everything you have, genuinely grateful, then you attract more to feel grateful about. "From our focus on lack, we can never attract the opposite. To attract whatever it is we want into our life, we have to change our focus, which will change our feelings, which will change our vibrations," says Grabhorn.

Cancer is so proficient with her emotions that it should be easy for her to work herself into an emotional lather—what Grabhorn calls "a warm fuzzy"—about something she wants. Perhaps Cancer has written a book that she would like to sell, but she doesn't have an agent and isn't sure how to go about finding one. The remedy? Cancer should concentrate on feeling so good about what she has written that the emotion originates in her gut. It has to be that deep to produce the emotional high that will attract what she wants.

An affirmation or visualization used along with this "feeling good" exercise is a valuable tool, but the words and visualization must mean something. Simply reciting a phrase or visualizing what she wants isn't enough; it must be backed with emotion, passion, desire.

Once Cancer knows what the emotional high feels like, she can produce it on demand. Then the next time she's beating herself up about something she's done—or not done—or when she's focusing on her problems or on what she doesn't have, she can switch into the feeling-good mode at the blink of an eye. Even if this process sounds simplistic or silly, Cancer should try it for just a week. When she's operating in her shadow mode, she tends to cling to the way she has done things in the past. Even if she's had success at whatever techniques she has used before, she should release them and aim for the feel-good technique. Better yet, read Grabhorn's book. Her methods work.

Cancer Traits That Enhance Creativity

EMOTIONS. Cancer's emotions are her most powerful resource. She's here to experience the vast spectrum of emotional experiences, good and bad. But because of her acute sensitivity, it's all too easy for her to get stuck in negative emotions. Quite often those negative feelings don't even belong to her. She has absorbed them from other people.

Vivian, a psychiatric nurse and a Cancer, works in an atmosphere that is emotionally chaotic and largely negative. To start her day on a positive, upbeat note, she gets up several hours before she has to leave for work, meditates for a brief time to bring in positive energy, walks her dogs, and may even do some tai chi movements to balance her energy. Her focus on surrounding herself with positive energy before she goes to work also functions as a protective device. Even the message on her answering machine reflects this focus: "Please leave a positive message."

If Cancer is working on a specific creative project, then, like Vivian, she might try starting her day with some sort of ritual that gets her creative energy moving in the right direction. A few minutes of meditation might help. She can affirm that all the creative ideas and feelings she needs for a particular project will flow into her without obstacle or impediment. Or she might create some other kind of ritual. The idea here is to immerse herself in the flow of creativity before she starts working on a project, or simply to start her day on the right path.

NURTURING. Cancer's ability to nurture others must also extend toward herself and her own creativity. In fact, she won't be able to nurture others unless she nurtures herself first. If her life is jammed with responsibilities (or even if it's crowded with just the usual responsibilities), she benefits from setting aside time for herself and her creativity.

Author Julia Cameron, in *The Vein of Gold*, notes, "When we are engaged in our creativity, we are in love with our process."

SAFETY AND SECURITY. These issues are important to most Cancers. The trick for Cancer is to nurture safety and security in her own life without draining herself or others in the process. Cancer should strive to create a niche for herself where she feels safe doing her creative work, whatever that is.

One Cancer friend of mine enjoys writing in cafés. She likes the noise, the clattering of plates, the scent of fresh coffee and warm pastries. She sits at a table in a corner of the café and scribbles away on yellow legal pads. She feels safe there, surrounded by scents and sounds and tastes and sights that trigger her creativity.

For Cancer, that niche may be a room in her house, a spot in her backyard, or, even more important for Cancer, near water. The body of water can be as large as the ocean or as small as an indoor fountain. There's something about the sound and smell of water that soothes Cancer's soul.

BELONGING. Vital to Cancer's creative process is a sense of belonging, a kind of tribal identification with some group or place. It may be her family or her friends or even the area where she lives. It may be her home or her belongings. Whatever it is, this tribal identification grounds her.

Cancer may want to expand this tribal identification by joining a group whose interests are similar to hers. If she's a budding writer, perhaps a writers' group is in order. If dance interests her, perhaps she should join a dance class or group. This type of belonging helps with her creative process. It's always helpful to be surrounded by people who can provide feedback and insight on her creativity.

GOOD MEMORY. Cancer's memory is so good that she can easily conjure up emotions from the past that can fuel her creativity. These emotions, whether positive or negative, may make her feel fragile and vulnerable initially. But creativity feeds on the power of memory and when she has strong emotional memories to draw on, her creativity flows.

INTUITION. Cancer's inner wisdom is one of her best guides—if she listens to it and follows its advice.

Cancer Traits That Deplete Creative Energy

CLINGING. When Cancer holds onto anything that has outlived its purpose, her creativity suffers. This includes relationships, habits, behaviors, thought patterns, beliefs, jobs, and belongings. Thanks to her finely honed intuition, however, she usually knows when it's time to release something. The challenge lies in the actual letting go—how to do it, when to do it, can she stand to do it. She should strive to remember that every time she releases something or someone in her life, she's making space for new experiences.

FEAR. We all have fears, so this isn't unique to Cancer. But because she lives so much within her feelings, her fears tend to be amplified. She wakes in the middle of the night, for instance, with a tightness in her chest. Her first thought? *Heart attack.* Forget indigestion, an incipient cold or the flu, or a pulled muscle. She cuts right to the worst possible scenario. Her fear overpowers her. Or it blocks her. Or it creates obstacles, distractions, hysteria, drama.

If she can turn her fears away from herself and redirect them into some type of creative venture, then they serve a purpose. Otherwise they are nothing but a hindrance to the creative process.

How Cancer Can Avoid Creative Burnout

For Cancer, burnout is most likely to occur when her emotional circuits are overloaded. She has absorbed so many emotions and so much energy from the people around her that it's as if she has no energy left for herself. Physical exercise helps: swimming, dancing, walking. Anything physical gets her out of her own head and out into the world.

At times like this, solitude may help, too, as long as she doesn't sit around and brood. If solitude is her choice, she must use the time constructively and creatively.

One of the first short stories I ever read by Cancerian Ernest Hemingway took place on a train. As I read the story, I had the sense that Hemingway was burned out when he'd written it. Then I realized it wasn't fiction at all, that it was true, that Hemingway actually had taken this trip, and that at the end of it he had walked away from his marriage. It struck me that he had done a very Cancerian thing with the experience: he had used it as fodder for his writing. And that's one of Cancer's strongest resources. Everything she experiences and feels can be used creatively, and it's one of the best ways to avoid burnout.

"Writers live twice," says Natalie Goldberg in *Writing Down the Bones.* They live their lives, and then they take bits and pieces of it and write about it.

The same is true of all creative people—and perhaps Cancers most of all.

Summoning the Cancer Muse

Meditation may be the best way for Cancer to summon her muse. This doesn't necessarily mean she has to sit in the lotus position and murmur *Om* for hours on end. Meditation is nothing more than a conscious effort to shift your awareness to a higher state, and there are any number of techniques for doing this.

Before she begins her creative work, she may try sitting quietly for a few moments and ask that her muse come forward and help her out as she works. Or she can take a walk beforehand, noticing the details around her—the color of the trees and grass, the texture of the flowers, the movements of her own body. Julia Cameron has extolled the powers of walking as a creative tool.

Cameron equates the creative process with spirituality, an idea that should appeal to Cancer's mystical soul. In fact, if Cancer can keep this thought in mind as she begins her creative work, the muse will surely rise to the occasion.

A ritual is also a great way to begin Cancer's creative work for the day. It can be something as simple as lighting a candle, incense, or aromatic oil or as complex as cleaning her work area. If she conducts this ritual whenever she's going to begin her creative work, her muse gets used to the idea that the ritual means she's ready to get down to business.

One Cancerian woman I know, a graphic artist, always brings a different plant into her room before she goes to work. The plant usually has brightly colored flowers on it that stimulate her hunger for color and texture. It signals her muse that the workday is about to begin and she had better be in attendance, thank you very much. "It started as a fluke, when I was trying to brighten up my work area. I realized I work better with plants in my room, and I work really well if at least one of the plants is new each day."

The fire muse thrives on action and doing; the earth muse comes alive through physical activities; the air muse is summoned through the intellect; and the water muse is summoned through emotions, intuition, and that which appeals to the senses.

The Cancer Muse Speaks

Symbols are the stuff of Cancer's inner world. She recognizes them for what they are—messages from the unconscious—and instinctively understands how to decipher them. No other sign has quite the appreciation for symbolism and symbolic gestures that Cancer does, so it isn't surprising that her muse often speaks to her in this way.

Perhaps she's thinking about opening her own business. She isn't fully committed yet; she's still toying with the idea. She walks into her local bookstore to check out resources on small businesses, bumps into a bookshelf, and only one book falls off the shelf—the exact book she needs. This incident is an example of her muse shouting to be heard. *Do it,* she yells. *Go for it.*

Cancer buys the book, reads it, and now she's really fired up about opening her business. But her need for security immediately rears up, whispering *Oops, taking risks is dangerous to your financial health.* And her enthusiasm instantly shrivels up.

But risk is exactly what she needs to take to get her muse stirred up and in her court on a regular basis. "Luck is something that happens to us," writes Julia Cameron. "Synchronicity is something that begins in our consciousness. Risk is something we undertake. Luck is passive. We *trigger* synchronicity. We trigger it through risk."

To take a risk involves faith that when you commit to a creative path, you're attracting everything you need for that path to work. *Everything*—money, opportunities, the right people, the right circumstances. "Faith moves mountains," isn't that how the adage goes? Take the leap of faith, Cancer, and watch what happens.

CANCER ACTIVITY ✳ Brainstorming with the Muse

CREATIVE PROJECTS

Each sign is invited to try a creativity activity. Aries made a wheel, Taurus wrote a poem. You, Cancer, are asked to list three creative projects you would like to tackle. It can be anything—redoing the interior of your house, writing a book, taking up painting, learning to play an instrument. Then list two ways for each project in which you might accomplish it.

The Project   *How to Accomplish It*

1. _____   _____

                                                _____

2. _____   _____

                                                _____

3. _____   _____

                                                _____

Keep this list posted where you see it often. Add to it if you want. Expand it to include synchronicities, dreams, and anything else you experience related to your creativity.

Another great activity to stimulate Cancer's creative adrenaline is to go through all those photo albums you've got stashed away in your closet. Select pictures that relate to particular time periods in your life and create collages with them. This brings up old memories and feelings and creates a certain vividness to the pattern of your life that is valuable fodder for creativity.

Cancer and Goals

Most of us have goals, even if we don't articulate them to other people. Some of us have time frames for our goals—by the day, month, year, or even five years. What you're going to do here is to set *creative* goals.

Start with a daily creative goal. If you want to write a book, perhaps your creative goal for a given day would be to write five hundred or a thousand words. Once you've accomplished your daily goals for a week, make weekly goals, then monthly goals. Then project yourself a year into the future and imagine what you would like to be doing a year from now.

Keep your goals flexible. Write them down. Somehow the act of writing them makes them more real. You may even want to have a large five-year goal that expresses your overall creative theme. Brainstorm with your muse. Dream on it. Then get busy.

Affirmation for Cancer

Post this where you'll see it often:

My creative risks pay off.

Leo, the Actor ♌

The next message you need is always
right where you are.
—*Ram Dass*

JULY 23–AUGUST 23

FIXED FIRE

SHADOW: THEY DON'T LIKE ME

Creative Theme

O*h, baby, let the good times roll. And roll. And roll.*
And to Leo, those good times are about performing. He is born
to express his creative thrust somehow, some way. Give him an audience and he'll entertain them. He hungers for the immediacy of this
kind of performance, when he can see and hear his audience, where
the boundaries between them blur, where feedback is immediate.

If there's no audience, he'll perform for himself. In front of a mirror.
At his computer. Singing in the shower. But if solitary performances are
all that Leo has, his creative drive soon withers. Like no other sign, he
needs to be recognized and applauded for his performance. *He needs an
audience.*

It should be no surprise, then, that so many performers are Leos.
Madonna and Mick Jagger typify the sign, performers who are so constantly *on* that we wonder who they are when they are *off*. Does Madonna
ever slop around in jeans and a work shirt? Does she ever go barefoot?
Who is the woman separate from the hype?

Dustin Hoffman and Robert Redford represent a different type of Leo in that they both seem to have a penchant for privacy that isn't evident with Madonna and Jagger. Jacqueline Onassis also had a fierce need for privacy and embodied Leonine dignity and regal presence.

Zelda Fitzgerald, wife of the writer F. Scott Fitzgerald, was also a Leo. But from the time she and Fitzgerald married, all that Leonine creativity failed to find a satisfying outlet and turned in on itself, resulting in Zelda's breakdown and subsequent institutionalization.

Leo's need for applause is evident in his flamboyant style. For some Leos this means flashy clothes or jewelry, a new, shiny car, or a grand home furnished in bold, dramatic colors. For others it may translate into being a publicity seeker or a big mouth or into mannerisms that call attention to himself. When the flamboyance is excessive, it's an example of the Leo who is literally crying out for attention, love, recognition. The main challenge for this kind of Leo is to learn how to celebrate himself even without an audience.

Leo's creativity often finds expression in teaching, which is a kind of performance, with the class as the audience. When I was in college I had an English lit teacher who was a Leo. Students loved his class because we never knew what to expect when we walked in. One day, for instance, we entered a dark classroom, where organ music played. The professor was lying on his back on the desk, his eyes shut, his hands folded on his chest. He held a single rose between his fingers.

None of us knew what it was about, so we simply took our seats and waited to see what would happen. After five or ten minutes, nervous whisperings rippled through the class. Then the professor suddenly sat up, swung his legs over the edge of the desk, and grinned. "I always wondered what it would be like to be at my own funeral."

Leos also make excellent therapists, counselors, and psychologists. Carl Jung, a Leo, is one of the world's best-known psychologists. Despite his numerous books and brilliant contributions to the field, Jung the man was the private kind of Leo. When he was eighty-one he was approached about writing his autobiography. He was hesitant about undertaking the project. As Aniela Jaffé writes in the introduction to that autobiography, *Memories, Dreams, and Reflections,* "Jung's distaste for exposing his personal life to the public eye was well known.

Indeed, he gave his consent only after a long period of doubt and hesitation."

What is particularly interesting about Jung's considerable creative output is what he had to say about writing, a remark that he made to Jaffe after the autobiography was under way. "A book of mine is always a matter of fate. There is something unpredictable about the process of writing, and I cannot prescribe for myself any predetermined course."

He had to feel an inner nudge before he could write. Even more, it had become an "inner necessity" for him to record his earliest memories. When he didn't do it daily, he experienced uncomfortable physical symptoms that ceased as soon as he started writing. This is how Leo's creativity functions when it's unfolding to meet its fullest potential. The creative thrust, whatever its target, moves through him like a force of nature, demanding expression.

Leo can be endlessly creative in work involving children and animals. Both appeal to the playful child in him, and they fulfill an audience function to some extent for him as well. Even people who have Leo Moons, Leo Ascendants, or Leo on one of the four angles of their natal charts tend to have this same approach toward kids and animals. If Leo doesn't have children of his own, there may be a niece, nephew, or even the child of a friend on whom he lavishes attention.

Most Leos tend to be naturally optimistic, with a buoyant disposition. But as soon as someone fails to appreciate or applaud them, as soon as they walk into a room and don't stop the conversation, they're plunged into a bad case of the blues. This is Leo's legendary ego rearing up, the part of him that is so focused on *me me me* that he just can't see beyond it. This is the Leo who is filled with opinions and eager to let you and everyone else know what those opinions are. This is the Leo you sometimes feel like punching in the mouth.

But Leo's friends—his *real* friends—overlook these ego lapses. These friends are in his life because his heart is as large as the outdoors.

Leo Creativity in Ordinary Life

Daily life sometimes seems to lack the pizzazz and flash that Leo craves. So when it's lacking, he creates it. These little dramas can occur anywhere—at work, at home, at school, in the car. *His creativity needs an outlet* and one way or another it will find expression, even in these minidramas that he brings on himself.

"How's your day going, Leo?" a coworker asks innocently.

And Leo tells him, because that's part of the drama, "You wouldn't believe it—on my way to work I got cut off by this jerk in a Corvette and I practically went off the road. There was an accident that held me up for twenty minutes, and then I had to rush to get here on time and a cop stopped me and I got a ticket and I was still late. Then as soon as I get here the boss hands me a new project and tells me it's got to be on his desk by six this evening. My wife's steamed that I won't be home until late, and my son's steamed because I won't be able to make it to his soccer game, and . . ."

Leo should now hit the PAUSE button and take a deep breath. When he woke this morning, his muse probably was running in high gear already, a million ideas racing around in his head. He knew all those ideas would have to wait because he had to go to *work*. And at work he can't be creative, not the way he would like. At work he's putting in time before his *real* life begins. So maybe he woke with a chip on his shoulder, anger in his gut, and well, as the saying goes, "Like attracts like." Sometimes the *like* he'll attract is disguised as the rude driver of a Corvette or a cop who needs his quota of tickets for the month or a demanding and unreasonable boss.

Let's try another scenario. It's the same morning. Leo wakes up with the muse breathing down his neck and races to his computer or darkroom or easel or the room downstairs that he's redecorating. He tackles his creative project and works feverishly for ten or fifteen minutes, works without a cup of coffee first, works without brushing his teeth or combing his hair, works for the sheer love of it. And when he finally glances up at the clock, he knows he's going to be late for work and *it doesn't matter*. The company won't fold if he's late. In fact, the company won't fold if he calls in sick.

In this scenario, he works until noon, then spends the rest of the day figuring finances, trying to estimate how soon he can quit his job to not only pursue his passion but earn his living at it. A major shift has taken place in his thinking. He has just realized that today may be all that's certain, but just in case he lives long enough to see tomorrow, he would like to be doing something he loves.

As Captain Picard on *Star Trek* always says, *"Make it so."* Each day, Leo should make one gesture that expresses his belief in his own talent—belief that comes from *him,* not from other people. He should accompany this gesture with a vivid visualization of himself doing what he loves *all the time.* He should back the visualization with emotion and create affirmations that express what he wants to do. It helps to write down the affirmations in the present tense and post them where he can see them often. If he does this often enough, regularly enough, his unconscious will get the message and go to work to attract what he wants.

Sound simplistic? Not to a Leo, who already trusts the process of life and all its inherent magic.

When Leo already makes his living doing what he loves, his creativity tends to be the focus of his life. Ed Gorman, a full-time writer and a Leo, is married to another writer, Carol Gorman. Ed, like most Leos, is generous. In fact, his generosity is practically legendary among the people who know him. He also seems to know just about every writer in the known universe, yet like so many Leos, he's a private man. Not many of the writers he knows have ever met Ed in person.

He used to be in advertising. Then in the early eighties he sold his first novel and has been writing full-time ever since. His most popular novels—*The Day the Music Died, Wake Up Little Susie,* and *Will You Still Love Me Tomorrow?*—are set in a small Iowa town in the 1950s. "Most of my novels and stories begin the same way, with some sort of emotional confrontation in the offing: man wants to tell off boss, child wants to confront abusive parent, woman wants to get out of marriage. I try to let the story line evolve from that—the boss the man wants to tell off happens to be his father-in-law; the child insists to his schoolteacher that he's being beaten but the parent is careful never to leave marks; the marriage the woman wants to get out of is marriage number four for her. Take familiar situations and give them little twists. One of my idols is John O'Hara, who was a master at doing this."

Leo Traits That Enhance Creativity

FLAIR. Leo has it, a flair that's as natural to him as the act of breathing. The trick is to take a good look at the area where his flair flows the most easily and effortlessly, then ask himself several important questions. Is this an area he would like to pursue creatively? Is it something he can do every day without his passion waning? Is he willing to commit himself to developing this area?

Perhaps he has a flair for color and decorating. Maybe he's the kind of person who can walk into a house and immediately spot what it needs to reflect the personalities of the people who live there. Is decorating something he wants to do professionally? If not, then how can he use this flair for color and decorating in a practical way?

Carl Jung had a flair for understanding symbols. Even though it was part of his work as a psychologist to understand symbolism in his patients' dreams, Jung allowed his natural ability to lead him into a lifelong study of symbolism in mythology and folklore, religion, primitive cultures, and psychic phenomena in general. As a result, he developed his theories of synchronicity and the collective unconscious and created new paradigms in psychology.

COURAGE. The Lion in *The Wizard of Oz* wants to ask the wizard for courage. He believes he's a coward, a disgrace to his species. In the course of his journey with Dorothy, the Tin Man, and the Scarecrow, however, he does many courageous things. When the wizard points out that he already possesses the very quality he's seeking, it's as if a light goes on in the Lion's head. He suddenly realizes he was always courageous, but because he didn't believe it, he acted in accordance with that belief.

The same is true for Leo. His courage is one of his strongest assets—not reckless courage like that of his fire brother Aries, but a dignified type of courage that rises from the very fiber of his being. He should draw on that courage to pursue his creative dream, whatever it may be.

TRUST. Like no other sign, Leo possesses an innate trust in the process of life. This is the kind of trust that allows him to "leap into the void" with absolute certainty that he will land on both feet. "I believe that as I have an impulse to create, the something I want to create has an impulse to want to be born," writes Julia Cameron in *The Right to Write*. To trust this feeling is what Leo does best.

If he wants to write, for example, then he should write instead of talking about it or spending endless hours preparing to do it. By simply setting aside time each day—fifteen minutes, thirty minutes, an hour, whatever he can fit in—he can accomplish his goal. Books are written one word at a time. The same is true for any creative endeavor. There's no time like right now to get started.

Leo Traits That Deplete Creative Energy

EGO. We all have one. We all need it. But ego often gets in the way of creativity. Ego is the voice in Leo's head that whispers, *You can't show that to anyone*. It's the part of him that pouts when his significant other passes judgment on something he has created and finds it wanting. It's the part of him that takes everything personally.

"Forget yourself," advises Natalie Goldberg in *Writing Down the Bones*. "Disappear into everything you look at—a street, a glass of water, a cornfield. . . . Don't worry—your ego will quickly become nervous and stop the ecstasy."

Ego doesn't like to be forgotten or shunted aside. But when you're involved in a creative process, when your right brain is turned on and humming right along, there's no room for ego. Leo needs to find a way to bundle his ego up into a little package and set it aside while he's creating.

I have a friend who wants to be a writer. She's bright, articulate, and fluent in several languages. But when she sits down to write, she can't seem to get past the first sentence before she reads it over again, obsessing about punctuation, word choices, verbs. . . . That's ego, the left brain speaking. If Leo can teach himself to create in the heat of passion, then his ego won't be able to get in the way. Later he can go back and let his ego have its say. Later he can edit or touch up or reshoot.

INSECURITY. All of us have bouts of insecurity, so Leo doesn't have any special claim on this territory. But when his ego is crying out to be noticed, it's usually because his basic insecurities have surfaced. The best way for Leo to lick long-standing insecurities is to make a daily list of everything he likes about himself—from the way he looks and acts and speaks to his talents and special gifts.

"No matter what the problem, the main issue to work on is LOVING THE SELF," writes medical intuitive Louise Hay in *You Can Heal Your Life*. "This is the 'magic wand' that dissolves problems." She advocates an affirmation that gets the process started: *I love and approve of myself*. Leo should say this a dozen times a day, a dozen times an hour. He should say it until his unconscious believes it. He should post it on mirrors, the refrigerator, in his car. Okay, so he's going to feel silly at first, walking around and saying these words out loud. But after a while, he'll start feeling so good about himself that he won't worry about how the words sound.

Hay suggests repeating the affirmation three to four hundred times a day. "Part of self-acceptance is releasing other people's opinions," she says. And if Leo thinks about it, really thinks about it, didn't his insecurities actually start way back in the past, with parents, teachers, or other authority figures telling him repeatedly that he wasn't creative enough to do what he loves? Or perhaps it started with the praise of these authority figures, whose approval and admiration he learned to depend on.

How Leo Can Avoid Creative Burnout

Scenario one: She's a singer. She's doing fifteen gigs in fifteen different cities in just twenty days. She's existing on a few hours of sleep a night and too much coffee, and her nerves are frayed. She knows she's approaching burnout, but short of canceling her tour, she isn't sure what she can do about it.

Now granted, most of us aren't singers on a fifteen-day tour. But intense creativity of any kind is like an internal circuit that has blown wide open. It sweeps us up in a kind of fever that just won't quit. Regardless of the type of creative process Leo is involved in, the remedies for burnout are the same across the board: sleep, balance, physical exercise, and solitude, not necessarily in that order.

Yes, this stuff is just common sense. But when Leo is *on* all the time, he has to take conscious steps to turn *off*.

I went through a period when I would get sick within a few days of mailing off a novel. It was never anything serious—a cold, the flu—but it invariably laid me up for a couple of days. I finally recognized this as a health pattern and went to my Louise Hay book to see what she had to say about whatever symptoms I had. Once I became aware of the pattern, I decided that when I finished my next book, this wasn't going to happen. I was going to give myself time while I was writing the book to see a movie, visit friends, go to the zoo with my daughter, or even take a vacation. I was determined to learn *balance*. After all, part of the creative process is experience, living, filling the creative well.

As soon as I brought my conscious awareness to the pattern, the situation improved. I realized I don't have to get sick just to take time off. I realized I don't have to drive myself relentlessly to get the work done; balance and pacing are far more effective in the long run.

By becoming conscious of your creative patterns, you can work to change the patterns you don't like.

Summoning the Leo Muse

Fire signs are usually too action-oriented to summon their muses through meditation. Where Aries may be able to summon his muse through physical exercise, Leo's best bet is simply to start doing whatever he's going to do. It may help, however, if he performs some small ritual before he gets started.

He can light a candle or a stick of incense. He can tidy up his work area, put on rock and roll music. Whatever the ritual, if he does it each time he's about to get down to the business of creating, his ego will learn that the ritual signals it's time to get out of Leo's way.

He might even give himself a suggestion as he's falling asleep at night that tomorrow's creative work will go well, seamlessly, with everything flowing easily together. If he's really feeling ambitious, he can request dreams that will solve some sort of creative challenge he has.

With practice, Leo will find other ways to summon his muse.

The Leo Muse Speaks

Impulses are the most direct voice of the fire sign muse. Any time Leo has an impulse to do something that breaks his established routine or that is otherwise out of the ordinary for him, he should follow the impulse and see where it leads.

Maybe one day on his way home from work he has an impulse to stop by the bookstore. He just intends to have a cup of coffee and browse. But while he's there he runs into an old friend he hasn't seen in years. They reminisce over coffee, trading stories about everything that has happened in the intervening time.

"Remember when we used to talk about opening our own bookstore?" asks Leo's friend.

He has never forgotten that dream. "We even designed the interior of the store. Sure, I remember."

"Well, I'm doing it. I've rented the space already. . . ."

And suddenly blood pounds in Leo's ears, pounds so loudly he doesn't hear the rest of what his friend says. All he can think about is that his friend has taken a leap of faith that he himself has never quite been able to muster. But the encounter changes something deep inside of Leo. He now realizes that he, too, can take this leap of faith. He, too, can live his dream.

Author Julia Cameron contends that creative people often feel guilty about owning up to their abilities. And guilt may be one thing that holds Leo back. He's afraid that if he shines too brightly, if he's too successful, the people who love him now will no longer love him because they'll be envious. Or disgusted. Or something else equally negative. This goes back to what Louise Hay says, which bears repeating. *"Part of self-acceptance is releasing other people's opinions"* about who and what we are.

Sometimes we delude ourselves into believing that we hold ourselves back because of other people when we're actually holding ourselves back because we're stalling. We are stymied by our fears. If that's the case—and only Leo himself will know for sure—then it's time to listen—really listen—when the muse speaks.

LEO ACTIVITY ✸ Brainstorming with the Muse

HAVING FUN

Your muse loves to play, Leo. So be playful when you brainstorm with her. Do it for fun, without becoming attached to results. Here's an exercise to help you do that.

In the space below, describe one thing you would like to do tomorrow just for fun. Let your imagination run wild. Provide details. Name names. Describe the place, the activity, how you're going to feel. Write it in the present tense, as though it's happening as you're writing it.

Better yet, go out and just enjoy yourself.

Leo and Goals

Setting goals can be difficult for you simply because you are so rooted in the *now*. But if you want to accomplish something creative, goals are essential. They make the creative practical.

What kind of goals? That depends on what type of creative project you're going to tackle. At first it's probably a good idea to make daily goals. *Today I'll start a painting. Today I'll shoot a roll of film down by the dock. Today I'll write two hundred words.* Whatever it is, make the goal realistic. You aren't going to write a thriller in a single afternoon (but if you do, I'd love to know how you did it!), and you probably aren't going to shoot your first documentary in a single afternoon, either. But you might write five fantastic pages on that thriller or shoot twenty minutes of terrific film on that documentary. You never know what's going to unfold once you set a daily goal and work to achieve it.

Once you're attaining your daily goals, set goals a bit further in the future—two weeks, a month, whatever feels comfortable. Keep the goals simple. Instead of setting a goal for yourself that involves ten different areas, pick one area. Write the goal succinctly. Say it aloud.

As a fixed sign, you should avoid falling into the rut of *I have to do this, come hell or high water.* Be flexible with your goals. Experiment with them. Approach them as a creative adventure.

Affirmation for Leo

Post this where you'll see it often:

> *I trust my creative process, and yes, I also love and approve of myself.*

Virgo, the Perfectionist ♍

I think it is our natural birthright to go from
success to success all our life.
—*Louise Hay*

AUGUST 23–SEPTEMBER 22

MUTABLE EARTH

SHADOW: I'M VERY PICKY

Creative Theme

Like Gemini, her head is busy. That steel-trap mind churns through endless pieces of data, collating details, sculpting them according to some inner blueprint of perfection. It's irrelevant whether the rest of us have any idea what she's doing. *She* knows, and that's all that matters.

Virgo and Gemini have some things in common because both are mutable signs ruled by Mercury. Their minds are quick, but their individual focuses are different. Where Gemini collects information and communicates it, Virgo collects information, sifts through it for the details that matter, and attempts to apply it in a practical way. Where Gemini is rarely discriminating in the information she collects, Virgo discriminates every step of the way. Whatever is deemed extraneous is tossed out, forgotten. Somehow her ideal of perfection is never compromised. It's as if it is coded into her genes, and it's this ideal that guides her every action, her every decision, her every interest.

Max Perkins has been called the greatest editor of the twentieth century. This is due, in part, to the fact that he worked with some of the greatest writers of his time—Hemingway, Fitzgerald, Thomas Wolfe, Marjorie Kinan Rawlings, Ring Lardner, and Taylor Caldwell. But his reputation is also due to the fact that his Virgo gift for perfection was finely honed.

In reading about Perkins, whether it's in A. Scott Berg's biography or in correspondence between Perkins and his writers, it's clear that he could see the finished product in a way the writers could not. He could zoom in on what was missing, what needed expansion, and what could be eliminated. He cared about his writers as people first, and he seemed pleased that he could provide them with a service, a notable Virgo trait. The service Perkins performed, of course, was to apply his editing genius to the creative work his writers produced.

Even more than this, Perkins seemed to be a genuinely nice guy. In 1930, the year of Zelda's first breakdown, she'd written several short stories that Fitzgerald sent to his agent, Harold Ober, asking him to forward them to Perkins for possible publication in *Scribner's Magazine*. Perkins's reply is included in Nancy Milford's biography *Zelda*. He begins by praising them: "They show an astonishing power of expression, and have and convey a curiously effective and strange quality." He felt, however, that they were for a limited audience (Virgo's ability to discriminate and discern) and that *Scribner's* would have to pass on them. Then he went on to praise them some more: "Descriptively, they are very rare, and the description is not just description. It has a curious emotional content in itself."

In just a few paragraphs, Perkins both embraced and rejected the stories, no small feat for an editor—unless that editor is a Virgo.

Perkins's job as an editor went well beyond his job description. He lent his writers money and offered moral and emotional support through their personal trials and tragedies. If he felt put upon, he rarely voiced it.

Every Virgo seems to have some special gift or ability that she willingly provides to others, without thought of compensation. Novelist Nancy Pickard, a Virgo, is a genius at interpreting symbols—in dreams, in the *I Ching*, or just in everyday experiences—and offers her insight to any friend who asks. When her writer friends have problems with plots and characters, they E-mail Nancy.

This Virgo trait is usually evident at a young age. From the time my daughter (a double Virgo, Sun and Moon) could crawl, she was caring for wounded animals—insects, frogs, birds, nothing was too small to be noticed if it was hurt. As she has gotten older, this need to help has extended to larger animals. It's not compassion, at least not in the way that we understand it, which motivates a Virgo in this way. It's a need to offer the most perfected part of herself.

Virgos are the absolute masters of details, and when this mastery is applied creatively, the results can be astonishing. In *Dear and Glorious Physician*, Virgo Taylor Caldwell wrote with such vividness about the life of Luke, a disciple of Christ who was a doctor, that the entire era springs to life. *You are there.* In one especially memorable scene, she describes a surgery with detail so convincing that she received letters from physicians asking where she had gotten her information.

Caldwell's grasp of details apparently emerged on intuitive levels as well. When Jess Stearn was researching and writing *The Search for a Soul: Taylor Caldwell's Psychic Lives,* he was blown away by the incredible detail she provided under hypnosis about her alleged past lives in Atlantis, at the time of Christ, and in ancient Greece. One can argue, of course, that since these eras were settings for some of her novels and therefore subjects she'd presumably researched extensively, it makes sense that convincing details about these time periods would emerge under hypnosis. On the other hand, perhaps she was writing from first-hand experience that her soul remembered.

Years ago I attended a library function at which Caldwell was a guest. Stearn's book about her past lives had been published shortly before this, and I asked her about the regression sessions that were conducted for the book. Did *she* believe the material proved that she had lived before? What did she believe about reincarnation?

At that time Caldwell was in her mid-seventies, still writing, still productive, but perhaps feeling the tug of her own mortality. I could almost hear that Virgo mind sifting through the details. She said that she had never been a believer in reincarnation and wasn't sure that she was now, despite the convincing material that had surfaced in the regression sessions. And yet, she said, reincarnation might explain how she was able to write a book about Atlantis when she was eleven or how she was able to write with such authority about surgery during the time of Christ. It might explain her predilection for historical fiction. But really, who could say absolutely whether it was true?

"I'm not as skeptical as I once was," she said, then gave a small, secretive smile and went on to the next question.

In the Virgo scheme of things, the mystery was still unfolding. And that means that until all the facts are in and all the details fit together, Virgo withholds final judgment.

Perhaps this ability to withhold judgment until the facts are in was the source of Max Perkins's genius. Perhaps it's the source of Stephen King's genius. In *Writers Dreaming*, King describes a dream he had when he was just a boy. "I came up a hill and there was a gallows on top of this hill with birds all flying around it. There was a hangman there. He had died, not by having his neck broken, but by strangulation." And typical for King, as he approached the gallows, the dead man grabbed him.

Many years later when he was writing *Salem's Lot*, he knew the story would be about vampires and would involve a spooky old house, and "as I was looking around for a spooky house, a guy who works in the creative department of my brain said, Well, what about that nightmare you had when you were eight or nine years old? Will that work?"

King decided it would work just fine. "I turned the dead man into a guy named Hubie Marston who owned a bad house and pretty much repeated the story of the dream in terms of the way he died." In other words, King didn't *judge* the dream; he *used* it. Taylor Caldwell didn't *judge* the material that emerged in her regressions; she allowed it to simmer, she mulled it over. When my daughter reaches out to an animal or a child in pain, she doesn't *judge*; she reacts. When novelist Nancy Pickard interprets symbols for friends, she doesn't judge; she simply offers her insight.

Virgo is layered. Just when you think you understand her, another layer is stripped away, exposing yet another mystery, another conundrum.

Virgo Creativity in Ordinary Life

All too often, Virgo's shadow—*I'm very picky*—can interfere with her ability to create. She becomes so obsessed with a single detail that she simply can't move forward creatively. In part the blame lies with her ideal of perfection, whatever that might be, and her need to express this ideal.

In many astrology books, Virgo is depicted as analytical, tidy to a fault, and fussy about details. That sounds about as exciting as a plate of lima beans. While these traits may be there on one level, they miss the point. Virgo's so-called shadow is part and parcel of her need to perfect *herself*. This is first and foremost her mission in life, her underlying motive for everything she does, even if she's not consciously aware of it. Her challenge on a daily basis is to develop a deeper awareness of how this ideal of perfection can cause her to be so nitpicky about her creative endeavors that she loses sight of the larger picture. In terms of creative projects, that larger picture includes the completion of the project and some concept of what she is working toward.

Virgo, perhaps more than any other sign, is constantly assailed by her inner critic. *What makes you think you're going to be the one out of a zillion wannabe writers who'll get your book published?* Or your art work or photography exhibited or your quilts taken on consignment? When the inner critic is especially dominant, it attracts experiences and people who seem to support its validity. Author Julia Cameron calls these people "creative snipers."

The snipers, says Cameron, are those people who find other people's creativity threatening because they aren't using their own creative potential to its fullest.

Cameron says the best way to deal with this kind of criticism is to use it in an artistic process of some kind. Make a collage or paint a picture or write a story about it. *Get rid of the way it makes you feel by transmuting the experience.*

Once Virgo begins to deal with the creative snipers in her life, she may find that her inner critic becomes less vocal as well.

As a mutable earth sign, Virgo needs to make her creativity practical. Suppose she's interested in feng shui, the Chinese art of placement. For her mutable Gemini cousin, it might be enough just to read about feng shui, to add that information to her general storehouse of facts and knowledge. But Virgo can't just read about it; she must apply it.

So suddenly she's squaring off the corners of her house. She's painting the front door red, adding purple and violet to her prosperity corner, and rearranging furniture to maximize the flow of chi. Perhaps she discovers she has such a flair for it that she begins to do it for friends, free of charge, because she enjoys it. Word gets around, and pretty soon strangers are calling and asking her to feng shui their homes, their offices, and, oh yes, what does she charge? Virgo eventually finds herself in a new profession.

This is one way the creative process can unfold for Virgo in ordinary life. In fact, to maximize her creative potential, Virgo would be wise to remember two rules: Allow her creative passion to guide her, and silence the inner critic through whatever means necessary.

Virgo Traits That Enhance Creativity

BELIEF. The type of belief we're referring to here is belief in the self. This is probably the most critical factor in enhancing Virgo's creativity. If she's been living her life with her inner critic breathing down her neck, it's imperative that she take steps now to silence the critic and allow herself to believe in her creative abilities.

Author and medical intuitive Louise Hay is an advocate of the power of belief. She discovered this power the hard way—by using her beliefs and her creative abilities to cure herself of vaginal cancer. Her journey through that healing process resulted in a wonderful and practical book, *You Can Heal Your Life,* which sold nearly four million copies and allowed her to start her own publishing company, Hay House. Her premise is wonderfully simple: "What we think about ourselves becomes the truth for us," Hay writes. "I believe that everyone, myself included, is responsible for everything in our lives, the best and the worst. Every thought we think is creating our future. . . ."

When you really think about this statement, its significance is astonishing and liberating. *Things don't just happen to us; nothing is random.* "The thoughts we think and the words we speak create our experiences," Hay continues. "We create the situations, and then we give our power away by blaming the other person for our frustration. . . . What we believe about ourselves and about life becomes true for us."

Hay's belief system can be frightening if you're in the habit of blaming other people for your problems, because these "other people" are mirrors of what you believe. Or, put another way, *like attracts like*. The bottom line for Virgo in terms of beliefs may be as uncomfortable as it is simple. She needs to ask herself: How and when did the inner critic gain such a strong hold on her life?

To banish the critic, repeat: *My point of power lies in the present. I love and approve of myself.* If you say this often enough and back the words with emotion, your critic will lose power over you. Try it, Virgo. Then pass judgment.

HUMOR. Most Virgos I know have a wry sense of humor and a quick wit. Virgo's creative energy is best served by a continued cultivation of humor in her life. Even in the bleakest times, when her creative energy seems blocked and nothing is going the way she planned, a bit of humor goes a long way toward mitigating the negative effects.

RISK-TAKING. To really grasp what this means creatively, take stock of your life as it exists *in this moment*. Are you happy? Do you love the work you do? How's your health? Do you like where you live? What would you like to change about your life? What are you willing to do to make that change?

Even though I'm not a Virgo, I know plenty of them. They are capable of taking *big risks*. How big? A number of years ago, a Virgo man was teaching drama at Yale. He didn't get tenure. After that he wrote for television but found the writing life too uncertain. He decided to become a literary agent.

His first office was in the lobby of a bank. He began to get clients. He was good at what he did, and the money started rolling in. He rented space for his agency, and his clientele continued to grow. He eventually bought a building for his agency, and today it's known as Writers' House.

Al Zuckerman once said that one of the best things that ever happened to him was not getting tenure at Yale. In essence, that event forced him to take a risk. His risk paid off. Today, Writers' House has more than fifteen agents and Zuckerman is one of the top agents in New York. *He found his creative path by taking a risk.*

I can do it, I will do it. That's Virgo's creative battle cry.

Virgo Traits That Deplete Creative Energy

ANALYSIS. It can be difficult for a Virgo *not* to analyze her creative process as it's happening. *The cat ate the rat,* she writes, then stops, puzzling over the sentence. Why does the cat eat the rat? How does the cat eat the rat? In a single gulp or does it take its time? Where is the rat when the cat finds it? Does the rat even belong in the story? By the time Virgo has finished with this sentence, the cat and the rat may not even *be* in the sentence anymore.

Analysis certainly has its place in the creative process, but it should be avoided when Virgo is in the creative flow. Remember Stephen King, in *Writers Dreaming:* "Part of my job as a writer is to dream awake." He notes that at the beginning and end of a morning's writing session, he's aware that he's writing. "But in the middle, the world is gone and I'm able to see better."

If the world is to vanish while Virgo is creating, her analytical voice must be silent.

SELF-CRITICISM. Nothing undermines Virgo's creativity as fast as self-criticism. Even though this trait may be a part of her quest for self-perfection, it is actually detrimental to that quest. Self-criticism is a tricky little devil, however. All too often it is habitual, so ingrained in who Virgo is that she barely notices it when she's criticizing herself.

"The main issue . . . is LOVING THE SELF," writes Louise Hay. "This is the 'magic wand' that dissolves problems. It is nearly impossible to really love yourself unless you have self-approval and self-acceptance."

To banish self-criticism from her life, Virgo has to become aware of how it is reflected in her thoughts and speech. Other people can be helpful in this regard. If Virgo has a significant other or a trusted friend, she might ask that person to identify self-critical remarks when she says them. Then she should try to trace the remarks to their origin. Hay suggests using a mirror when doing affirmations designed to banish self-criticism because mirrors reflect how we feel about ourselves. "They show us clearly the areas to be changed if we want to have a joyous, fulfilling life."

Virgo may initially feel self-conscious when she stands in front of a mirror and says, *"I love and approve of myself."* But the degree of her self-consciousness is the surest measurement of just how deeply she needs the affirmation.

How Virgo Can Avoid Creative Burnout

Virgo can easily become a workaholic and not even notice it until she gets run down or sick or until her creativity becomes blocked. To avoid creative burnout, balance is essential. Periods of intense creative activity should be followed by periods of relaxation.

A regular physical exercise program of some kind is especially beneficial to Virgo. This program, whatever it is, should be something that is fun. Otherwise Virgo may make it a chore. Daily walks can be a good choice. While walking, we tend to notice details that otherwise escape us. There are cracks and slopes in the sidewalk, flowers are pushing up out of the earth, and when did the sky get so blue, anyway? We also become more aware of our bodies—how the muscles in our legs stretch, how our feet negotiate the terrain, how our hearts beat more quickly. Colors are brighter, we breathe more deeply.

If you don't enjoy walking, then try bike riding. Whenever I'm stuck in my writing, I find that a long bike ride takes me far enough outside myself so that I can find my way back into whatever I'm working on. I have forged certain paths on these bike rides and allow my instincts to guide me to the right path for a particular ride. Sometimes I simply need the movement, the scent of the air to clear my head. Other times I need the dirt roads that are lined by horse farms, the wooded areas where a family of stray cats lives, or the back route to another neighborhood, where the tallest pines nod and sway in the breeze.

If Virgo can approach her exercise program as an adventure or as fodder for her creativity, the benefits can be enormous.

Meditation may also be a good way for Virgo to avoid creative burnout. She is nowhere near as restless as Gemini, but whether meditation appeals to her depends to some extent on the type of creative work she does. If she's a writer, then the last thing she may want to do is spend another ten or fifteen minutes sitting in quiet silence. But if her creativity is oriented more toward physical activity, then meditation may be exactly what she needs.

Summoning the Virgo Muse

There's something magical about summoning what we can't see or hear, taste or touch or smell. But how can magic be channeled into something as practical as a time frame without losing the magic itself? For Virgo, the secret lies in habituation. If Virgo has a day job, then perhaps she sets aside a couple of hours every evening for her creative projects. If her creative passion *is* her day job, then she probably has a set time that she works: nine to noon, one to five. Some kind of set schedule encourages the muse to arrive when she's needed and to stick around for the duration. But what happens when Virgo is ready to work and the muse is a no-show?

This is where the summoning comes in. This is when Virgo has to figure out some way to coax the muse out of hiding. Rock and roll music blasting from the CD player might do it. A stick of freshly lit incense, a bouquet of flowers, a few moments of meditative silence, even screaming in desperation might do it. Given the ephemeral nature of creativity, there aren't any hard-and-fast rules about how to summon the muse when she's in hiding. Sometimes, though, if the muse proves to be especially stubborn, Virgo should just set out alone. The creative output on that day may not be her best, but at least she'll get her time in. *She'll follow the schedule.*

But as Stephen King says, the muse has the inspiration. And that's what we're after.

The Virgo Muse Speaks

Sometimes the muse hollers, sometimes she whispers, and sometimes she speaks through other means, rather like a New Age channeler speaking for the dead. In any kind of creative endeavor, the best kind of help from the muse comes when Virgo is *plugged in*—to the novel, the painting, the photograph, the colors, the texture, the role, whatever form her creativity takes. It's what Stephen King means when he says that in the middle of his writing day, the world vanishes. He merges with whatever he's doing. The boundaries between them disappear. Virgo and her muse are one.

We see this kind of merging in great acting, when an actor playing a role ceases to be the actor and becomes the character he or she is playing. We see it in terrific writing—Taylor Caldwell creating her cast of characters in *The Captain and the Kings*. We see it when magician David Copperfield performs before live audiences.

Merging.

The muse also speaks to us through our experiences, good, bad, and in between. Virgo's car breaks down in a bad neighborhood in the middle of the night. Her cell phone is at home. The closest pay phone is four blocks away, and between her and that phone are two thugs with lead pipes. Regardless of how she gets out of this potentially bad situation, her muse is already busy with what she's feeling and experiencing, filing it away for future reference. Two weeks or a year from now, she may be casting around for an idea and her muse will toss out this experience and the emotion—*terror*—that went with it. Virgo seizes it and is off and running.

Creativity doesn't exist in a vacuum. It needs fodder—*stuff*—with which to work. And that stuff is our experiences—not just the experience itself but the emotions, the situations, the people, the thoughts, the whole bundle. So from time to time, Virgo needs to take a break and replenish the well. Then, when the well is replenished, the muse is likely to come on strongly, and that's when the fun really begins.

VIRGO ACTIVITY ✳ Brainstorming with the Muse

DETAILS

Earth cousin Taurus was invited to write a poem. You, Virgo, are asked to list ten details about your creativity. Are you meticulously tidy about your work space? Do you have a particular time of day when you're most creative? Do you like live plants in your work area?

1. _____

2. _____

3. _____

4. _____

5. _____

6. _____

7. _____

8. _____

9. _____

10. _____

What do these details tell you about yourself and your creativity? What do they reveal about your creative goals? Is there something in this list that speaks to you more loudly than anything else? If so, it may hold a vital clue about the direction in which you should move.

Virgo and Goals

Put together a realistic schedule for your creative work. Follow it faithfully for a week. At the end of that week, evaluate the schedule and make whatever changes that are in keeping with how closely you were able to maintain it. Use the new schedule for another week; then evaluate it. Do this for two more weeks, for a total of a month. By then you should have a realistic and practical schedule for your creative projects.

Keep creating!

Affirmation for Virgo

You've probably already guessed what this one is going to be. Post it where you'll see it often:

| *I love and approve of myself.* |

12

Libra, the Harmonizer ♎

One cannot have a single thing without
its opposite.

—*Frank Herbert*

SEPTEMBER 23—OCTOBER 22

CARDINAL AIR

SHADOW: PEACE AT ANY COST

Creative Theme

Put a Libra in a room filled with people who can't agree and watch harmony gradually settle over them. It's the Libran magic at work, the ability to mediate disagreements and bring harmony and peace to virtually any situation.

It's ironic that a sign connected with balance and harmony has such difficulties himself with these very qualities. Not that the rest of us could guess it by looking at him, because Libra has mastered the art of social camouflage. He often speaks quietly and looks like a paragon of calm, centered decorum. It seems that nothing ruffles him. Inside, however, a battle ensues that usually boils down to his most chronic issue: how to maintain harmony without compromising so completely that peace comes at any cost.

His sphere is relationships. He is here to form deep and abiding bonds that allow him to confront and deal with the dichotomies and contradictions in human nature. More than any other sign, he is able to see the many sides of an issue. He understands that your truth and his truth may not be the same, but both are right. He can live with this paradox. It's his gift.

But in living with this paradox, Libra is compelled to find the calm center of his own essence, the place where the paradox can't touch him. Even for a self-aware Libra, this can be a difficult challenge. So Libra seeks distractions in what is aesthetically pleasing and calming to his finely honed senses. Music. Art. Dance. Prose that flows with luscious simplicity. He surrounds himself with beauty—beautiful things, beautiful people. He seeks the calm center of the storm.

F. Scott Fitzgerald was this kind of Libra. At the age of twenty-four, he became an overnight celebrity when *This Side of Paradise* was published. A week later he married the young beauty from Montgomery, Alabama, who would become the love of his life, his inspiration, and his nemesis. Their extravagant lifestyle was hardly conducive to the sort of tranquillity that Fitzgerald's Libra energy craved. They eventually settled in New York City, where he wrote *The Beautiful and the Damned*. After Zelda became pregnant with their first child, they went to Europe, then settled in Saint Paul, Minnesota, for the baby's birth.

Thanks to his raucous lifestyle, Fitzgerald had difficulty finishing his third novel. He began to drink heavily—and yet allegedly wrote only when he was sober—and tension between him and Zelda increased. Zelda, a Leo, apparently craved an attention that Fitzgerald didn't give her. While in Europe again, where he was trying to finish *The Great Gatsby,* she supposedly had an affair with a French naval aviator. This incident, coupled with the commercial disappointment of *Gatsby,* did nothing to strengthen the Fitzgeralds' marriage.

In 1930 Zelda had her first breakdown, and Fitzgerald's novel went on the back burner. He wrote short stories to pay Zelda's bills at the expensive Swiss clinic where she was being treated. In 1932 she suffered a second breakdown and spent the last sixteen years of her life as a resident or an outpatient of mental institutions. But 1932 was also the year that she wrote *Save Me the Waltz,* her autobiographical novel. It resulted in considerable bitterness between the Fitzgeralds because he was using the same material in the novel he was writing at the time, *Tender Is the Night.*

From an astrological point of view, Zelda's breakdowns were desperate attempts to seize the attention she craved (Leo). Fitzgerald, who staked out their marriage as his exclusive creative territory, rationalized his actions on the basis that he was paying for her treatment and writing was his livelihood. He justified it in his own mind—then spent the rest of his life feeling guilty about it. And because he was a Libra, for whom relationships were pivotal to his creative life, it isn't surprising that he fell in love with movie columnist Sheila Graham at precisely the point where his estrangement from Zelda was at its peak.

Frank Herbert, author of the science fiction classic *Dune,* as well as nearly thirty other novels, was also a Libra, but of a very different sort from Fitzgerald. His relationship with his wife of thirty-seven years was, by all accounts, a Libran ideal. She was his first editor and worked for years as an advertising writer so that Herbert could write his fiction. It took him six years to research and write *Dune,* a perfect example of the way Libra's cardinal energy can stay focused on a single track until the desired result is achieved. Ironically, *Dune* was rejected twenty-three times and finally sold for $7,500. To date it has sold more than twenty million copies.

There's a certain duality in Libra's psychological makeup that isn't mentioned very often. It isn't due to a penchant for secrecy or to deviousness but to something simpler: a reluctance to hurt anyone's feelings. As a result, Libra sometimes finds himself paralyzed by indecision. Should he take the new job or keep the old job? He doesn't want to hurt his old boss, with whom he has shared many wonderful years, but the new job offer is very attractive. . . . Or the more usual dilemma: He loves woman A, but he also loves woman B. He can't stand the thought of hurting either of them, so he maintains both relationships, running himself ragged, trying to remember what he has told to which woman.

In some ways Fitzgerald's relationship with Sheila Graham fell into this category. He could never bring himself to divorce Zelda, but he loved Graham and remained involved with her until the end of his life. In Graham's autobiography, *Beloved Infidel,* she makes reference to Fitzgerald's guilt about not being able to marry her because of his obligations to Zelda. This, too, is right in keeping with Libra, a kind of accidental duplicity that stirs deep feelings of guilt and remorse.

When Libra finds his creative path, his focus and clarity may astonish him most of all. Author and past-life researcher Carol Bowman, a Libra, found her creative path through her son, when as a young boy he developed an aversion to loud noises. Instead of taking a conventional route (doctors) to get to the heart of the problem, she took him to a friend who was a professional hypnotist and uncovered a past life in which he had been a black Civil War soldier.

Bowman began to research the area and several years later was invited to appear on *Oprah* with her son and daughter to talk about what she had discovered. This led to her first book, *Children's Past Lives,* a Web site, speaking engagements, and more cases. Her second book, *Return from Heaven,* concerns reincarnation within the same family where there is physical evidence from one life to the next. In other words, your grandmother may return as your daughter or son. The creative path that she discovered serendipitously has become her life's work, an example of how flawlessly this sign's creative energy can unfold when Libra is paying attention.

Libra Creativity in Ordinary Life

The above examples are simply that—examples of how Libra's creative energy can be expressed. None of it implies that Libra is creative only when he is following a particular path. Each of us, regardless of our sign, is inherently creative. We're creative when we rearrange furniture in a room or when we listen to music. We're creative when we relax. This may seem contradictory to society's definition of creativity, but only if we're allowing society to define what creativity means.

When author Julia Cameron is asked by other people what they should "make art about," she tells them: "What you care about; what you think about." When my Libra father was much younger, he used to invent things that made life easier for his family. This was one of the things that he cared and thought about. When my sister was born, for instance, he invented a contraption that would rock her to sleep at night, using an old-fashioned record player and a bassinet. I have a Libra friend who loves diamonds and used to sell them for a living. To this day she can talk about diamonds like no one else I've ever met—their value, their shapes and sizes and colors, their purity, their brilliance.

To be creative on a daily basis, Libra must first identify what he cares and thinks about most of all. Is it social issues? Animals? Kids? Art or music? Gossip? Jewels? Then he has to determine how he can use these interests in a creative way. One Libra woman had spent ten years as the owner of an art gallery. Around the age of fifty-six she discovered that her heart was no longer in it. Her real passion, which had been only a hobby all these years, was horses. So she sold the gallery, and she and her husband moved to their country home full time and began to breed and raise horses.

"Do what you love and the money follows": isn't that the adage? To this, add: Do what you love and your creativity explodes from the starting gate. But for Libra, the trick lies not only in identifying what he loves but in getting out of the way so that his intuition can lead him onto the path where he can fulfill his creative passion.

How does intuition do that? By offering clues.

For the most part we live in a primordial soup of symbols. They speak to us in our dreams, trail us like friendly dogs in our waking lives, and often get right in our face until we acknowledge them. These symbols contain messages that tell us whether we're on the right or wrong track, whether we're hot or cold or lukewarm. Sometimes the message is couched in our relationships with other people—*My boss treats me like a slave, my coworkers ignore me, I don't earn enough money doing what I do.* . . . Well, the message here might be that it's time to get out of your line of work and find something else to do. Chances are the thought has already occurred to you, but fear is holding you back.

Sometimes the message is positive. When Bowman was asked to appear on *Oprah,* she knew she'd received a stamp of approval from the cosmos. *Go for it,* the invitation seemed to be saying. After all, she was just a young woman gathering stories from other mothers about their kids; she was simply looking for common patterns. When Libra John Lennon started jamming with Paul McCartney, Ringo Starr, and George Harrison, he was having fun, doing what he loved. Then doors opened.

Doors opening—perhaps that's the first sign. Things seem to flow effortlessly together. The right people and circumstances appear at the right time. *Click click click*—everything hums right along. The message? You're on the right track.

Sometimes the messages are quite literal. You're doing 75 mph on the freeway, and as you hit the exit ramp your brakes fail. You're fortunate that you get out of it with just a fender bender. What's the message? You're moving too fast in some area of your life. It's time to hit the brakes and smell the roses.

"In a sense," asserts Julia Cameron in *The Right to Write,* "our creativity . . . is . . . a natural function of our soul. . . . What we need is the intention to allow creativity to create through us."

What, exactly, does that mean?

Read on.

Libra Traits That Enhance Creativity

BALANCE. Okay, this one can be challenging for Libra. It's precisely what he's compelled to develop in his life, and it's the one quality he needs above all others in his creativity. In fact, if he has balance, he can have everything else.

For every Libra, *balance* means something different. For one it might mean learning to say no to people who impinge on his creative time. For another it may mean clearer divisions between his professional and personal lives. For yet another it may mean carving out a place to create that is quiet, peaceful, aesthetically pleasing.

Libra's first question to himself should be: *Where is my life lacking balance?*

INDEPENDENCE. Just as cooperative adventure doesn't compute for Aries, independence may not compute for Libra. But at the start of a creative adventure, Libra should strive to work alone. This way he won't be tempted to seek peace at any cost, which usually serves the other person. This adventure is about Libra's creativity, *his* creative space, *his* creative odyssey.

ACKNOWLEDGING YOUR OWN UNIQUENESS. Whatever the thrust of his creativity, Libra has to recognize that he brings a unique slant to the work. Libra Anne Rice brings qualities to her writing that aren't usually associated with the sign: sex, death, immortality. And under a pseudonym, she has written soft- and hard-core porn. In reading Rice, there's no question that she acknowledges the unique slant she brings to vampires, witches, mummies, and other supernatural entities.

"I want each book to be a risk," Rice says in *Writers Dreaming*.

Which brings us to the next trait.

RISK-TAKING. To take a risk means to do something you may not have done before, to extend yourself in some new way, to go out on a limb. For one person this may entail something as simple as traveling alone. For another it may be learning to rock climb. Translated into creativity, a risk may be something like the one Bowman took when she turned a personal story into a larger quest and then went out on a limb and wrote about it. Or it might be the feverish burst of writing that Rice did in the wake of her daughter's death from leukemia, when she wrote *Interview With the Vampire* in a matter of weeks.

Libra has to define what creative risk means to him, and then go for it.

Libra Traits That Deplete Creative Energy

PEACE AT ANY COST. This is probably Libra's weakest point. In his need for harmony, he all too often bends over backward to accommodate everyone else's needs, and his own needs become submerged. Creatively he must follow his own heart and instincts. He must be *selfish.*

Selfish isn't a popular word in our society. It has become equated with greed, arrogance, and other negative qualities. But without a bit of judicious selfishness, creativity falters. Besides, what Libra views as selfish probably isn't, so the best advice on this score is that Libra should carve out time for himself that is free of obligations to anyone else. It's not selfish, Libra. It's *necessary.*

INDECISIVENESS. At the crossroads, Libra panics. It's a quiet panic and may find expression initially in insomnia, lower back pain, or some other chronic ailment. But it's panic nonetheless, and its source is indecision. *Should I write a romance or a mystery? Should I quit my day job? What about health insurance and benefits? No, no, I can't quit my job. But I hate what I'm doing, hate it. . . .*

This endless mental loop strikes at the worst times—in the middle of the night, on the freeway, over breakfast. It's relentless. But as soon as Libra makes a decision, he sleeps like the proverbial baby, his back is fine, he feels better than he has in years. The hard part is the decision. So many choices, so many possible roads to where he hopes to go. Fine. Then he should examine the choices, let his intuition guide him. But one way or another, sooner or later, he must *commit*.

How Libra Can Avoid Creative Burnout

Music. Libra needs a dose of music daily, and it doesn't matter whether it's Mozart or Ottmar Liebart or The Grateful Dead. Whatever his pleasure in music, he should put it on, crank it up, and lose himself.

When I was growing up, one of my greatest pleasures was walking into my father's den in the evening to chat, to get help with homework, or just to spend time with him. I liked his study not only because he was in it but because music was always playing. He's a Libra, and for as long as I can remember, music has been intrinsic to his well-being. Even though he never played an instrument or had any musical training, he finds in music what all Libras seek: peace and balance and harmony. It's his refuge, his solace.

Another way Libra can avoid creative burnout is to visit museums. I've yet to meet a Libra who doesn't feel, at the very least, a kind of awe when he walks through room after room of van Goghs, Picassos, Monets. Art whispers to him. Art calms him. The ballet, opera, a Broadway play, a gourmet meal, an evening with close friends: all these pursuits allow Libra to ground and center himself, to find the calm in the midst of the storm.

Rent a movie or settle in with a book: either of these pursuits can help Libra avoid creative burnout. But they have to be the right movies, the right books. A movie like *Titanic* may appeal to the romantic in Libra. A novel like Graham Greene's *The Comedians* will appeal to the part of him that needs to be taken outside of himself, whisked away to some foreign shore and culture.

If Libra has an exercise routine, great. If not, then he should create one. A brisk walk through a park or some sort of natural sanctuary appeals to Libra's aesthetic side. The solitude is a relief and gives him the opportunity to mull things over, to open his senses to his environment.

For a Libra, walking can be a remedy for everything.

Summoning the Libra Muse

Libra, unlike Aries, doesn't expect the muse to be around when she's most needed. Libra knows the muse is ephemeral and moody, that she is, in fact, a lot like the muse that Sharon Stone plays in *The Muse*. She must be placated, lured, coaxed, cajoled. Libra must bargain with her: *If you come through for me on this project, then I'll give you a two-week vacation.*

Libra, unlike his restless air cousin Gemini, usually enjoys meditation, so this could be one method he uses to summon the muse. But how, exactly, is this done? There are no hard-and-fast rules on this, but here are some suggestions:

* As Libra goes into meditation, he should request communication with his muse. He should ask that ideas and solutions concerning his creative projects come to him with clarity.

* If it helps him to have a mental picture of his muse, then by all means he should request that an appropriate image come to mind as he's meditating. There are no rights and wrongs; the image that comes is unique to him.

* He should meditate for whatever length of time feels comfortable to him.

The muse can be summoned any time Libra is in an altered state of consciousness—as he's falling asleep or waking up, during long walks or some other physical activity, even as he sits down to do his creative work. Some muses seem to like ritual. Libra might consider lighting a stick of incense or making some other ritualistic gesture before he goes to work, a signal that he's ready and is requesting the help of his muse.

As silly as some of this may sound, most creative people have small rituals that mark the beginning of their creative time. One writer I know simply shuts her door. The trick is to be consistent about it. The muse gets the hint.

The Libra Muse Speaks

Libra's muse sometimes announces her arrival through other people. This isn't as much of a contradiction as it may seem. Rick, a Libra electrician who sketched cartoons as a hobby, put together a portfolio of his work to submit to a local newspaper. But he couldn't bring himself to mail it off. He was afraid the sketches weren't good enough, that they would be rejected.

One day at a job he was eating lunch with a couple of other electricians who were talking about how much time they had left until retirement. *Going to buy a camper and see the country . . . Going to buy my farm . . . Going to Europe . . .*

Then one of them asked Rick what he was going to do when he retired. He took a long slow look at each of their faces and it struck him that these men had delayed their dreams, put them all on hold until that *someday* in the future when retirement freed them. He spun the cap on his thermos, got up, and drove downtown to the post office to mail off his sketches. It was as if his muse had spoken directly to him through these other men. He knew he had a chance to live his dream *now*, but not unless he mailed off the sketches. If he didn't at least mail them, he would never know for sure how good or bad a cartoonist he was.

Sometimes the muse is more direct. She rises up inside of Libra shaking herself free of sleep, and gives him exactly what he needs when he needs it. At times like this, it's as if the muse has downloaded the information directly into his brain. It's one of those *Aha!* moments, a creative epiphany, and Libra seizes it and runs with it.

When Libra is blocked creatively, it's a good idea for him to determine whether the source of the problem lies in the way he thinks and feels about his muse. Libra, of course, will insist that he loves his muse, that she is everything any creative person could ever want. But when he's sitting around with his creative friends, he may make remarks like "My muse is out to lunch." Or "My muse went south for the winter." And then his creative friends will nod, "Yeah, I know just what you mean, amigo." And then he wonders why his muse really is out to lunch when he gets down to the business of creating.

Whenever my husband and I catch each other talking negatively about something, we mention it. *What's the belief behind that remark? What are you really saying? What kind of message is that to send out into the universe?* We talk about the universe as though it has ears—and maybe it does. Maybe the law of attraction works so flawlessly that if we really believe that our muses—or our finances, our relationships, our jobs—are messed up, we attract experiences that support this belief.

Like attracts like.

Scary, huh?

LIBRA ACTIVITY ✳ Brainstorming with the Muse

ANOTHER VERSION OF THE WHEEL

Aries was invited to create a wheel that will enable him to be creatively productive the next time he has to get results fast. You're invited to do the same wheel with friends, under relaxed and social conditions. A group of four to six people is best. Consider it a party game. On a blank sheet of paper, everyone in the group is asked to jot down one belief they hold. That's it. One belief. It can be something as simple as *I believe the sky is blue*. Or something personal: *I believe I have talent*. Or *I don't have anything new to say*.

The only rule is that the belief you jot down has to be *true*, as opposed to something you write to impress your friends. Draw twelve lines that radiate in a circle from this phrase. At the end of each line, you're going to write something that relates to this belief. How has it helped or hindered you? Where did this belief originate? In childhood? In your family? With your boss? If the statement is negative, how can you phrase it in a positive way? If the sentence is positive, how can you enhance it?

The idea is that it should be done quickly, without much thought—which means it should be coming from your right brain. When you're finished, put all the papers together, mix them up, then everyone in the group should pick out a sheet and comment on what has been written.

If nothing else, you're going to have some laughs. But if you gain insight into how your deepest beliefs operate in your life, you may be shocked into getting rid of the beliefs that are repressing your creative expression.

Libra and Goals

Here's the deal. Pick a time frame. Two weeks, a month, three months, a year. Longer than five years and less than twenty-four hours probably aren't realistic, but if you feel compelled, use them.

List three creative goals that you have for this time period. They can be about anything. But make them genuine. Be sincere. No one sees this but you.

Give some thought to how you might accomplish these goals. Stick to the broad strokes. If you get too specific, you limit yourself. Post the goals where you'll see them often. They're a form of visualization, a way of letting the universe know that you're serious about your creative life. Then proceed to set these goals in motion by making decisions, by acting on whatever it takes to make these goals happen.

As simplistic as it may sound, the universe—or the higher mind, soul, whatever name you want to use—responds to your desires. It doesn't just respond sometimes; it *always* responds. So as the adage goes, "Be careful what you wish for." You may just get it.

Affirmation for Libra

Post this sentence where you'll see it frequently:

| *It's okay to take time for myself.* |

13

Scorpio, the Transformer ♏

Dying is an art, like everything else. . . .
—*Sylvia Plath*

OCTOBER 23–NOVEMBER 21

FIXED WATER

SHADOW: I'M IN CONTROL

Creative Theme

It's the late fifties. Life is as clear as a black-and-white photograph, with good guys (the United States) and bad guys (Russia) and strict gender roles—men work, and women, for the most part, do not. There are a million taboos, topics that are never mentioned in polite conversation.

Now imagine two young women, both of them aspiring poets. They meet at Boston University, where they are taking Robert Lowell's class in poetry. Lowell has already drawn analogies between the two students' poems, perhaps noting that both women seem to share a fascination with death. As the friendship between these young women deepens, they share intimate details of their individual suicide attempts.

Their bond, this dangerous fascination with death, is incomprehensible to others. But after the younger of the two women killed herself, the other poet told her psychiatrist: "She took something that was mine, that death was mine. Of course it was hers, too. But we swore off it, the way you swear off smoking."

The women, Anne Sexton and Sylvia Plath, were both Scorpios, the most emotionally intense sign in the zodiac. Transformation at the deepest levels: that's what the sign is all about. For these two women, there were no transformations as significant as creativity and death. Of the two, however, Sexton tackled taboos the way few other female writers had at the time. Her poems covered the gamut from abortion to menstruation, incest and adultery, masturbation and drug addiction. These days such topics are the stuff of TV talk shows. But in Sexton's era, propriety didn't look kindly on open discussion of them.

Break the taboos, dig deeper, get to the heart of it—this is the Scorpio terrain. Like Cancer and Pisces, Scorpio *feels* her way through life. Her emotions define who she is. Yet unlike the other two water signs, Scorpio plays for keeps. If she says she comes from a family of spies, then it's probably true. Even more importantly, though, is that whoever she tells this to should realize this confidence is never to be broken. Scorpio is secretive, she demands loyalty from whomever she calls friend, and her creative talents, whatever they are, run deep.

Jodie Foster, Michael Crichton, Bill Gates, Pablo Picasso, Kurt Vonnegut, Margaret Mitchell: What do we really know about any of these people apart from their press releases and their official bios? Nothing. Zip. Nada. What we do know is that their creative talents are considerable and, in some way, smack of *transformation*. Gates *transformed* the way we use technology. With every character Foster plays, she *transforms* some aspect of our understanding about who *we* are. In his books, Crichton has brought us a UFO hidden beneath the ocean (an appropriate symbol for a water sign), dinosaurs, abortion, time travel, and *ER*. Picasso transformed the art world with Cubism, and Vonnegut rewrote our concept of what a novel might be. You get the idea. Scorpio isn't like the rest of us, and hey, guess what? That's fine with her.

When Scorpio finds her creative niche, she may lock herself in a room for months until she gets it right. Until she gets it the way *she* wants it. Until she feels she is in complete control of her creative material. In an interview some years ago, Crichton talked about the way he works. First there's the research. Scorpio is good at this, at digging, at excavating. In Crichton's twelve novels, he has delved into primatology, neurobiology, biophysics, international economics, Nordic history, and genetics. Then there's the writing. When Crichton begins a book, he gets up early to write, breaks for lunch, then returns to his writing. As the book moves forward, he gets up earlier and earlier until he isn't sleeping at all. This keeps the momentum rolling, and he usually finishes the book in about a month.

Crichton, born on October 23, 1942, is a very early Scorpio—his Sun is at 0 degrees and 9 minutes. Being so close to the cusp of another sign, Libra, suggests that he has attributes of both signs. In his memoir *Travels,* this Libra voice emerges several times. During a session with a psychiatrist, the doctor points out that Crichton can't seem to say no to other people.

"In general, you feel you have to please people or they won't like you," the shrink says.

"Right."

This alone is so typically like a Libra that when I first read it, I went onto Crichton's Web site to see if I had gotten his birth date wrong. I hadn't.

"Well," he said, "you're a doctor. If you were presented with a person who never received praise and encouragement, no matter how hard he worked, who felt that what he did was never enough, and who as an adult was very unsure of himself, and easily manipulated by total strangers, what kind of person would you say that was?"

Crichton was stunned with the conclusion that he was an insecure person. "This was a new idea to me, that there might be some things about myself that I couldn't see without outside help. But it obviously was true," Crichton writes.

As I read the book, I found myself dividing Crichton's experiences into Libra moments and Scorpio moments. The Libra felt insecure, didn't want to hurt anyone, and felt ambivalent about many things. The Scorpio sought intense, transformative experiences through travel, spiritual inquiry, meditation, channeling, seeing auras, mystical experiences of all shapes and types. It's this energy that Crichton brings to his fiction.

Scorpio, like Taurus, brings intense focus to her creativity and keeps at it until it's finished. Like Taurus, her polar opposite, she doesn't give up. But because Scorpio's emotions are so vested in the creative process, her focus is often more powerful than Taurus's and probes much more deeply. It's as if she has X-ray eyes that allow her to see and find what others miss entirely. Her intuitive perceptions are so acute and so much a part of who she is that she often makes decisions based on nothing more than a hunch. And if she's ever asked why she made that particular decision, she probably won't be able to articulate it. *She knows why*, and that's all that matters.

Scorpio Creativity in Ordinary Life

Water signs tend to be introspective, but with Scorpio, that introspection can be utterly ruthless and relentless. Even when she's doing something mundane like driving to work or cooking a meal, a part of her is analyzing her emotions, picking them apart, digging for the kernel of absolute truth. Like a bit of sand in an oyster's shell, this process eventually renders a pearl, a creative product of exquisite beauty. But the process that occurs between the scrutiny and the pearl is propelled by Scorpio's bottom line: We are all going to die. Our mortality unites us at the deepest, most transformational levels, and everything else is a moot point.

To people of other signs who approach life in a more lighthearted way, this kind of thought on a daily basis is incomprehensible. This isn't suggesting that Scorpios are morose, depressed people. All this mulling and introspective thought goes on within the privacy of their own skulls. The rest of us perceive it as intensity, charisma, a kind of radiant magnetism. But for the most part we don't have a clue what's really going on inside her.

When Scorpio turns that relentless introspection outward, onto other people, she's asking the same questions of others that she asks of herself: *What motivates him? What secrets does he have? Who is he in the deepest ocean of his private self?* Her intuitive powers are so great that she is capable of finding these answers about others and about herself. Quite often her creative expression reflects this probing.

During Anne Sexton's first psychiatric hospitalization, her psychiatrist encouraged her to resume writing poetry as a kind of therapy. She wrote some of her best poetry then, part of which became her first published book, *To Bedlam and Part Way Back*. Most of Sexton's poems reflect the probing intensity typical of Scorpio. Her fame grew out of her need to understand herself. By turning her emotions inside out, she won a Pulitzer Prize and was the first woman ever awarded an honorary Phi Beta Kappa from Harvard.

Once Scorpio finds her creative path, she often *becomes* that path, so that her life and her work are inseparable.

Creativity, of course, isn't just about acting and dancing, singing and writing and painting. It's about how we create our lives from breath to breath. It doesn't hurt to take stock every so often, either. What does she see in her life? Happiness? Misery? Or something in between? Are her relationships stable and fulfilling? Does she like her job, the place where she lives, the direction in which her life seems to be moving? Her world is a loyal reflection of her beliefs, thoughts, and emotions.

Scorpio usually has an instinctive understanding of what those particular words mean. But in the event that she has never thought about it (unlikely) or has forgotten it (even more unlikely), she should try the experiment at the end of this chapter and prove it to herself.

The shadow part of the sign—*I'm in control*—is probably the most difficult challenge Scorpio faces. Even if she believes that her deepest beliefs create her experiences, she shares the world with six billion other people and, to some extent, shares their reality as well. If she doesn't conquer her shadow—or at least learn to live with it—she invariably reaches a point in her life where circumstances teach her that some things are *not* within her control. Her father is diagnosed with Alzheimer's. Her brother goes to prison. Can she stop any of these events? Can she reverse them? No. She can fold them into the fabric of who she is and attempt to use the experiences creatively.

Pluto, as ruler of Scorpio, demands nothing less than a full commitment to the adage "Know thyself." And know herself Scorpio must, if she is to successfully navigate the minefield of her creative powers.

Scorpio Traits That Enhance Creativity

TRUST. A stranger sits beside Scorpio on the train. She instinctively draws into herself, making it clear by her body language that she wants no contact. An hour later, she's sitting over coffee with a friend and the same withdrawal is there. *Prove yourself,* that withdrawal seems to say. *Show me you're worthy of my friendship and trust.* With stranger or friend, Scorpio has a tough time trusting.

At a dinner party one night I met a young woman who insisted that she was a Libra. But everything about her—the way she moved, talked, and listened, the questions she asked and didn't ask—said that she was a Scorpio. Later that evening I did tarot readings for a couple of the people at the party, including the young woman. Except that I didn't really read for her. I couldn't. I felt completely blocked. I looked at the cards, kept trying to fit them together into a story, but it was as if I were trying to read Chinese. She glanced up with a gleeful expression and said, "I'm hard to read for, aren't I?"

I agreed that she was.

"It's because my life is perfect," she replied, and proceeded to explain the ways in which her life was perfect, all the things I would expect to hear from someone who is fiercely private. I simply picked up the cards and that was that. Later I got her birth information from her mother and did her chart. She was a Scorpio, all right, on the cusp between Libra and Scorpio, and the one thing that struck me was that she had the talent to be a surgeon.

It turned out that she had wanted desperately to go to medical school, but then she'd gotten married and that plan had gone south. I felt that she regretted her decision not to go to medical school and it would become an issue for her again around the age of twenty-eight. Then she would have to act on it or accept that it was one of those roads not taken. I sensed the issue of medical school was a sore point between her and her husband, who hadn't gone to college, because it would create such a wide educational gulf between them. That was the source of the block when I'd tried to read for her.

All trust begins with trusting the self, the most important ingredient in the creative process.

AWARENESS OF THE BODY. Some sort of physical exercise routine is beneficial for Scorpio. Not only does it help her pace herself, but it's an excellent creative device as well.

Scorpio only has to decide on a time frame that fits into her life—

fifteen minutes, thirty, whatever she can carve out—and do it regularly. Once she gets into the rhythm of her routine, she may find that it's essential to her creative process, that she sees and hears things that stimulate her creativity in new ways, that push her in new and different directions. Over a period of days and weeks, her physical stamina will increase, and that, in turn, will increase her creative output.

EXPLORING METAPHOR. Scorpio does this so easily and naturally that she often takes it for granted, which is precisely why it behooves her to develop a conscious awareness of how metaphor functions in her life. What kind of metaphors? Here's a story.

Several years ago a writer friend and I attended a conference at which we were supposed to do a book signing. We felt vaguely uneasy, however, because Mercury was retrograde, a period during which communication often goes awry, travel plans collapse or are suddenly rearranged, and details should be confirmed and double-checked. Despite the fact that we are both astrologers, we hadn't done any of the things you're supposed to do to prevent snafus. But the drive was uneventful, the setting was superb, and our room overlooked the ocean and was spacious enough so we didn't get in each other's way. All the signs auguring a productive weekend seemed to be in place.

The morning after we arrived, Phyllis suddenly came running out of the bathroom, a wet washcloth pressed to a finger. "You won't believe this. I picked up a washcloth off the edge of the sink and a wasp stung me in the finger. What do you think that means?"

"We're going to get stung."

We just looked at each other, I remember, and simultaneously blurted, "They won't have our books."

Sure enough, our books hadn't arrived and never did.

In looking at the incident rationally, it seems, well, *strange*. What are the odds that a wasp would fly into a room on the fourth floor of a hotel and take refuge under a damp washcloth at the edge of the sink? It wasn't there the night before.

One could argue, of course, that the wasp *was* there the night before, perhaps in some other part of the room, and that it landed near the sink because it was thirsty. Maybe it fell asleep under that washcloth and slept through the night and woke at the precise moment that Phyllis picked up the washcloth. Who knows? The only thing that can be said with any certainty is that it stung Phyllis, and when we looked at the *metaphor*—the sting—we immediately knew what it meant.

So what practical use is this kind of metaphor? It didn't change anything; we still didn't have books for our signing. But it reminded us that we hadn't done our part, which was to call ahead to make sure our books would be there.

This is the kind of metaphor that Scorpio understands instinctively. If she can turn her high-resolution consciousness on such events, she will always be one step ahead of the game.

RELINQUISHING CONTROL. Okay, this is a biggie for Scorpio. It may be bigger than the trust issue. Or it may be that the two are so intimately woven together that when she works on one, she is also working on the other.

Every Scorpio has control issues, even when she swears *No way.* They can crop up in any area of her life, and regardless of what that area is, it has an impact on creativity. The Scorpio who tries to control the lives of her adult children, all of whom live three thousand miles from home, is wasting creative energy that might be better used developing her personal interests and passions. The Scorpio who tries to control her significant other may discover eventually that her significant other has gone elsewhere for comfort and love.

The trick is to get at the root of the need to control whatever it is she is trying to control. Fear is usually the culprit, and when it comes right down to it, that fear usually centers around mortality. Perhaps, in her heart of hearts, Scorpio feels that if she can control her immediate world, ultimately she will be able to control death as well. Absurd? Not to a Scorpio.

Scorpio Traits That Deplete Creative Energy

A TASTE FOR REVENGE. Take a look at the symbol that represents Scorpio. See that point at the end of the glyph? That's the scorpion's stinger. When she's angry, when she is beside herself with a smoldering rage, the first thing she thinks about is revenge. Maybe the thought simply flits through her mind, as ephemeral as a whisper of wind. Or maybe it takes root. Astrologically, it's not a coincidence that Scorpio rules the Mafia. In fact, a Scorpio somewhere sometime is probably the source of the adage "Don't get mad. Get even."

Forget getting even. Instead Scorpio should figure out why she attracted circumstances that made her feel she needed to get even in the first place. Then she should turn that need for revenge in more constructive—and creative—directions.

OBSESSION. This can actually work for or against Scorpio. It depends on the object of her obsession and her motive for the obsession. Creative obsession can be a good thing when it's used to help herself or someone else. It can be a bad thing when it's used to destroy something or someone. The terrain is tricky, and only Scorpio can decide what kind of obsession she has and how she's going to use it.

DEFENSIVE BARRIERS. All of us build barriers to protect ourselves from emotional pain and injury. Some of us learn how to do this when we're young, some of us learn how to do it as we grow into adulthood. But only Scorpio is born with the knowledge.

Imagine a castle surrounded by a moat. The castle is Scorpio, the moat is the barrier. What does it say? *You must fight to know me. You must overcome incredible odds to reach my heart. You must come to me, I won't go to you.* When this kind of barrier is applied to the creative arena, it doesn't just falter. *It fails completely.*

If you're a novelist, it means you will never penetrate to the heart of your characters. If you're an artist, it means you will never convey an emotion that will touch other people. If you're a musician, it means you won't ever allow your soul to emerge. Regardless of your creative arena, barriers only stifle your talent.

How Scorpio Can Avoid Creative Burnout

One of the best ways for Scorpio to avoid burnout is to approach creativity as a spiritual practice that can be expressed in anything she does. Whether she is hiking or cooking, running kids to soccer games or reading a book, it is all creative and can be spiritual as well. This kind of approach can relieve Scorpio of the relentless internal pressure she often feels where her creativity is concerned. She realizes it's okay to be creative in whatever she does, that the point is to *live creatively.*

Scorpio, like other water signs, usually enjoys meditation and yoga, and both pursuits are excellent ways to avoid burnout and stimulate creative thought. There are many excellent books on both topics, and Scorpio should experiment with different techniques to find which ones suit her.

My husband teaches Astro-Yoga, a form of yoga in which the various positions are geared to particular Sun signs. The idea in Astro-Yoga is that the body can be used as a vehicle for visualization and affirmation and that by doing postures for particular signs, you can pull in the energy for that sign. If you were in need of creative stimulation, for instance, you would do the series of postures related to Leo, which rules creativity. If you were in need of some nurturing in your life, the series of postures related to Cancer would be just the ticket. If this type of yoga is something that appeals to you, check out *The Lotus and the Stars: The Way of Astro-Yoga* by Rob and Trish MacGregor (Contemporary Books, June 2001).

Summoning the Scorpio Muse

This should be easy for Scorpio to do, as long as she doesn't try to control the process. The best methods involve a touch of ritual. Before she begins her creative work, she might light a stick of incense, meditate for a few minutes, put on her favorite CD, tidy up her work area. The idea is that whatever ritual she uses, she should do it consistently so that her muse connects the ritual to the beginning of her creative work.

Sometimes the muse can be summoned simply by going to work. Even if Scorpio doesn't feel fully plugged into her creativity when she does this, if she pretends that she is, eventually she will be. At times like this the muse is like a spoiled child who doesn't like to be ignored. If she thinks Scorpio is ignoring her, she comes out of hiding loaded up with great ideas and plenty of adrenaline to drive Scorpio forward.

Here are some other effective methods:

✳ As you drift to sleep at night, request that your muse be in attendance when she's needed tomorrow.

✳ Request a dream that will answer some creative problem or challenge that you face. This method can produce astonishing results if you are good at dream recall.

✳ Devote a few minutes to meditation before beginning your creative work.

✳ Take a walk into creativity.

✳ Work late at night or early in the morning, when life is usually quieter. Ideally, the muse will follow whatever schedule Scorpio sets up.

✳ Take outings to get the creative flow going. You might try an outing to your favorite aquarium, park, museum, beach, or anywhere else that you enjoy. One Scorpio I know makes monthly trips to a place that has thousands of live butterflies that often touch down on your head or shoulders as you walk through. "Just being around these beautiful, ephemeral creatures makes me perceive differently," he says.

✳ Go see a movie. There's nothing quite like a good movie to whisk Scorpio out of her own head and into some other world.

The Scorpio Muse Speaks

The muse speaks to us in many different ways, and those ways aren't always as direct as we would like. Although we would prefer her to be constantly whispering in our ear, dictating that best-seller or the great American novel or seizing control of our hands as we sculpt or paint, the muse usually has her own agenda. Sometimes that agenda is to make us work for what we need.

Synchronicities seem to be one of the muse's favorite ways to communicate. Elizabeth, a photographer, was planning a trip to Sedona, Arizona, to photograph the incredible canyon landscapes. For a period of several weeks before she left, it seemed that everywhere she turned she found references to Arizona—in bookstores, on television, in casual conversations with friends. Many of these references dealt with the Hopi Indians. There were so many synchronicities involving the Hopis, in fact, that she altered her itinerary so that most of her time would be spent on the Hopi reservation. These photos turned out to be some of the most compelling in her portfolio.

Scorpio is so naturally intuitive that it shouldn't be a stretch for her to tune in to synchronicities like these and use them to her creative advantage.

SCORPIO ACTIVITY ✳ Brainstorming with the Muse

THE DREAM

Each sign is invited to brainstorm with the muse in a way that capitalizes on the strengths of the particular sign. Your invitation, Scorpio, is to request a dream that relates to your creativity. Transcribe it in the space provided here, and then interpret it.

My Dream

_____

_____

_____

My Interpretation

_____

_____

_____

When you interpret your dream, look for underlying themes, repetitive symbols, and note anything that strikes you at a gut level. This exercise can be done once or many times. It's especially useful when you're feeling lost or creatively blocked.

Scorpio and Goals

Fixed water. The fixed part of the equation means that you can usually stick with any goals you set. You aren't a quitter. The water part of the equation means that the goals that mean the most are those related to your inner life. Without giving it too much thought, jot down three possible projects that you would like to develop creatively. Give yourself a time frame. Then decide how you can best go about achieving at least one of those goals.

Affirmation for Scorpio

Post this where you'll see it often:

I trust the process of life.

14

Sagittarius, the Traveler ♐

. . . all serious daring starts from within.
—*Eudora Welty*

NOVEMBER 22—DECEMBER 21

MUTABLE FIRE

SHADOW: I'M RIGHT, YOU'RE WRONG

Creative Theme

Picture this. A man, a doctor by profession, sits in a room lit only by candlelight and night after night stares into a brass bowl filled with water. Gradually visions unfold before him, a mental movie of future events. Some of the visions are so frightening that he hesitates to reveal them. Other visions are beyond his capacity to grasp, and he realizes they belong to a time so far in the future that he can't possibly interpret what they mean.

When the man finally transcribed the prophecies for the general public, he couched them in four-line poems called quatrains, many of which have survived to the present day. The man was Nostradamus, a Sagittarian who encompasses the true meaning of the sign's theme: *the Traveler.* He literally traveled into other realms to find truth.

As a mutable fire sign, Nostradamus's creativity found expression in many ways. He was not only a doctor and a seer but also an astrologer with a knowledge of alchemy and magic. He absorbed information from every source available to him, and this storehouse of facts, in turn, fueled his visions.

True to the Sagittarian archetype, he saw the big picture—his final predictions extend to 6000 A.D. True to the mutable nature of the sign, he gave two possible versions of the Age of Aquarius that are contradictory. In the first version, nuclear war destroys the planet in 1999, which obviously didn't happen. In the other version, the Aquarian Age marks a golden age of enlightenment.

What is especially interesting about these two possible versions of the Aquarian Age is that Edgar Cayce and other psychics throughout history have predicted that a rise in humanity's consciousness is capable of mitigating the predictions or canceling those predictions altogether, thus creating new paths of probability. This idea bears uncanny parallels to the Many-Worlds theory of quantum physics, which basically says that for every decision we make, individually and collectively, reality splits off into multiple tangents.

In other words, there may be a reality in which the world was devastated by nuclear war, another in which Atlantis rose off the coast of the United States, and yet another in which the British prevailed in the American Revolution or where Gore won the election. Sagittarius is capable of grasping all these tangents even when he doesn't understand how to connect the dots that create this mind-boggling "big picture."

Thanks to Jupiter, the planet that rules Sagittarius, no other sign is as creatively expansive. Even when a Sag (pronounced Saj) has a singular passion, he doesn't confine himself to just *one* thing. He can't. Part of his journey as a Sagittarius is to expand his awareness through experiencing what is unfamiliar and strange. He is a nomad, a philosopher, a spiritual seeker, a student, a stranger in a strange land, searching for Truth, whatever and wherever it might be.

Although Sagittarius isn't considered one of the dual signs like Gemini and Pisces, which are symbolized by two of something, there's nonetheless a curious duality about these individuals. The symbol for Sagittarius is the centaur, a mythological creature that was half horse, half human, and perhaps that's where the duality comes in.

Writer Shirley Jackson is a prime example. As the mother of four kids,

Jackson did carpools, recitals, laundry. But she was also a professional writer, something of an anomaly for a woman in the forties and fifties, and her daily life was erratically divided between these two callings.

Duality also dominated her fiction. On the one hand she wrote light-hearted domestic fiction for women's magazines that accurately reflected her own chaotic life in the midst of the staid, supposedly safe world of a small town in the fifties. On the other hand she wrote fiction that still terrifies us today because it reflects our darkest fears. Her short story "The Lottery," which first appeared in the June 28, 1948, issue of *The New Yorker,* remains one of the most controversial and disturbing pieces of short fiction ever published.

The story's premise is shockingly simple: In a small New England town, the residents gather every year for an annual ritual and celebration, the lottery. This tradition is overseen by the town fathers, whose job is to make sure the whole thing runs smoothly. In the story, the family that wins the lottery goes through another lottery, and that family's mother is stoned to death.

In Jackson's novel *The Haunting of Hill House,* a lonely middle-aged woman who has had many bizarre psychic experiences is invited to spend a weekend at a haunted house. In the end, the spirits of the house become her lover, her friend, her nemesis.

Jackson once wrote to a friend: "I delight in what I fear." As a Sag, she took that fear and expanded it, magnifying it with such genius that her fears ultimately connected with our own. Whatever Sag tackles creatively is born from the place inside of him that yearns to understand where he fits in the bigger scheme of things. In some area of his life, he demands the freedom to explore that particular issue. And that's precisely where the duality is born.

The duality that was so apparent in Jackson's life and work might be defined in twenty-first century terms as the wild man (or woman) versus the conformist. The wild man or woman is the horse half of the centaur; the conformist is the human half. One part of Sag operates from pure raw instinct; the other part is acculturated. One way or another, Sag is invited to experience both.

Sagittarius Creativity in Ordinary Life

In the daily world, Sag seems to come in two broad creative types. The first type has an unquenchable thirst for *experience*. He's the traveler, the truth seeker, the spiritual iconoclast who samples a little of this, a little of that, and tries to fit it into a coherent picture of who he is. He's a Nostradamus or an Arthur C. Clarke or a Beethoven (also Sagittarians). He's Jonathan Swift, showing us through satire where we fail, where we triumph. Or he's Dave Brubeck or Margaret Mead. This first type, in other words, is a wild card, a complete original.

The second creative type is the Sag who falls into the shadow category. He already has experienced everything there is to experience and is therefore in a better position than anyone else to decree what is true and what is correct. He's been there, done that, and he isn't the least bit shy about telling everyone else that his way is the only way. When the Sag shadow is railing fast and furiously, you just want to cover his mouth and shout, *Enough already!*

In the end, creativity in daily life for a Sag comes down to a simple choice—to maintain that almost childlike innocence in his pursuit of experience or to descend into a kind of jaded cynicism that already has all the answers.

Sag shines most brightly when he's doing what he loves. Millie Gemondo, a Sagittarian psychic from West Virginia, tells you what she sees, nothing more, nothing less. And when she doesn't understand what she sees, she tells you that, too, in the hopes that *you,* at any rate, will know what she's talking about. She has lived in West Virginia all her life, but her journeys are the kind that Nostradamus took. By allowing herself the freedom to do what she loves best, she travels into truth through her clairvoyance.

Sagittarians, whether they are celebrities or simply ordinary people going about their lives, understand that the "bigger picture" is the global village, that what affects one affects all. This perception often results in a humanitarian expression of their creativity. Rose, one of my Sag neighbors, has a regular job at a hospital, but her creative passion, the pursuit that brings her the most pleasure, is animals. She volunteers for a pet rescue organization that fosters cats and dogs until they can be placed in suitable homes. Most evenings and weekends she's making the rounds of various neighborhoods, feeding and befriending strays so they can be brought into her organization to be neutered, fostered, and adopted. She considers her volunteer work to be her "real" life, the place where her creativity shines.

In 1985 Sagittarian singer Dionne Warwick teamed up with Gladys Knight, Stevie Wonder, and Elton John to record "That's What Friends Are For," profits to be donated to the American Foundation for AIDS Research. In 1990 she joined other singers at Radio City Music Hall for the That's What Friends Are For benefit and raised $2.5 million for various AIDS organizations. She is also spearheading the development and production of a history book that will detail African and African-American history for use in schools and libraries.

Sagittarius Steven Spielberg does more than bring us movies that we love. In 1994, after filming *Schindler's List,* Spielberg established the Survivors of the Shoah Visual History Foundation. His purpose? To chronicle firsthand accounts of survivors, liberators, rescuers, and other witnesses of the Holocaust. This huge undertaking is intended to create a multimedia archive for use as an educational and research tool. Already it contains more than 200,000 videotapes that include more than 100,000 hours of testimony. If you watched the entire collection straight through, it would take more than thirteen years.

Granted, this kind of undertaking may lie beyond the capabilities of most of us. But it illustrates the humanitarianism of which Sagittarius is capable and the way creativity can be channeled to benefit not only the self but others.

Sagittarius Traits That Enhance Creativity

RISK-TAKING. Sag usually doesn't have any problem taking creative risks, but he can get into ruts just like the rest of us. When this happens, the best route out lies in action, something with which he's intimately familiar. Rather than action just for the sake of action, however, Sag might try creating a strategy, a plan, some sort of blueprint for his creative exploration.

Ian, a Sagittarian teacher whose creative passion was travel, wanted to cram as much of South America as he could into six weeks during his summer break. When he'd gone to Europe the previous summer, he'd had a hotel reservation for his first night in London, his Eurail pass, and his ticket home. Beyond that, he simply went with the flow. He assumed he would do the same thing in South America. Then a friend informed him that getting around South America wasn't as easy as getting around Europe and suggested he do some research if he wanted to make the best use of his time.

It quickly became apparent to Ian that getting around South America wouldn't be as easy as flashing a pass and hopping a train. So for the first time, he actually planned a trip. He *created a strategy and gathered information*. Without realizing it, he drew on the strength of his opposite sign, Gemini, by gathering information before he left on the trip.

By the time he was ready to leave, he knew exactly where he wanted to go, what he wanted to see, and how he would get to all the points in between. And being a Sag through and through, he also left enough unscheduled time in his itinerary so that he could still go where the spirit moved him. The result? He saw everything he had wanted to see and also connected with a local tour company and airline—and is now leading travel tours through Peru as a full-time job.

Sag should set his sights, gather information, set up a time frame, then go for it.

ASKING WHAT-IF QUESTIONS. There's no surer way for Sagittarius to get into a creative frame of mind than to ask himself *what-if* questions.

What if he were at the end of his life and looking back? What regrets might he have for what he didn't do? For the path not taken? *What if* he knew he had only a year to live? What creative projects would he tackle in that year? Not all what-if scenarios have to be so black-and-white, so final. But when Sag presents himself with a what-if scenario like one of the above, his perceptions tend to move in new and unexpected directions.

In Stephen King's memoir on writing, he discusses what-ifs. "The most interesting situations can usually be expressed as a *What-if* question," writes King. Yes, he's talking specifically about writing, but the statement can apply to all kinds of creative endeavors. Perhaps Picasso, while painting one day, asked himself what would happen if he used cubes as a motif. Or perhaps Spielberg, way back when, asked himself, *What if I direct a movie about a lovable alien who befriends a young boy?* Regardless of Sag's creative arena, he probably won't go wrong by asking *What if. . . .*

TRUTH-SEEKING. This can be a touchy area for all of us, not just Sagittarius. In our society, "creative worth" is too often equated with money. If you sit around long enough with a group of writers, for instance, the conversation invariably turns to the subject of advances. *Hey, did you hear Crichton just got a two-book contract for thirty million?* From there the conversation turns a little closer to home, to a writer everyone in the room knows or has met who has just gotten a big six-figure advance for a new novel. It's not Crichton, but hey, it ain't bad. Then these writers feel depressed for a while because they aren't getting six-figure advances and that must mean they aren't that talented or creative. As a result, perhaps a couple of these writers decide *they* are going to write a blockbuster by following *a formula*. This is where the trouble starts.

As many experts on creativity advise, passion shines when we're creating from what *interests* us or moves us or from what we find intriguing, humorous, or mysterious.

It's essential for Sag to create from *his* truth—what Cameron would call his *vein of gold*. To do that, however, Sag has to know what his truth is, has to be able to define it to himself. He can then use that truth to allow his creativity to unfold.

BEING GENUINE. As Sag creates from his personal truth, his creative work becomes more genuine. One trait really can't be separated from the other. If Sag loves animals (and many of them do) and knows a great deal about a particular kind of animal, that animal may be part of his creative genuineness. If one of his interests is fear, as Shirley Jackson's was, perhaps the exploration of fear is part of his genuineness.

The trick lies in mining these passions and interests for nuggets Sag can use in his creative work. My friend Renie Wiley, a Sagittarian, has been mining her passions for years: art (she was a commercial artist at one time); astrology (she can read a chart backward and forward and in-side out); metaphysics (she's a practicing psychic). She's especially adept at reading *patterns*—symbols in an astrology chart, hexagrams in the *I Ching,* the art on tarot cards, or symbols she might pick up clair-voyantly. This is *her* vein of gold.

Sagittarius Traits That Deplete Creative Energy

I'M RIGHT, YOU'RE WRONG ATTITUDE. Here it is again, that shadow. Nothing depletes creative energy faster.

SELF-INDULGENCE. Blame Jupiter. As the planet of success and expansion, Jupiter often urges us to extend ourselves in ways that may not be in our best interests. *Oh, man, does that fudge look great. I'll just have one piece.* Or Sag is shopping and sees something he simply has to have now, this instant. Never mind that he's in debt up to his eyeballs and won't be paid till next week. He charges the item. When this type of self-indulgence appears in creative expression, it often has unpleas-ant repercussions.

I knew a Sagittarian who could build anything—a chair, a table, a house. His carpentry work approached the caliber of great art. He could also fix anything that needed fixing and usually managed to fix it so that it worked better than it had when it was new. He was an entre-preneur by profession, one of those whiz kids who was able to sell in-vestors on an idea and then make things happen.

But he was the most self-indulgent man I've ever known. He was al-ways in debt. Every time he went into a store he saw something he sim-ply had to have that moment. He owned the most expensive cars, electronics, and appliances. He lived in a mansion furnished with only the best of everything. He drank only the most expensive booze, and when things started to collapse in his life, he drank more and more of that expensive booze until he became a full-blown alcoholic. The strict religious beliefs that he had once professed so strongly—and by which he judged everyone else—went straight out the window. He lost his job, his wife, his family, his mansion. His entire life collapsed.

This is the sort of grim scenario that aptly illustrates the expansive nature of Jupiter. The expansiveness works on many levels, and not all of them are positive. But when Sag is aware of the potential pitfalls, he can easily avoid them. What's the adage? "Know yourself."

How Sagittarius Can Avoid Creative Burnout

For some Sagittarians, creativity *is* the remedy to burnout—general burnout. But for the Sag who is creative on a daily basis, by either profession or avocation, there is only one remedy that *really* works: to experience something new and unfamiliar.

If Sag has never climbed a mountain, then a mountain may be in order. If Sag has never set foot in the wilds of Africa, he should renew his passport. If Sag has intended to work on his master's or a doctorate but never found the time, he should head over to the local college and talk with an expert. The idea here is that new experiences replenish the creative well, which in turn replenishes Sag's physical body, which vanquishes burnout.

"We do not learn by our experience but by our capacity for experience," said Buddha. For Sagittarius, this means that the experiences he chooses in order to avoid creative burnout aren't nearly as important as the fact that he is yet capable of and willing to have new experiences. And ultimately this is the source of his genius.

One of my writer friends has a Sagittarian son. He's nearly seventeen and already well traveled. Europe, South America, the Mediterranean, Central America: he's seen them all. When asked about his trips, he offers, "It was great," but not much else. Yet beneath that simple remark, I always sense he's integrating these experiences into who he is and who he is becoming. As his mother says, "By the time he's an adult, he'll be able to handle himself in any situation." That's vital for a Sag.

Summoning the Sagittarius Muse

For Sagittarius, this is fun. He gets to conjure something that he can't see, hear, taste, touch, or smell. He has the chance to do a little magic.

Summoning the muse *is* a bit like pulling the proverbial rabbit out of the hat. But in this case, Sag is both the hat and the rabbit.

Meditation works for some signs, but it's probably too passive for Sag. He needs action, movement, a sense that he's a participant rather than an observer. Walking or running may be exactly what Sag needs to shift his awareness to the place where his muse lives. And that may be the key: Instead of summoning the muse, instead of inviting her to visit in *his own* space, Sag must meet the muse where *she* lives.

So let's assume that Sag decides a daily walk is in order. While he's walking, he might give himself a suggestion that he is going to visit his muse, that he is, in fact, walking into her domain, her territory, her country, her frame of mind. If Sag does this over a period of several days, the muse will get the hint and be ready for him when he arrives.

Summoning the muse should be no more difficult than brushing our teeth in the morning. After all, she really isn't a separate being. She's just us, camouflaged, disguised, playing a game of hide and seek.

The Sagittarius Muse Speaks

Sometimes her voice is so soft it's barely a whisper in the wind. Other times you just can't shut her up—she's ranting, she's raving, she's a high-maintenance babe who just happens to have the answers you need.

Assignment, Sag: rent *The Muse* at your local video store. Sharon Stone plays the part of the muse and she's got it down pat. Once you see the movie, you'll get the message. The muse—*your* muse—is every bit as independent as you are. She has moods, she has worries, she has *issues*. She has a *life*. But even when she's in the midst of *her* life, she doesn't forget you.

Her messages appear in the strangest places, at the strangest times. Sag is blocked. He just can't get moving on his creative project. Every idea he has goes nowhere, and the sheer weight of gravity is pulling him down. Then, while he's out running errands one morning, a song comes on the radio and a refrain catches his attention: *Do what you want to do.* . . . All day this phrase runs through his mind, and finally that night it happens. His muse has shown up, his creative adrenaline rushes through his veins, he is *plugged in.*

Plugged in. Think about that phrase for a moment. We plug our appliances into sockets that power them through the miracle of electricity. We may not have a clue how electricity is generated or how it fires up a light bulb or computer. In the same way, we may not have a clue how the muse works or what language she speaks. But we know when we're *plugged in* to the creative flow. Once Sag experiences this flow, this being *plugged in,* he instinctively knows what to look for and, with a bit of practice, how to make it happen.

No one can explain this to Sag. He must *experience it for himself.* So get busy, Sag. Get plugged in.

SAGITTARIUS ACTIVITY ❋ Brainstorming with the Muse

THE JOURNEY

Aries was asked to draw a circle, Taurus was asked to compose a poem, and you, Sag, are asked to take a journey. This journey doesn't have to be to Greece or some other far-flung corner of the world—although it can be if you have the time and the money. But a twenty-minute walk around your neighborhood will do the job, too.

On this walk, details count. Take it all in—the smell in the air, the people and sights, the colors, everything. The point of this activity is to stimulate your awareness of details—the dots in the big picture—and to connect them by writing about your experience.

Your Walk

_____

_____

_____

_____

_____

_____

Whenever you get into a creative bind, take a walk or a bike ride through a neighborhood you've never been in. Then write about it. Even if your creative arena isn't the written word, the activity does wonders for your creative adrenaline.

Sagittarius and Goals

Since you're so good at seeing the big picture, setting creative goals shouldn't be a problem for you. Choose two or three goals that fall within a short time frame—two weeks, a month—things you can achieve fairly quickly. Set aside time each day to work toward these goals. Once you get into the rhythm of it, you'll be shocked at how quickly your time frame flies by and how easy it really is to accomplish what you set out to do.

At first keep your goals small and simple. As you attain these goals, you'll feel more confident and more willing to create larger and more ambitious goals for yourself.

Affirmation for Sagittarius

Post this where you'll see it often:

> *I create from my truth, no one else's.*

15

Capricorn, the Achiever ♑

Without discipline, there's no life at all.
—*Katharine Hepburn*

DECEMBER 22–JANUARY 19

CARDINAL EARTH

SHADOW: THE END JUSTIFIES THE MEANS

Creative Theme

In 1968 a young man skyrocketed to fame with the publication of his first book. The Vietnam War was in full swing, cops were clubbing demonstrators on the streets of Chicago, Martin Luther King and Robert Kennedy had been assassinated, bell-bottoms and flower children were everywhere. The United States was in the midst of a major paradigm shift, and readers were hungry for the kind of searching this book described, a spiritual quest into the nature of reality and consciousness.

Yet the author never sought the spotlight. His life, like his birth and his death, was veiled in enigma. According to immigration records, Carlos Castaneda was born in Cajamarca, Peru, on Christmas Day in 1925. But according to his ex-wife, Castaneda was born somewhere in Italy on Christmas Day 1935. Either way, that means he was a Capricorn. The thematic heart of this sign—the Achiever—certainly fit Castaneda.

His first book, *The Teachings of Don Juan: A Yaqui Way of Knowledge,* was published by the University of California Press and became a best-seller after an enthusiastic review in the *New York Times*. A mass market edition subsequently sold over 300,000 copies in 1969. Eight books followed between 1971 and 1993, with *The Art of Dreaming* as his last book.

The shadow part of the sign—success at any cost—seems to have bypassed Castaneda entirely. Or did it? Keith Thompson, who interviewed Castaneda for an article in *New Age Journal* in 1994, remarks that "contradiction is the force that ties his (Castaneda's) literary Gordian knot." In other words, if Castaneda had appeared with Oprah and Letterman and made the rounds on the lecture circuit, there would be no mystique. By doing the opposite of what many celebrities do, by maintaining the mysterious aura about who he really was, Castaneda became more famous than he might have otherwise.

But was it a ploy?

The interview took place after weeks of negotiation with Castaneda's agent, who claimed that arranging it was complicated because he had no way of getting in touch with his client. No tape recordings or photos were permitted. This restriction was apparently in keeping with Castaneda's belief that "To slip in and out of different worlds you have to remain inconspicuous. The more you are identified by people's ideas of who you are and how you will act, the greater the constraint on your freedom."

Even though Capricorn may deny it, there's a certain secrecy about people born under this sign. It doesn't seem to be a defensive mechanism, as it is with Scorpio, but simply a penchant for privacy. A great deal has been written about Edgar Allan Poe, another Capricorn, and yet certain areas of his life remain shrouded in mystery. After several months at West Point when he was getting good grades, Poe suddenly racked up sixty infractions in a one-month period and was court-martialed. There's a two-week period after he left West Point when nothing is known about what Poe did or where he was.

J. R. R. Tolkien, author of the *Lord of the Rings* trilogy, is another enigmatic Capricorn. What is known about Tolkien consists of facts: that he was born in South Africa, that he married his childhood sweetheart and had four children, that he was a long-time professor at Oxford. We also know that the trilogy originated in a story he told one of his children about a creature called a Hobbit. But who was Tolkien the man? Who was Castaneda the man? Who was Poe the man? Perhaps one of the traits endemic to creative Capricorns is that who they are is less important than what they create. Or to put it another way, *the message is greater than the messenger.*

The penchant for privacy is mitigated somewhat if the Capricorn Sun is combined with a Leo Moon or a Leo Ascendant. Author Jack London was a Capricorn with a Leo Moon. Astrologically speaking, this may explain why London was a full-blown celebrity in his time, a flamboyant and controversial figure who frequently made the news. It explains why he was such an eloquent speaker. His discipline as a writer, however, came from that Capricorn Sun. He wrote a thousand words every morning, and in sixteen years that amounted to over fifty books, hundreds of short stories, and numerous articles.

Capricorn is a builder, and nowhere is this more apparent than in her creative expression. Tolkien "built" the world of Middle Earth. It has its own language, history, and mythology. Within this world the characters play out archetypal struggles between good and evil. Castaneda also built a world, one in which a shaman and a seeker embark on a heroic quest together. The world Poe built in his creative works is consistently dark and scary.

As a cardinal earth sign, Capricorn values what is practical, tangible, sensible, even in her creative endeavors. In Castaneda's writings, for instance, the mysticism and magic appeal to us at a mythological level. But what makes the books fascinating is how Castaneda continually tries to connect sorcery to the tangible everyday world. He tries hard to make sense of it. His need to understand becomes our own—and that's the real power of Capricorn's creations. We identify with the struggle because it is our struggle, too.

Capricorn Creativity in Ordinary Life

Building anything creative is a step-by-step process. A book is written one word at a time, a painting is created one stroke at a time, a quilt is stitched one square at a time. Capricorn is methodical and consistent in her creativity and is one of the most disciplined signs in the zodiac. When she undertakes a task—any task—she does it with utter commitment and moves forward one step at a time.

Capricorn is an expert at finding what she needs. Whether it's a job, the ideal house, or people who can further her creative goals, she instinctively understands how to back intense desire with active visualization to attract what she wants. Yet if she's asked how she did it, she'll shrug and write it off as luck or being in the right place at the right time. While either of those explanations may be true, they aren't the whole story.

My sister, a divorced Capricorn with three boys, wanted to move from the town where they had lived for fifteen years. They found a house on a lake that they liked, but the commute to work would be considerable for her. "So create a job for yourself in the new town," I told her.

She laughed. "What do you mean by that?"

"Put out feelers, do some networking. That's all it'll take."

Sure enough, within three months of her purchase of the house, she found a job two minutes away. A year later, she and her family wanted to move back to the town where they had lived before. When she expressed misgivings because she didn't have a job in that town, I reminded her that she'd created a job for herself a year ago and could do it again.

So she put out feelers and started to network, and within three weeks she had a job offer from her previous employer for more money. This illustrates Capricorn creativity in action, when intense desire and need bring about change.

Capricorn, of course, isn't the only sign that gets what she wants. But when her focus and ambition are crystallized, she raises the ability to an art form.

The shadow side of the sign, that the end justifies the means, is an easy trap for Capricorn to fall into unless she's careful. It may start when she lies awake at night worrying that her career isn't moving along rapidly enough or in the direction she would like. Or she may lie there thinking about her unfinished novel or screenplay, her incomplete portfolio, her abandoned darkroom. And then a kind of hard-edged determination takes root. This is precisely the point where Capricorn gets into trouble. She parks her emotions and compassion at the curb, and everything but the goal dims in importance. *Naked ambition,* that's what her shadow side is all about.

At some point an internal system of checks and balances kicks in. The more nakedly ambitious she is, the more elusive her goals become. This is when she may find herself fifteen feet from the summit of her achievement and surrounded by obstacles so insurmountable that she's forced to take another, perhaps longer route to reach the top. If she's smart, she uses this detour to reevaluate her creative goals, and quite often her life veers in some new and better direction. If she simply keeps shoving and pushing against the obstacles, she may find herself back at ground zero.

One of the best ways for Capricorn to take stock of where she is and where she would like to go creatively is to begin with her immediate life, her immediate surroundings. Is she satisfied with her personal relationships? Is her job or profession fulfilling? Does she like where she lives? Are her goals clear? Is she drawing on the full potential of her creative gifts? If she answers no to these or similar questions, then here is where she should focus the full force of her attention. In fact, the only rule of thumb she should keep in mind is: *If Capricorn can imagine it, she can make it happen.*

Capricorn Traits That Enhance Creativity

DISCIPLINE. Regardless of what creative goal Capricorn is trying to achieve, discipline is vital to her success. This is something she understands. For Capricorn, though, it's a fine balance. Her tendency is toward overwork, but if she goes too far in that direction she may stumble into the shadow part of the sign. The adage "Know thyself" may be altered slightly to fit Capricorn's need in this area: "Know your limits."

GOAL ORIENTATION. Even though there's a section on goals at the end of this chapter, it bears mentioning here. Capricorn is great at setting and achieving goals, and if there's any point where she doubts this, she should set small bite-size goals for herself, the kind of goals that can be reached in a day or a week. Once she gets into the habit of achieving these smaller goals, the big ones won't be a problem.

AWARENESS OF THE PHYSICAL BODY. Capricorn, like fellow earth sign Taurus and fellow cardinal sign Aries, is a physical sign. Any regular kind of physical exercise benefits Capricorn creatively, particularly when it's done regularly, as a pleasurable pursuit rather than an obligation.

As an earth sign, Capricorn might also respond well to some type of yoga. Yoga's physical benefits are well known: increased flexibility and blood flow and general conditioning of muscles and joints. Yoga is also considered a spiritual practice, and when Capricorn connects with her spiritual beliefs, she also connects with her creative source.

Since Capricorn's knees are the weakest part of her body, jogging or running aren't recommended as a physical routine. But virtually anything else will do—as long as Capricorn enjoys it. Walking is an excellent choice.

EMOTIONAL AWARENESS. Frequent emotional checks are important for Capricorn; her emotions are the barometer for the rest of her life. When she is out of synch with herself, her emotions will tell her how and why. When she's fallen into her shadow mode, her emotions will tell her that, too. Pay attention to your heart, Capricorn. It has stories and secrets to tell.

Also pay attention to your anger, Capricorn. When you're mad, don't hold it in, don't bite your tongue. Say it, express it, scream, beat your fists against the table. *Get it out.* Then get on with the rest of your life.

Capricorn Traits That Deplete Creative Energy

INGRATITUDE. When Capricorn is moving relentlessly forward on her creative path, heat cranked up and ambition burning, she forgets to appreciate all that she has—family, friends, loved ones. Whatever her life, it is *her* life, and gratitude for it should play a part in her daily thoughts.

ACCEPTING RESPONSIBILITY. Capricorn is always willing to accept responsibility. If there's a project at work that needs to be done, Capricorn volunteers or is tapped. If there's something at home that needs to be done, Capricorn gets the job. And pretty soon she's up to her eyeballs in responsibility and can't eke out enough time for her own creative passions.

If she can learn to lighten up on herself, the creative payoff can be tremendous.

LACK OF HUMOR. Blame Capricorn's ruling planet for this one. It's tough to maintain a sense of humor when Saturn, the taskmaster, is breathing down your neck. One way for Capricorn to mitigate the effect of Saturn is to look at the humorous side of everything. Perhaps that's easier said than done, but Capricorn simply has to look at it as one more challenge to be met. Daily doses of laughter put her creative goals in the proper perspective.

If there's nothing in her life at the moment that strikes her as particularly humorous, she might rent comedies from her local video store. Or find columnist Dave Barry's newest book. Better yet, she should track down a copy of Norman Cousins's book *Anatomy of an Illness,* about how he laughed himself back to health after he was diagnosed with a serious illness.

HOLDING GRUDGES. Capricorn, like Scorpio, rarely forgets a slight. The bigger the slight, the more difficult it is to forget, and the more difficult it is to forget, the more difficult it is to forgive. Not forgetting is one thing; not forgiving is something else entirely, a major block to creativity. "We may not know how to forgive, and we may not want to forgive, but the very fact that we say we are willing to forgive begins the healing process," writes author and medical intuitive Louise Hay. Although Hay is referring to health and healing, the statement is true for creativity as well.

Sometimes, to draw fully on her creative gifts, Capricorn must forgive herself first of all.

How Capricorn Can Avoid Creative Burnout

Creative burnout for Capricorn occurs when she is physically exhausted and emotionally drained. It often goes back to the responsibility she has assumed, leaving little time for herself and her creative endeavors. This personal time is such an important facet of her creative health that to ignore it invites problems and complications.

"When I'm really feeling overwhelmed, I get off by myself," says Elena, a Capricorn dance teacher. "I head to the beach with a book, take a hike with my dog, or simply find a shady spot outside and chill for a while. When I get off into nature by myself, I feel my creative reservoirs filling up."

Jeff, a Capricorn writer, takes long naps when he's burned out. "When I'm physically exhausted or emotionally whipped, I stretch out in a hammock with a book and eventually just fall asleep. During these naps, I have the most amazing dreams, and in some weird way, these dreams replenish my creativity."

Dreams can be valuable creative tools regardless of your sign. Writer Reynolds Price says that sometimes when he doesn't know what he's going to write the next day, he simply goes to sleep—"and the next morning the answer will be there," he says in *Writers Dreaming*.

"I think dreams are important in terms of how they assist you creatively," says writer and artist Maurice Sendak. "They can help clarify an emotional condition."

The metaphysics of dreaming and its link with creativity are perhaps best expressed by Seth, the entity for whom author and mystic Jane Roberts spoke over twenty years. "Some inventors, writers, scientists, artists, who are used to dealing with creative material directly, are quite aware of the fact that many of their productive ideas came from the dream condition."

Once Capricorn trains herself to remember her dreams, she can request dreams that provide solutions to her creative challenges and dilemmas. She can use her dreams to tap into her creative well. Creativity is all about opening up the channel between you and your muse. Try different techniques. There's no right or wrong way.

Summoning the Capricorn Muse

As an earth sign, Capricorn may have trouble with the concept of summoning something that has no basis in physical reality. But if she thinks of the muse as some force or energy within herself, the concept is easier to work with.

To summon her muse, Capricorn has to do the most difficult thing of all: find her passion. For Tolkien, it was storytelling. For Joan Baez, it's singing. For Jack London, writing was another expression of the way he lived his life, with zest and a sense of profound adventure. For Paul Cézanne, the passion was painting. These passions may seem obvious, but in every instance the Capricorn in question had to find that niche.

For Capricorn, the passion may be folded into some hobby or interest that she pursues in her spare time. For one Capricorn woman I knew, this passion was rare books. She collected them, read them, and knew more about them than most bookstore owners. She wanted very much to go into business for herself, but fear that she wouldn't succeed held her back. *She didn't believe in herself.*

Once Capricorn has identified her passion and believes in herself deeply enough to reach for her dream, summoning the muse is fairly easy. Some sort of consistent ritual can bring the muse out of hiding; done consistently over time, it signals the muse that Capricorn is committed and ready to get right down to it.

The ritual can be as simple as putting on her favorite music or something as complex as prayer or meditation. Any activity that puts Capricorn in an altered state of mind can be a vehicle for her creativity. As author Julia Cameron notes, creativity needs two things: stamina and openness.

Capricorn has plenty of stamina. But how open is she? This depends on her belief system. "[W]e are closed or blocked when we have belief systems that hamper the flow," says Cameron. If Capricorn's belief system includes a fundamental lack of belief in her own creativity, then her muse may stay hidden regardless of how many rituals she performs. Sometimes this lack of belief stems from childhood, when Capricorn was told that she wasn't creative or when she got the idea from parents or other authority figures that creativity was "dangerous." Or wild and unpredictable. Or that decent people don't make a living like that.

Before Capricorn can successfully summon her muse, she should know what she believes about creativity and specifically about *her* creativity. If negatives show up in those beliefs, she needs to vanquish them. She can go the expensive and time-consuming route—therapy—or she can use alternative methods like affirmations, visualizations, general belief work—or she can *pretend*. She can *pretend* she believes in herself. She can *pretend* by pursuing her creative passion. If she pretends long enough, her inner censor eventually gets the hint and recedes.

The Capricorn Muse Speaks

As a cardinal sign, Capricorn may hear her muse speak most directly through impulses, just like Aries and Cancer. Fine, impulses. But what does that have to do with the muse speaking? Everything.

An impulse is a signal to do something different. In *Cast Away* the final scene shows Tom Hanks at a crossroad in the middle of nowhere. Fields stretch in every direction. The sky is so blue your heart aches. The world seems ripe with possibility. Hanks glances up one road and down another, considering his options. Which direction should he take? Which *possibility* should he pursue? We are left with the sense that he will follow the impulse that will connect him with the person who kept him going during the four years of his isolation. We are left with *hope*.

When we follow an impulse, we're answering a summons from the muse—or the soul or the higher, wiser self. Muse. Spirit. Divine Self. Buddha or Moses. It all amounts to the same *source*.

An impulse is an invitation to plug into your creativity, to be daring and adventurous.

But I'm not the adventurous type, laments Capricorn.

You're not being asked to climb mountains here. All you have to do is follow an impulse. Perhaps on the way to work tomorrow, you'll have an impulse to take a different route. Instead of squashing the impulse, decide to follow it. Along this new route, you may see or experience something that urges you to perceive in a different way. That perception may open a new door to your creativity. Sometimes it's just that simple.

If following an impulse is too adventurous, then you might get in the car and just start driving, noticing the landscape, the weather, listening to music. This distracts your left brain and allows you to hear the muse when she speaks.

Then there are dreams, one of the muse's favorite methods of communication. I keep a notebook next to the bed with a pen that has a battery-powered light in it. Over the years I've dreamed bits and pieces of plots and characters, found ideas, opening sentences, and endings to novels. Once I woke with a single word running through my head that turned out to be the title of a novel I hadn't written yet.

While in an altered state of consciousness, author and mystic Jane Roberts (a triple earth sign) used to find herself in a place she called a "psychic library." She was able to access information contained in this library, and a lot of material from her book *Psychic Politics* came from this place. When I was stuck while writing a novel some years ago, I decided to try the psychic library idea in a dream state. I gave myself the suggestion that I would go to a library in a probable future where the book I was struggling with was already written.

In a dream, I found the library and located the shelf with my published books. I found the novel I was working on and opened it to the section that was giving me trouble. As soon as I tried to read what was written, though, everything blurred and I lost track of the rest of the dream. The next day, however, I was able to breeze through the section that had tied me in knots. Now, whenever I'm in need of a new idea or having trouble with a book, I simply give myself the suggestion to go to the library.

Mine your dreams, Capricorn.

CAPRICORN ACTIVITY ✸ **Brainstorming with the Muse**

ONE GOAL

At the top of a blank sheet of paper or using the space provided below, jot down one goal that relates to your creativity. Then set a timer for sixty seconds and quickly list everything that comes to mind about how you might achieve this goal. Don't ponder, don't mull it over, just make a list. By doing the list quickly, your right brain—your muse—has a chance to speak.

Now look over the list. Each day try to implement at least one item on the list.

My Goal

_____

My List

1. _____

2. _____

3. _____

4. _____

5. _____

Capricorn and Goals

Capricorn people tend to be goal-oriented, but it's helpful to write down your goals and give yourself a time frame for achieving them. In the beginning create small goals for yourself with small time frames. *Today I'll write five hundred words on my novel. Today I'll spend thirty minutes brainstorming for ideas.*

As you achieve these small goals, create larger goals with larger time frames. Creativity needs structure, but the structure can't be so rigid that the creativity gets edged out. Bring a sense of play to the process.

Affirmation for Capricorn

Post this affirmation where you'll see it frequently:

| *My creativity unfolds smoothly, effortlessly.* |

16

Aquarius, the Paradigm-Buster ≈

We are all, in our consciousness, one.
—*Joseph Campbell*

JANUARY 20–FEBRUARY 18

FIXED AIR

SHADOW: MY MIND IS EVERYTHING

Creative Theme

Now that the Age of Aquarius is finally here, most Aquarians should feel right at home in the world. We are in the midst of a collective paradigm shift in nearly every segment of society, from health care to education, finances, science, spirituality, and communications. We are learning to create and live our personal myths, to understand our spiritual needs and the role those needs play in the rise of global consciousness. Our personal and collective belief systems are changing, and as the old paradigms collapse, the new ones are rising from the ashes. In short, the world is rapidly catching up to the Aquarius vision.

Aquarius has always been a paradigm-buster. He sees the way something is and says, *I don't believe it just because the experts say it's true. So I'm going to find my own truth.* Then he does exactly that. Or he doesn't like what he sees and sets out to change it. Or he finds a better way of doing something. This attitude is true across the board for Aquarians, regardless of their creative endeavors and passions. Just look at some of the people in the lineup: Abe Lincoln, Thomas Edison, Amadeus

Mozart, Clark Gable, Charles Darwin, Jules Verne, Toni Morrison, Charles Lindbergh.

Aquarius is the true visionary of the zodiac, and in some area of his life, that visionary talent spells genius. Linda Smith, an Aquarian friend of mine, has a genius for seeing through other people's camouflage. Phyllis Vega, an Aquarian writer and astrologer, has a genius for taking complex abstractions and making them easy to understand. Editor and Aquarian Kate Duffy has a gift for knowing what works or doesn't work in a novel, and she's a whiz with titles. "It's like having perfect pitch," she says. "But my pitch is with titles rather than notes."

The theme for Aquarius actually encompasses much more than paradigm-busting. After all, the point of busting a paradigm is so that something bigger and better can take its place. For Aquarius, a new belief system must be better for everyone—not just a select few. It must serve the larger tribe of humanity. Unless it does, paradigm-busting is just empty rebellion, like that of the revolutionary who continues to fight old battles long after the war has been lost.

This inner commitment to humanity is at work when Aquarius hears that the friend of a friend—someone he has never met—is living on the streets of Manhattan, and sends a check to help out. This same commitment is operating when Aquarius becomes a vegetarian and a spokesperson for animal rights. In whatever area Aquarius commits himself to the larger world, it must first make sense to him mentally (the air), and then his commitment is usually total (the fixed nature of the sign).

Aquarius is always easy to talk to and, like Gemini, can talk about a great many things. He enjoys lively exchanges about ideas and concepts, ideals and creativity. His depth of knowledge is usually much greater than Gemini's, however, and there's a certain eccentric edge to everything he says. This eccentricity is due to Uranus, the sign's ruling planet, and is often evident from a very young age. Before Aquarius hits high school, the eccentricities are likely to show up in appearance— streaks of green and pink in the hair, for instance—or in behavior, as in rebellion for the sake of rebellion. Later on, they may be manifest as unusual interests.

Jules Verne, for instance, ran away from home when he was a young boy so that he could work on a merchant ship. He was caught and returned to his parents, but his rebellion didn't stop there. When he was in law school in Paris, he decided the theater interested him more and that law wasn't for him. His father found out and refused to pay his expenses in Paris, so Verne turned to writing stories to support himself. His eclectic and restless intellect devoured topics as diverse as geology and astronomy, all of which eventually went into the books for which we know him best: *Twenty Thousand Leagues under the Sea*, *A Voyage to the Center of the Earth*, *Around the World in Eighty Days*.

Charles Darwin went off to medical school at the age of sixteen but was so repelled by the sight of surgery performed without anesthesia that he left to become a clergyman. Even though he received a degree, the most influential event in his life was an invitation to serve as an unpaid naturalist on the HMS *Beagle* for a five-year scientific expedition to the Pacific coast of South America. He was twenty-two years old at the time. The research from his voyage formed the basis for his book *Origin of Species*, which in true Aquarian fashion caused considerable controversy and transformed the scientific thought of his era.

With both men, early rebellion led them to their creative path. This isn't to say that every Aquarian has to rebel to find his creative passion. But most Aquarians find and define their creative path by breaking with the tradition in which they are raised.

Yet, as a fixed sign, Aquarius can be as stubborn as Taurus about changing his opinions and beliefs. He must be convinced intellectually that the new opinion or belief makes more sense than the old one. This is the point where Aquarius may move into his shadow: *My mind is everything. I already have the answers I need*. The irony is that for a sign so visionary and oriented toward the future, there can be deep pockets of resistance to new ideas. If Aquarius notices these pockets of resistance in himself, it's to his advantage to explore them and uncover their source because they could prove to be blocks to his creativity.

Aquarius Creativity in Ordinary Life

Freedom is Aquarius's prime directive, as intrinsic to his life as breathing. He needs complete freedom to explore what interests him, to find his own path, and to express his creativity in his own way. It behooves Aquarius to be as clear as possible on that score. This may entail taking a risk—quitting a dead-end job or a job that simply doesn't interest him, or ending a relationship. It may mean he has to carve time out of each day for himself and his creative endeavors. He may have to rearrange his life so that he's able to use his time more effectively. He may have to dig in his heels and stubbornly refuse to allow people and other responsibilities to infringe on his creative time.

When writer Toni Morrison worked as a full-time editor at Random House, she used to write in the evenings, after her sons had gone to bed. Her first project was to expand a short story she'd written several years earlier for a small writer's group to which she belonged. *The Bluest Eye* was published in 1970 to critical acclaim, but wasn't commercially successful. Three years later her second novel, *Sula,* was published. It focused on a friendship between two adult black women and in 1975 was nominated for the National Book Award for fiction.

Morrison left Random House in 1983, after nearly twenty years there, and was named the Albert Schweitzer Professor of the Humanities at the State University of New York in Albany. While at SUNY, she wrote her first play and her novel *Beloved,* which won her the Pulitzer Prize and was also a best-seller. In 1987 she was named the Robert F. Goheen Professor in the Council of Humanities at Princeton, the first black woman writer to ever hold a named chair at an Ivy League university. Here she began her next novel, *Jazz,* which was published in 1992. A year later Morrison won the Nobel Prize in Literature, another first as she was the first black woman to ever win in that category.

By following the pulse of her own creative spirit, Morrison is living the creative theme of her birth sign.

Aquarius tends to be an excellent strategist. Once he finds his creative path, he lays down a strategy for moving forward along that path. He may not do this in a literal sense, plotting everything from A to Z on a sheet of paper, but the strategy is bright and vivid in his own mind, and that's what counts. At his best he is constantly absorbing, taking in anything and everything that might be useful to him in his creative life. He is doing what writer Jack Kerouac advised: "Be submissive to everything. Open. Listening."

Aquarius, when he is open and receptive in the way Kerouac meant, absorbs knowledge and information just as Gemini does. He becomes a sponge, soaking up information from everything and everyone who surrounds him. But Aquarius and Gemini use the information differently.

In college I had an Aquarian roommate who created vivid mental images just by the way she spoke. One night while we were out walking, we got into one of our esoteric discussions about life and death, life after death, life on other planets, all the usual cosmic biggies. She suddenly hunched over and held her right hand as though it were clutching something. She emitted an odd little cackle. "Who am I?" she asked.

Against the street her stooped shadow looked ancient, like that of some wizened old woman with tales to tell. "Beats me," I replied. "Who are you?"

"Diogenes in search of an honest man. I'm holding a lantern that lights my way. That's us—now and fifty years from now."

The connection was pure Aquarius, the abstract made tangible. I still see her, hunched in the moonlit dark, cackling, holding that imaginary lantern. I expect this image will be with me until the end of my life.

Aquarius, despite his forward, progressive thinking, has a steel-trap memory capable of conjuring up vivid detail about an opera he saw with his parents when he was nine years old or the scents in his grandmother's house when he was five. It's the vividness of these memories that he calls on to create.

Aquarius Traits That Enhance Creativity

CURIOSITY. This trait is one of the most obvious for the enhancement of creativity. It applies to every sign, but particularly to the fixed signs—Taurus, Leo, Scorpio, and Aquarius. It's so easy for fixed signs to become entrenched in their own opinions and beliefs that maintaining curiosity is of primary importance to their creative process.

Lindbergh wasn't just an aviator. He and a Nobel Prize–winning physician designed a perfusion pump, described in a book called *The Culture of Organs,* published in 1938. "As I look back from the vantage point of time, I realize that my intuitive interest in life's mysteries was strong and fundamental in my early childhood and that it increased, at least subconsciously, to the point where even my fascination with aviation was unable to hold it down," wrote Lindbergh.

Curiosity—that's where all creativity really begins.

OBSESSION. This may sound odd, but many creative people create out of their obsessions and their fears and in doing so vanquish the powers these things hold over them. The inverse, of course, is also true, that our obsessions and fears often hold us back, providing drama in our lives so that we don't feel compelled to create anything.

This is one area where Aquarius himself should make the call. Only he knows at which end of the spectrum he falls.

EMOTIONAL AWARENESS. Aquarius can be emotionally remote and cold at times, a trait that invariably baffles the people around him. It isn't the kind of duality found among Geminis, nothing that pronounced. It's as if Aquarius has gotten up on the wrong side of the bed and simply can't be bothered with anyone else. Some astrologers refer to it as indifference, others call it detachment, but it amounts to the same thing: a withholding. An Aquarian isn't likely to give you a bear hug as you walk in the door.

Yet to create from a deep inner place, emotional reality is vital because it connects us to our personal mythology. "In days when there was a strong body of belief in myth, we had a way through life," says writer Anne River Siddons in *Writers Dreaming*. "We had a pattern to follow and things to show us how we were connected to the wild and to the natural world." We now need to find the mythology within ourselves.

Emotions, to a large extent, define our "bliss," what author and mythologist Joseph Campbell called living the "mythologically inspired life."

Aquarius might ask himself, *What is my myth? What myth am I living? What myth would I like to live?* These questions often hold vital clues to Aquarius's creative passions.

THINKING OUTSIDE THE BOX. Aquarius has a natural predisposition for doing this. The more he can do it, the sharper his perceptions become and the greater his creative drive.

Aquarius Traits That Deplete Creative Energy

CLOSING OFF. This goes back to the fixed nature of the sign and is a propensity that Aquarius shares with Taurus, Scorpio, and Leo. It can happen in any area of life where he is certain that all the answers and evidence are in, that there's nothing new to learn.

Oddly, this is a trait that Aquarius also shares with the shadow side of Sagittarius, yet the expression differs. Where Sag operates from the premise that *his* truth is the only truth, so what's the point of investigating, Aquarius closes off because he thinks all the answers are in.

STUBBORNNESS. While this trait can be a creative asset for Aquarius and other fixed signs, it can just as easily become a liability.

FRIEND: Hey, did you ever see the movie *Resurrection,* with Ellen Burstyn?

AQUARIUS: C'mon, I'm an Aquarian. The mind interests me, not the body.

FRIEND: Actually, it's about how a woman who has been crippled uses her mind and her will to heal herself and then goes on to heal other people.

AQUARIUS: Sounds boring.

When Aquarius stubbornly resists something, it would be to his advantage to ask himself the following questions: Where does this stubborn resistance originate? Why does a particular subject cause him to erect walls around himself? What is the resistance telling him? Against what is he protecting himself? By brainstorming in this way, he opens himself to other possibilities and frees up creative energy that would otherwise go into continued resistance.

How Aquarius Can Avoid Creative Burnout

Over the years I've heard various descriptions of creative burnout:

The well went dry.

I feel scorched from the inside out.

I've run out of ideas.

I'm empty.

I feel parched inside.

I'm used up.

The common thread here is that there's nothing left in the creative well. It's a terrible, helpless feeling. You want desperately to turn on the magical faucet and get the flow going again.

When I was first making my living as a writer, I used to fall into a kind of postpartum depression whenever I finished a novel. I often came down with a cold or the flu that laid me up for a couple of days. Invariably while I was sick I would dig into the stack of books next to my bed and go through it in a sort of fury, reading for hours on end. After writing my sixth or seventh novel, I dreaded finishing a project because I could feel the depression and a cold just around the corner.

I decided it would be easier to break the pattern than to get sick, and realized that one of the reasons this pattern existed was that I didn't allow myself time to read and do other things that I enjoyed while I was writing fiction. In other words, my life was short on balance. Once I recognized the pattern and took steps to create some balance in my life, things started to change. I no longer *needed* to get sick to have time to read. I didn't *need* the depression.

There are still times when I finish a book and the old pattern returns. Now that I'm aware of it, though, it's a rare occurrence. As I got to know more writers and met other people who were involved in creative projects, I discovered that my pattern wasn't unique. An intense creative period may be followed by insomnia, a kind of chronic restlessness, or a sense of feeling directionless. Sometimes it's followed by a major shift in an intimate relationship, a move, or even a career change. It's as if all that adrenaline that got you through the creative period needs an outlet.

"I like writing to be something that fits into cracks and crannies," says Julia Cameron in *The Right to Write.* "I don't like it to dominate my life. I like it to fill my life."

This can be said of any creative endeavor and is the secret to avoiding creative burnout—not just for Aquarians but for people of any Sun sign.

Part of the problem for Aquarius is that its ruler, Uranus, is a highly charged planet. It rules lightning and sudden explosive events. It's the astrological equivalent of a live wire that swings down from an electrical pole, sparks flying from it, and ignites a field of dry grass. In the blink of an eye, a catastrophe is in progress. Apply this kind of energy to the human nervous system and you have some inkling of how creative burnout can affect Aquarius. Nerves are frazzled; the brain goes haywire.

Travel can be a great anodyne to creative burnout for an Aquarian. Foreign travel is best because by immersing himself in a culture alien to his own, Aquarius is taken out of himself. When foreign travel isn't possible or convenient, just a few days away can work miracles.

The other thing that seems to work for Aquarius is to take a workshop or seminar in something that interests him. As an air sign, his mind is always eager for new knowledge, new information, new vistas.

Summoning the Aquarius Muse

This shouldn't be a problem for Aquarius. Even if he gripes and complains that the muse is out to lunch, that he simply isn't getting anywhere with his creative projects and endeavors, that's just a stall for time. The truth is that he can summon her any time he wants.

He only has to shut his eyes and make a request. It's the equivalent of what used to happen on the TV show *I Dream of Jeannie.* Rub that lamp, ask for help, and voilà, the muse appears and she's ready to help.

If it makes Aquarius feel better, he can create a ritual that communicates his intent. Or he can tidy his work area, say a prayer, go for a walk. *Anything that signals his intent will work.* For Aquarius, that's all it takes. *Intent.*

The Aquarius Muse Speaks

Tonight on the evening news, Tom Brokaw talked about menopause. That in itself was astonishing. Even more astonishing was that menopause was approached as a creative wakeup call. I don't think the word *creative* was actually used, but it seemed to be what Dr. Christiane Northrup was saying.

It's the time to reevaluate your life, Northrup said, and then the image cut to a woman sketching a child. Menopause had "shown" her that she had a dormant talent as an artist. The woman was also keeping a journal on menopause for her daughter, and one line in particular caught my attention: "It's just one more thing women have to endure."

Endure? Hello? Red flags popped up. That sentence revealed tomes about a negative worldview in which certain things must be *endured* as a result of gender. This is the same kind of worldview that says creative people are unstable, crazy, alcoholics, poor, suffering—you get the idea. If, in a weak moment, Aquarius buys into this kind of worldview, he had better escape it fast. This belief system makes it very difficult to be creative and nearly impossible to summon the muse when she is most needed.

So if Aquarius encounters deep and continued resistance in summoning his muse, it's time to go back to basics. He needs to uncover what his worldview *really* is.

"I am spirit masquerading in matter's form," wrote Charles Lindbergh in his *Autobiography of Values.*

Here we are talking about spiritual issues related to creativity. And ultimately, this is what may make the most sense to Aquarius. Visionary and paradigm-buster, Aquarius must feel a higher purpose in everything he undertakes. If his worldview can accommodate a spiritual approach to creativity, his muse will definitely speak to him when he shuts his eyes.

AQUARIUS ACTIVITY ✸ Brainstorming with the Muse

BELIEFS

"Know thyself." This ancient adage fits all the fixed signs well. To know himself, Aquarius should know what he believes.

In the space below, list five to ten beliefs that you have about creativity. No one sees this except you, so be honest. If you were taught that creativity is "too wild" or "unpredictable," include it. For each belief that may hold you back, rewrite it in a positive way. If you write, for instance, that "Creativity is too wild and unpredictable" (and therefore bad), you might rewrite it as "My creativity is one of my greatest assets."

In doing this activity, it can be helpful to try to identify the source of the negative beliefs. Where did they start? When did they take root?

_____

_____

_____

_____

Post your positive rewrites where you work, and read them out loud frequently.

Aquarius and Goals

Setting creative goals helps to define what you want to accomplish. Consider the goals as the big picture, and the time frame and strategy you create as the smaller picture.

Start with small goals and small time increments—a day, a week, a month—so you can see your progress quickly. Many professional writers, for example, set daily goals—five hundred words, a thousand words. Once you achieve these small goals, set larger goals for longer time frames. In this way, you become accustomed to creating every day.

My friend Phyllis, the Aquarian writer and astrologer, tackles new projects by setting a time frame for herself—four months, six months, whatever seems realistic. Then she constructs the backbone of the book. Where does it begin? Where will it end? How will each chapter be structured? By applying their organizational skills to their creative projects, Aquarians are then able to let their imaginations soar within the structure they've created.

Affirmation for Aquarius

Post this where you'll see it often:

| *My creativity flows.* |

17

Pisces, the Healer ♓

... the only courage you really need is the
courage to begin.

—*Julia Cameron*

FEBRUARY 19—MARCH 20

MUTABLE WATER

SHADOW: LET ME ESCAPE

Creative Theme

For decades she wrote in utter obscurity, recording the minutiae of her inner life with the free-flowing prose of a poet. She wrote about everything—writing and creativity, music, the arts, women, relationships, love and sex, flowers and birds, dreams and symbolism, living on a houseboat, her childhood and her adulthood, her husband and her lovers and her lovers' lovers. Life was her fodder. Nothing was sacred, and yet it was all sacred.

"I feel like a fugitive from the mysteries of the human labyrinth I was trying to pierce," she wrote during a trip to Mexico in 1947. "I escaped my patterns. I escaped familiar and inexorable grooves. The outer world is so overwhelmingly beautiful that I am willing to stay outside, day and night, a wanderer and a pilgrim without abode."

The "patterns" or habits that Anais Nin mentions in the quotation above pertain to the type of Pisces whose inner life provides the material for creativity. Nin's inner world was often more real to her than the outer world and was recorded in her voluminous diaries—some 35,000 pages by the end of her life. The diaries provided her with a buffer against the outer world and also served as a meticulous chronicle of the various stages of her life, her many love affairs, her creative aspirations and dreams, her analysis with renowned psychologist Otto Rank, and her friendships with many of the prominent writers and artists of her time. Nin lived out the Pisces creative theme.

Pisces perceives primarily through emotions and the subjective lens of her own consciousness. She is born with an inner sense of the inter-connectedness of all things, her awareness dreamlike, mystical, and in-timately linked to the collective unconscious. This is true whether the Pisces is Nin, Albert Einstein, Salvador Dali, Tom Wolfe, Rob Reiner, Billy Crystal, Liz Taylor, Edgar Cayce, Mickey Spillane, Michelangelo, John Irving, or Gabriel Garcia Marquez. The way one Pisces differs from another is in the form of her creative expression.

A lot has been written about Pisces as victim and martyr. Although it's true that she's a sucker for a sob story and her deep compassion can get her into trouble, I haven't found there to be more martyrs and vic-tims among Pisces than among other Sun signs. When they do act out those particular roles, there's usually some grasp of the deeper issues involved.

As a mutable water sign, Pisces is emotionally adaptable, so it's of-ten difficult to pin her down on what, exactly, she feels. Is she happy to-day, or is she just saying she is because she figures it's what you want to hear? Like her mutable cousins Gemini, Virgo, and Sagittarius, she can be a chameleon at times, impossible to pigeonhole.

Pisces tends to create in an organic, holistic way. That is, she isn't very good at strategy, planning, outlines. She intuitively perceives the entirety of what she's trying to create and trusts that it will come out just fine in the end. Intuition, in fact, is one of her strongest creative gifts, and if she listens to its whispers and follows its cues, she will rarely go wrong.

When Pisces is in her creative groove, the rest of the world vanishes. Imagine Michelangelo as he sculpted the *Pietà*. Did he break for lunch? Probably not. It's likely that he worked in a kind of fever, sculpting, per-fecting, driven by an inner vision of what he was trying to create. When Pisces is functioning at full creative tilt, the fever and the inner vision are all she needs. When her creative drive falters, she stumbles into the shadow part of the sign, *Let me escape*. This escapism can take many forms and is all too often addictive—alcohol, drugs, food, sex.

Anais Nin, after her first meeting with Aldous Huxley, reacted badly to his belief that drugs were a necessity for everyone. She wrote, "I still feel, as I always have, that the effort made to live, love and create without artificial stimulus is part of the enrichment." Her one LSD experience, she says, proved to her that the drug "only opened the same realms which one can have access to by way of dreams, poetry, writing."

Spoken like a true Pisces.

So where does the healing theme fit into the creative picture? It runs like a current through everything that Pisces does. For Rob Reiner, that healing is found in humor: he makes us laugh. For Michelangelo, that healing was found in creating art so exquisite that it transforms and transports the viewer. For Einstein, the healing lay in his relativity theories, which forever changed the way we looked at the world. For Liz Taylor, the healing lies in her charity work, notably in raising money for AIDS research.

I've met a number of Pisces individuals who work in hospitals, nursing homes, behind the scenes, caring for other people. This is the other side of the Healer, the Pisces with profound compassion.

A few years ago my daughter made a friend in our neighborhood whose mother, Eileen, is a Pisces. She has the huge, liquid eyes that many Pisces people have and a heart as big as the outdoors. She has the kind of natural artistic talent that some people spend years trying to learn, is the mother of three girls, and is happily married to a Canadian whom she met in her native Scotland. Her life is full, yet Eileen feels a need to return something to the community. She started a community drive to raise money for migrant workers and is the first person her church calls when a child is in trouble. Charity is where her creative energy goes. This, too, is Pisces.

Pisces, like Gemini, is a dual sign. It's symbolized by two fish swimming in opposite directions. Every astrologer has his or her take on what those fish represent. To me, one fish symbolizes the heart and the other symbolizes the head, which is why Pisces is often torn in two directions. Her heart says one thing, her head says another. Her compassion is constantly struggling against her need to escape, to be left alone, to simply drift in the labyrinth of her consciousness, her own awareness.

Sometimes one wins, sometimes the other. The big question is which fish dominates her creativity?

Pisces Creativity in Ordinary Life

According to medical intuitive Carolyn Myss, intuition is "the ability to use energy data to make decisions in the *immediate moment*. Energy data are the emotional, psychological, and spiritual components of a given situation. They are the 'here' and 'now' ingredients of life, not nonphysical information from some 'future' place." This is a perfect definition for how Piscean creativity works in daily life.

Here's one possible scenario: Pisces has a hunch that says she should be looking for a new job that is more rewarding. But she doesn't really want to go through the hassle of job hunting, and besides, her present job isn't all *that* bad. So she ignores the hunch. But her creativity is endlessly inventive, and pretty soon someone offers her a job that would be more rewarding, have better benefits and pay, and would give her a lot of creative freedom. Her hunch is to take it.

But her head is screaming, *Give me proof, give me evidence, give me an assurance that the new job is better than the old. . . .*

She turns the job down. Two months later she is fired.

Another possible scenario: Pisces follows that first hunch and not only finds a more fulfilling job but finds her dream job, and an entirely new chapter of her life opens up.

This is the daily creative challenge that Pisces faces. Which fish does she listen to? Her head or her heart?

Under ideal conditions, the Piscean creativity rises from a blend of mind and heart, reason and intuition. To attain this blend, Pisces must develop a deep awareness of how her reason and intuition can work together instead of against each other. She must learn to weigh her creative choices. She may notice a change in her creativity when she approaches it as a spiritual practice.

"Creative energy," writes Carolyn Myss in *Anatomy of the Spirit,* "breaks us out of habitual patterns of behavior, thoughts, and relationships. . . . If allowed to flow, creative energy will continually reshape our lives and reveal more meaning for why things happen as they do than we could determine on our own."

In daily life, then, the challenge for Pisces is to use her creative energy *consciously*. This often entails identifying her fears, recognizing the ways they hold her back, and making a conscious effort to vanquish them. One of the simplest methods of doing this is to become aware of the thoughts that drift through her mind and to listen to herself when she talks. When she encounters a negative thought or hears herself say something negative, she should attempt to get to the root of the negativity and the fear that's causing it.

Negative thoughts and remarks provide all of us with clues about limiting beliefs we have that may be blocking our creativity. Glance through the list that follows and check the ones that resonate for you:

* Artistic people are always poor.

* It's who you know that counts, not what you write.

* I'm not creative enough to make my living doing what I love.

* To get published, you have to know someone.

* The odds are against me.

* Creativity entails suffering.

* It's the luck of the draw.

* I'm never lucky.

* I hold grudges.

* I can't help it.

* I don't have choices.

* I have no imagination.

* I don't deserve it.

* I'm not very creative.

Many of our negative beliefs originate in childhood, when we adopt them from our parents and other authority figures. They become so ingrained in who we are that we "forget" they're even there, and yet daily we are confronted with the consequences of those beliefs. Pisces, with her deep intuition, should be able to ferret out these negative beliefs and understand that they no longer serve a purpose in her life.

Jupiter is co-ruler of Pisces, which means that the planet's expansiveness can work for or against Piscean individuals. What Pisces fears may be amplified beyond reason; what she dreams may also be larger than life. When Pisces learns to use Jupiter's expansive energy so that it works to her benefit, she's won half the battle.

Pisces Traits That Enhance Creativity

IMAGINATION. Pisces has this trait in such abundance that she can create anything she can imagine. Her dreams are an important source of inspiration and allow her access to the richness of her imagination. Even during sleep, the Piscean mind is busy making intuitive connections and dipping into the deeper recesses of her imagination to find the solutions and answers she needs.

One of the more popular stories about Einstein concerned sleep. After months of working on his relativity theories, he still hadn't come up with the answers he needed. He lay down for an afternoon nap, and when he woke he had his answer. The history of invention is filled with anecdotes like this. In the act of releasing the quest for whatever it is that's needed, the inventor or the writer or the artist or the candlestick maker falls asleep, and when he wakes, the missing piece is "found."

Many of the writers I know have similar experiences with sleep. They may be blocked on a particular scene, a plot point, perhaps a character. Discouraged, they get away from the writing by going to sleep, and when they wake up the block is gone and they know exactly where to go with the story.

"I'll wake up with ideas, specific plot ideas, scenes," says Elmore Leonard in *Writers Dreaming*. "Very, very often what was a puzzle, what was a problem at six o'clock, having worked all day, gets solved overnight."

INTUITION BALANCED WITH REASON. No question that Pisces has an abundance of natural intuition. It allows her to access the deeper recesses of her imagination and her soul's "higher wisdom." But once Pisces has listened to her intuitive guidance, she must gather the facts, the left-brain information, that she needs to set the guidance in motion.

HUMOR. All of us need more of it. But the Pisces brand of humor is unique because it focuses on the general absurdity of life. Pisces benefits if she allows her humor to spill over into her creativity.

COMPASSION. Without it, Pisces is just going through the motions. When she allows herself to feel it straight down into her soul, there's no telling what her creativity may do with it.

Pisces Edgar Cayce, called the most documented psychic of the twentieth century, had an abundance of compassion. By following where it led him, he was able to tap into creative wells that far surpassed anything seen in his day and age. Cayce would go into a trance, his wife or his secretary would give him a name, and he would proceed to "read" that person. In his lifetime, Cayce gave more than 14,000 such readings, pinpointing the origin of health problems, patterns of behavior, and the soul's purpose in this life.

When Pisces creates out of compassion and love, using the tools with which she is born, there are no limits to her creative expression.

Pisces Traits That Deplete Creative Energy

VACILLATION. Blame the usual conflict between the head and the heart, intuition and reason. Pisces can spend days weighing one against the other and still not make up her mind. This eats up creative energy that could be better used elsewhere. The next time she finds herself vacillating, she should give herself just five minutes to make up her mind and commit to one course of action or another.

I don't recommend doing this if Pisces is facing a major life decision, however. In the beginning, stick to smaller issues. *Should I work on my portfolio tonight or watch TV? Should I go out with friends or finish that chapter in my novel?* In these examples, neither choice is better than the other. It may be that Pisces needs a night out on the town with friends or that she needs to kick back and relax in front of the tube. Some of her best ideas come to her when she's relaxed. The idea here is for Pisces to become accustomed to making quick choices about small issues, then gradually work her way up to larger issues and concerns.

ESCAPISM. *Oops, I don't like what I see or what I have to deal with, so bye, I'm outta here.* That's the kind of escapism Pisces is good at when she feels cornered and incapable of resolving issues in the real world. It can lead to addictive behavior, excessive sleeping, losing herself in a fantasy world. It's not that all escapist behaviors are good or bad; they may be simply another form of creative expression. But they probably aren't going to fulfill Pisces's enormous potential. The big question for Pisces boils down to whether escapism is where she wants to expend her creative energy. And that's a choice no one else can make.

How Pisces Can Avoid Creative Burnout

"I'm blocked."
"My idea isn't working."
"I can't seem to move past a certain point."
"I've hit a wall."
"I can barely breathe."
"I'm exhausted."
"I've hit a drought."
"I'm out of fresh ideas."

All these remarks are indicative of creative burnout, negative beliefs, or both. Sometimes the two are synonymous. Pisces will be moving along in her creative endeavors and then slam into a wall. When this happens several times, at the same point each time, it may suggest a belief pattern. If it happens during or after a particularly intense creative period, it's probably burnout.

The best way for Pisces to avoid creative burnout is to approach her creativity as a spiritual practice. This may be true of all of us, but it's especially true of mystical Pisces. If she can connect with her own divinity through her creative endeavors, then she knows instinctively how to pace herself and what she should do to avoid burnout.

"An artist exudes vitality; a spiritual person exudes peace," writes Natalie Goldberg in *Writing Down the Bones*. And in the end, peace is what Pisces is after.

Summoning the Pisces Muse

Water signs rarely have trouble with the concept of summoning something that can't be seen, felt, heard, touched, or tasted. They live in a world of emotion and imagination, and they can conjure a monster just as easily as they can conjure their muses. Pisces in particular has a gift for this, thanks in large part to her wonderful imagination.

In fact, to summon her muse it may help if she has some sort of idea what her muse might look like. Is the muse male, female, an animal, an angel? Is it some mythological figure? Is it a goddess?

Years ago I knew a Piscean pianist who believed that his muse was Merlin, Arthur's fabled magician. He had little statues, drawings, and paintings of Merlin around his place, books on Merlin, and paraphernalia related to Camelot. Whenever he sat down at his piano to practice or to write music, he had only to glance at the three-foot-tall statue of Merlin that stood nearby to become inspired. His creativity was rarely blocked. Although I couldn't put it into words at the time, I realize now that music was the spiritual center of his life.

Once Pisces knows what her muse looks like, summoning her is as easy as shutting her eyes, taking a deep breath, and requesting that the muse appear. Another method is for Pisces to request the muse's help while falling asleep at night and having a notebook and pen nearby to record whatever dreams she has.

Weather permitting, Pisces might try going swimming before she taps into her creativity. It's only natural that a water sign would gravitate toward water for inspiration. She can swim in it, walk beside it, listen to it, soak in it, float on its surface, whatever her pleasure. The point is that water connects Pisces to her deepest self.

The Pisces Muse Speaks

"I write out of my deepest fears," admits one Piscean writer. "The way I see it, if I write about the stuff that terrifies me, then it won't happen."

This is one way the muse speaks to Pisces, through her deepest fears, her private terrors, the secrets she can't confide in other people. Another way the muse speaks is through symbols—in her dreams, her daydreams, her fully conscious life. It also speaks to her through her passions.

Cameron believes that art begins "in the heart." When I first read this in *The Vein of Gold,* two books immediately came to mind: Judith Guest's *Ordinary People* and Sue Miller's *The Good Mother.* Both books left me choked up in the end because I felt the loss and helplessness that the characters felt. The same is true for movies that touch an emotional chord. Every artist creates from the inside out. The muse is merely the vehicle.

When an artist writes genuinely from the heart, from any emotion— fear, paranoia, joy, nostalgia, pain, whatever it might be—it touches other people. It becomes larger than itself. It transcends itself and spills into the realm of the spiritual, the divine.

PISCES ACTIVITY ✺ Brainstorming with the Muse

DREAMING

Your brainstorming activity, Pisces, is to keep a dream journal for one week. Before you fall asleep each night during this week, request that your muse provide you with ideas, guidance, and anything else you need creatively.

At least once during this week, try to come awake in your dream and consciously manipulate the action. This is known as lucid dreaming. Chances are you have had lucid dreams in the past. They probably happened spontaneously. Now you're going to bring your intent to the endeavor.

According to Stephen LaBerge, one of the pioneers of lucid dreaming, lucidity often occurs when the dreamer recognizes some inconsistency or glaringly weird element in a dream. The recognition brings the dreamer awake within the dream. Here are some tips for inducing lucid dreams:

* As you're falling asleep, clarify your intent to have a lucid dream. Intent, says LaBerge, is vital in inducing lucid dreams.

* Focus on one thing in particular as you're falling asleep—your breath, a mental image, your heartbeat, how relaxed your body feels. "If you keep your mind sufficiently active while the tendency to enter REM is strong, you feel your body fall asleep but you, that is to say, your consciousness, remains awake," says LaBerge.

* Use a familiar object as a trigger to wake up inside a dream. When Carlos Castaneda was training with the Yaqui shaman Don Juan, he learned to find his hand in dreams. This became a trigger for lucid dreaming.

* Once you begin lucid dreaming, manipulate the dream so that you are working on a particular creative project.

Remember, keep a dream journal for seven days, recording what you've dreamed. What did each night's dream tell you about your creative life?

Pisces and Goals

Pisces generally isn't one for setting goals, at least not consciously. It's a good idea, however, to set creative goals and post them in your work area. Keep them small at first and easily attainable. Instead of listing a yearly goal as *Get novel published,* you might have a daily goal to write five hundred or a thousand words on your novel. Or you might have a weekly goal of ten or twenty pages. Once you attain your daily and weekly goals, set monthly goals, then yearly goals.

Goals shouldn't be rigid, but they should be strong enough to provide a structure for your creative life.

Pisces Affirmation

Post this where you'll see it often:

| *My creativity flourishes today and every day.* |

18

Your Ascendant

> . . . myth is the revelation of a divine life in man.
> —*Carl Jung*

How do other people perceive you and your creative endeavors? What kind of image do you project? What kind of creative energy do you radiate? The sign that was rising at your birth not only answers these questions but sets up the layout of houses for your horoscope.

The only way you'll have an accurate Ascendant is if you have your chart drawn up by an astrologer (or a computer). However, it's possible to estimate your rising sign by using the chart on the next page. This won't give you the degree of the rising sign, but you should be able to estimate the house placement of your natal Sun and Jupiter.

CHART 8 · Your Rising Sign

Rising Signs

♈ ♉ ♊ ♋ ♌ ♍ ♎ ♏ ♐ ♑ ♒ ♓

Sun Signs — **Time of Birth**

Sun Signs	♈	♉	♊	♋	♌	♍	♎	♏	♐	♑	♒	♓
♈ Aries	5 a.m.	7 a.m.	9 a.m.	11 a.m.	1 p.m.	3 p.m.	5 p.m.	7 p.m.	9 p.m.	11 p.m.	1 a.m.	3 a.m.
	7 a.m.	9 a.m.	11 a.m.	1 p.m.	3 p.m.	5 p.m.	7 p.m.	9 p.m.	11 p.m.	1 a.m.	3 a.m.	5 a.m.
♉ Taurus	3 a.m.	5 a.m.	7 a.m.	9 a.m.	11 a.m.	1 p.m.	3 p.m.	5 p.m.	7 p.m.	9 p.m.	11 p.m.	1 a.m.
	5 a.m.	7 a.m.	9 a.m.	11 a.m.	1 p.m.	3 p.m.	5 p.m.	7 p.m.	9 p.m.	11 p.m.	1 a.m.	3 a.m.
♊ Gemini	1 a.m.	3 a.m.	5 a.m.	7 a.m.	9 a.m.	11 a.m.	1 p.m.	3 p.m.	5 p.m.	7 p.m.	9 p.m.	11 p.m.
	3 a.m.	5 a.m.	7 a.m.	9 a.m.	11 a.m.	1 p.m.	3 p.m.	5 p.m.	7 p.m.	9 p.m.	11 p.m.	1 a.m.
♋ Cancer	11 p.m.	1 a.m.	3 a.m.	5 a.m.	7 a.m.	9 a.m.	11 a.m.	1 p.m.	3 p.m.	5 p.m.	7 p.m.	9 p.m.
	1 a.m.	3 a.m.	5 a.m.	7 a.m.	9 a.m.	11 a.m.	1 p.m.	3 p.m.	5 p.m.	7 p.m.	9 p.m.	11 p.m.
♌ Leo	9 p.m.	11 p.m.	1 a.m.	3 a.m.	5 a.m.	7 a.m.	9 a.m.	11 a.m.	1 p.m.	3 p.m.	5 p.m.	7 p.m.
	11 p.m.	1 a.m.	3 a.m.	5 a.m.	7 a.m.	9 a.m.	11 a.m.	1 p.m.	3 p.m.	5 p.m.	7 p.m.	9 p.m.
♍ Virgo	7 p.m.	9 p.m.	11 p.m.	1 a.m.	3 a.m.	5 a.m.	7 a.m.	9 a.m.	11 a.m.	1 p.m.	3 p.m.	5 p.m.
	9 p.m.	11 p.m.	1 a.m.	3 a.m.	5 a.m.	7 a.m.	9 a.m.	11 a.m.	1 p.m.	3 p.m.	5 p.m.	7 p.m.
♎ Libra	5 p.m.	7 p.m.	9 p.m.	11 p.m.	1 a.m.	3 a.m.	5 a.m.	7 a.m.	9 a.m.	11 a.m.	1 p.m.	3 p.m.
	7 p.m.	9 p.m.	11 p.m.	1 a.m.	3 a.m.	5 a.m.	7 a.m.	9 a.m.	11 a.m.	1 p.m.	3 p.m.	5 p.m.
♏ Scorpio	3 p.m.	5 p.m.	7 p.m.	9 p.m.	11 p.m.	1 a.m.	3 a.m.	5 a.m.	7 a.m.	9 a.m.	11 a.m.	1 p.m.
	5 p.m.	7 p.m.	9 p.m.	11 p.m.	1 a.m.	3 a.m.	5 a.m.	7 a.m.	9 a.m.	11 a.m.	1 p.m.	3 p.m.
♐ Sagittarius	1 p.m.	3 p.m.	5 p.m.	7 p.m.	9 p.m.	11 p.m.	1 a.m.	3 a.m.	5 a.m.	7 a.m.	9 a.m.	11 a.m.
	3 p.m.	5 p.m.	7 p.m.	9 p.m.	11 p.m.	1 a.m.	3 a.m.	5 a.m.	7 a.m.	9 a.m.	11 a.m.	1 p.m.
♑ Capricorn	11 a.m.	1 p.m.	3 p.m.	5 p.m.	7 p.m.	9 p.m.	11 p.m.	1 a.m.	3 a.m.	5 a.m.	7 a.m.	9 a.m.
	1 p.m.	3 p.m.	5 p.m.	7 p.m.	9 p.m.	11 p.m.	1 a.m.	3 a.m.	5 a.m.	7 a.m.	9 a.m.	11 a.m.
♒ Aquarius	9 a.m.	11 a.m.	1 p.m.	3 p.m.	5 p.m.	7 p.m.	9 p.m.	11 p.m.	1 a.m.	3 a.m.	5 a.m.	7 a.m.
	11 a.m.	1 p.m.	3 p.m.	5 p.m.	7 p.m.	9 p.m.	11 p.m.	1 a.m.	3 a.m.	5 a.m.	7 a.m.	9 a.m.
♓ Pisces	7 a.m.	9 a.m.	11 a.m.	1 p.m.	3 p.m.	5 p.m.	7 p.m.	9 p.m.	11 p.m.	1 a.m.	3 a.m.	5 a.m.
	9 a.m.	11 a.m.	1 p.m.	3 p.m.	5 p.m.	7 p.m.	9 p.m.	11 p.m.	1 a.m.	3 a.m.	5 a.m.	7 a.m.

Rising Signs and Their Ruling Planets

The planet that rules the Ascendant also rules the chart. Refer back to chapter 4, chart 7, for a list and description of the rulers for each sign. If your rising sign is Aries, for instance, then Mars rules your Ascendant and your chart. This means that Mars figures prominently in your creative process.

Once more glance at Stephen King's chart. He has Cancer rising at 29 degrees and 52 minutes. Cancer is ruled by the Moon. His Moon in Sagittarius falls into his fifth house. Just this information tells us that other people (Ascendant) see him as a creative man (fifth house). They also see him as a private individual (Cancer rising) who is protective of his family's privacy.

His Moon trines his Midheaven, indicating that his creative expression finds public favor and recognition. His Moon also sextiles his Mercury in Libra in the fourth house (☿15♎02), which is in a close conjunction to the IC, or cusp of the fourth house. This indicates that his emotions (Moon) feed his intellect and communication skills (Mercury). With that Mercury sitting so close to the cusp of the fourth house, it's safe to say that communication is lively around his house and that books, education, and communication figure prominently in his home life and personal environment. (See chapter 25 on aspects.)

Again, this merely shows how one bit of information in a chart connects with other bits to deepen the understanding of the individual.

ARIES RISING

Ruled by Mars

You project a confident self-image, that of a person who takes creative risks. You're viewed as something of a creative pioneer, someone who forges into unknown territory with relentless energy and enthusiasm. Your creative passions are varied, and no matter what you tackle, you do so with a sense of adventure.

Examples: Paul McCartney, Joan Baez.

TAURUS RISING

Ruled by Venus

You project a stable, grounded self-image. Other people consider you to be creatively reliable, a person who completes what you start. You may not be the fastest worker in the zodiac, but you're consistent and often visionary. Others may see you as somewhat stubborn, too, which can be both an asset and a liability in creative work.

Examples: George Lucas, Carlos Castaneda, Carlos Santana, Toni Morrison.

GEMINI RISING

Ruled by Mercury

You project an image of versatility, restlessness, and intellectual curiosity. People see you as a lively, interesting individual whose creativity wears many faces. You may also be construed as having two distinct moods or sides, and this can be intimidating to people who don't know you well. You have seemingly inexhaustible reserves of creative energy.

Examples: Jack London, Michael Caine.

CANCER RISING

Ruled by the Moon

A number of people in my database on creative people have Cancer rising. It's one of the most intuitive Ascendants, which is a plus in any type of creative endeavor.

Other people tend to see you as a caring, nurturing, and compassionate individual. You take emotional risks in your creative work and are known to do whatever has to be done to get the job finished.

Examples: Meryl Streep, Cher, Steven Spielberg, Albert Einstein, Bill Gates, Vincent van Gogh.

LEO RISING

Ruled by the Sun

You project an image of self-confidence, generosity, and tremendous warmth. People admire your creative drive and stamina. There's a certain dramatic air about your public persona, which is probably why so many people who are in the public eye have Leo rising.

Examples: J. R. R. Tolkien, Ernest Hemingway, Zelda Fitzgerald.

VIRGO RISING

Ruled by Mercury
You project an image of a meticulous, precise person, who is well-rounded and often analytical. Others consider you to be dependable. You may not take a lot of creative risks, but the ones you do take are usually planned and possess some type of strategy.
Examples: Agatha Christie, Margaret Mitchell, Mozart.

LIBRA RISING

Ruled by Venus
You project an image of graceful self-confidence. The creative risks you take are balanced, often artistic, and sometimes broad in scope and vision. People see you as a refined individual.
Examples: Jacques Cousteau, David Copperfield, James Dean, Sally Field, John Lennon.

SCORPIO RISING

Ruled by Pluto, Co-ruled by Mars
You project an intense self-image that often smolders with sexuality. Other people perceive your creativity as a powerful emotional force in your life but may be puzzled by your secrecy.
Examples: George Harrison, Paul Cézanne, Clint Eastwood.

SAGITTARIUS RISING

Ruled by Jupiter
Not surprisingly, my database has a number of people with Sagittarius rising.
You project a charismatic self-image. Even if you're quiet when you enter a room, people notice you. Others believe you have abundant creative abilities, that you're able to perceive the big picture, and hopefully

they realize you need the freedom to pursue your creative endeavors according to *your* agenda. Your wry sense of humor often takes people by surprise.

Examples: Jodie Foster, Clark Gable, Frank Herbert, Herman Hesse, Marilyn Ferguson.

CAPRICORN RISING

Ruled by Saturn

Others see you as a serious, responsible person who always gets the job done. You aren't known for the creative risks you take, but when you do take them, they shock you as much as they do the people around you. You're quietly ambitious and have the patience to achieve your creative goals.

Examples: Charles Darwin, Harry Houdini, Susan Sarandon.

AQUARIUS RISING

Ruled by Jupiter, Co-ruled by Saturn

Other people see you as an independent visionary, someone who plays by your own rules. You are well known for your humanitarian concerns and for your individualistic views. Your creativity is rarely predictable and always finds unique expression.

Examples: Abe Lincoln, Michael J. Fox, Richard Wilhelm, F. Scott Fitzgerald.

PISCES RISING

Ruled by Neptune, Co-ruled by Jupiter

You project an aura of compassion, caring, and quiet idealism. You are known for seeing the best in any situation. Your creativity stems from deep faith and a vision that pierces the camouflage of ordinary life.

Examples: Alfred Hitchcock, Robert Redford, Ringo Starr.

Entire books have been written on rising signs. These brief descriptions are the equivalent of snapshots.

PART TWO

Jupiter and Creativity

We can be anything
because we are all.

—Mary Greer

19

The Role of Jupiter ♃

In the middle of difficulty lies opportunity.
—*Albert Einstein*

Imagine you're twelve years old, on a camping trip with your family, and you get lost in the woods. Not just a little lost, but major lost. All the trails twist like pretzels through the dense forest, you don't have much water left in your canteen, it's getting dark, and you're terrified. Just when you think things can't get any worse, you stumble and twist your ankle and it starts to rain. The rain comes down harder and harder, a cold, unforgiving rain that drenches you to the bone. You hobble over to a tree, huddle beneath it, crying and shivering, and squeeze your eyes shut.

And when your eyes open again, the hazy beam of a flashlight pierces the wet darkness. You realize that if you'd been on the other side of the tree, you wouldn't have seen the beam of light. Your frenzied shouts lead the search party straight to you. What do you feel? Elation, euphoria, relief, gratitude, lucky beyond belief, and utter faith in this miraculous thing called life. In astrological terms, you have just experienced the blessings of Jupiter, the very paragon of luck, expansion, and synchronicity.

It's fitting that the largest planet in our solar system, eleven times the size of Earth, was known to the Greeks as Zeus, the greatest of all the gods. In mythology, he's depicted as a bearded, muscular man sitting on a throne with a thunderbolt in one hand and lightning in the other. He was considered the father of gods and men and was the founder of royal power, justice, the rule of law. He presided over the Olympian community and also over the human community, his larger family. He was the god of weather, the one who caused the rains to fall and who, when he was angry, hurled lightning from the heavens. In short, Jupiter had it all—charisma, humanity, and power.

The planet Jupiter has a diameter of nearly 89,000 miles, but despite its massive size, its density is only slightly greater than that of water. Its inner core is 90 percent hydrogen and about 10 percent helium. It radiates 1.6 times as much energy as it receives from the Sun. In fact, if Jupiter ignited and became a sun, it could become its own solar system because of its numerous moons. In astrological terms, this accounts for the warmth of the Jupiterian personality—warm and radiant like the sun—and, on a less positive note, the posturing that may be evident in some Sagittarians—Jupiter, after all, is the biggest guy in this corner of the universe.

The pressurized hydrogen in the planet's mantle is thought to generate electrical currents, which in turn create its powerful magnetic field. Jupiter's magnetic field extends millions of miles into space and has some influence on the asteroid belt.

Jupiter's distance from Earth varies between 365 and 600 trillion miles. Its orbit around the Sun takes about twelve years, so it moves through a single sign in roughly a year. Sometimes it moves more slowly or quickly, so its stay in a particular sign may be slightly less or slightly more than a year. Despite its distance from the Sun, its size and luminosity make it visible to the naked eye. It often appears to be striped, due to the swirling gases that make its atmosphere less dense than the atmosphere of Earth.

Jupiter's most famous feature—the Great Red Spot—is a high-pressure storm that is believed to have raged for at least seven hundred years. It varies in size and color from year to year, extending from 17,000 to 25,000 miles in length and some 9,000 miles in width—three times the size of Earth.

Galileo first discovered Jupiter's largest four moons in 1610, and the discovery caused quite a stir in the Church. If Jupiter had four moons in orbit around it, that meant that the Earth couldn't be the center of the universe, as was believed at the time. Galileo paid for his discovery by spending much of the rest of his life under house arrest. Today Jupiter is known to have seventeen moons. Ganymede, the largest moon, has a diameter of 3,280 miles, making it the largest moon in the solar system and also larger than Mercury and Pluto. The smallest moon, Leda, is a wisp of a thing, just 64 miles in diameter.

Even from this brief description of Jupiter, it's apparent why it's the planet linked to expansion. Whenever I'm doing a chart, one of the first four elements I look at is Jupiter. Its sign and house placement and the aspects that are made to it provide an enormous amount of information about a person: disposition; area of life in which an individual feels lucky and blessed; hints about worldview and spirituality; how a person learns; the areas in which the individual is likely to succeed and to expand in his life; and how serendipitous factors and synchronicity play into his creativity.

In many ways Jupiter forms the very core of our creative thrust in life. Yes, other planets play a role in our creativity, but only Jupiter gives us an immovable faith that life is not only worth living but worth living well, to our fullest creative potential. Only Jupiter provides us with the opportunities we need to fulfill that potential—the lucky break, the right person or people to help us along our creative path, the opportunities for experiences and events that shape our spiritual beliefs and our creative passions.

As noted, Jupiter takes nearly twelve years to circumnavigate the zodiac, so it stays in a single sign for about a year. But the year doesn't run from January to January. Anyone born between September 25, 1946, and October 23, 1947, for instance, has Jupiter in Scorpio. Thanks to the sign, creative expression for all these people will involve some type of investigation that takes them into the so-called taboo areas of sex, death, the occult, deep psychological motivations, reincarnation. Anyone born between January 17, 1995, and February 2, 1996, has Jupiter in Sagittarius, the sign that it rules. These people tend to be truth seekers with an itch to travel, and they're the true positive thinkers. In some way their creativity will reflect this.

Whatever sign it's in, Jupiter also interacts with the rest of the planets, angles, and points in a chart. Someone with a Virgo Sun and a Jupiter in Scorpio, for example, would make an excellent investigator or researcher. No detail would be too small to escape this person. Creative expression might revolve around communication, the health field, life-and-death issues, the occult, sexuality, or other "taboos." Individuals with the Sun and Jupiter in visionary Aquarius might fulfill their creative potential through humanitarian efforts, in the legal, political, or education arena, or even in some type of spiritual pursuit.

Since Jupiter rules Sagittarius and is the co-ruler of Pisces, astrologers also look at the houses with Sagittarius and Pisces on the cusp. Glance again at Stephen King's chart in chapter 4. King's Jupiter (♃) in Scorpio (♏) falls in the fourth house: ♃23♏48'. Translated, that means his Jupiter is in Scorpio at 23 degrees and 48 minutes. The sign of Sagittarius (♐) is on the cusp of King's fifth house, and Pisces (♓) lies on the cusp of his ninth house.

Even if I didn't know whose chart it was, that Jupiter in Scorpio in the fourth house indicates a fundamental need for creative expression and the ability to do it in a way that taps into the collective unconscious. It suggests that his early childhood had a tremendous impact on his spiritual beliefs and worldview and that his mother (represented by the fourth house) was instrumental in the formation of that worldview.

With Sagittarius on the cusp of the fifth house—which symbolizes creativity, pleasure, speculation—King's creativity is the source of his greatest pleasure in life. With Pisces on the cusp of the ninth, that creative urge involves higher education, foreign travel or cultures—or publishing.

Glance at the aspectarian—the graph that accompanies King's chart. This provides the angles, or *aspects,* that the planets make to each other. Locate Jupiter in the first vertical column on the left-hand side and the Sun in the diagonal column. Now find the square where Jupiter and the Sun intersect. The mark in that box resembles an asterisk (✱). It's an aspect called a sextile. It means that King's Sun in Virgo at 27 degrees and 24 minutes forms a 60-degree angle with his Jupiter in Scorpio at 23 degrees 48 minutes. The sextile isn't exact—a bit less than 4 degrees. It's still considered a sextile, however, because astrologers work with *orbs,* several degrees of latitude allowed on either side of the aspect.

A sextile is a point of ease in a chart, where the energies between the two planets function smoothly, effortlessly. With a sextile between his Jupiter and his Sun, King's creativity isn't just his passion, it's a powerful force in his life and about as close as it gets to a guarantee for success.

Retrograde Jupiter

When a planet moves retrograde, it appears to be moving backward through the zodiac. The key phrase here is "appears to be." This backward motion is actually an optical illusion. It's similar to what happens when you're in a train going in one direction, and another train, moving in the opposite direction, speeds past you, and *you* feel as if you're moving backward. Only the Sun and the Moon never go retrograde.

When Jupiter is retrograde in a natal chart, the nature of the planet is driven inward—that is, you must expand inward first and discover your personal truth, your worldview, your belief system. Once you've found it —and there will always be an inner resonance about this belief system—then you can turn it into the outward world and use it creatively.

The Shadow Side of Jupiter

Thanks to Jupiter's reputation as the luckiest and most expansive planet in the zodiac, it seems almost snide to mention its shadow side. But let's take a look.

On the one hand we have all these wonderful descriptions: expansiveness, luck, truth seeking, faith in a larger plan or higher power, optimism. On the other hand we have laziness, overconfidence, boastfulness, preachiness, overextending oneself, promising what can't be delivered, scattered energies, hypocrisy. These shadow traits aren't limited just to Sun signs.

Any planet, house cusp, or angle that falls in Sagittarius or Pisces is prone to excess. If, for instance, Sagittarius or Pisces lies on the cusp of

236 ✷ CREATIVE STARS

the second house of money, then look for a profligate spender. Money goes out as fast as—or faster than—it comes in. With a Sag or Pisces Moon, there may be emotional excess of some kind. With Sag or Pisces on the Ascendant, there may be claims of possessing "the full and only truth." A Mercury in Sag may manifest itself as someone who never shuts up or someone who has a strong message to get out to the rest of the world. A double whammy like a Sun in Sag and a Moon in Pisces can spell alcoholism unless the person is self-aware.

"Waste is the sin of the negative Sagittarius," wrote famed astrologer Grant Lewi. "Waste of personal powers . . . of money and material things . . . and lack of respect for property." He might just as well have been talking about Jupiter's shadow side. The shadow side of expansion, after all, is excess.

Jupiter's excess tends to show up early on in some people. It's evident in the kid who walks into the toy store with Mom and immediately wants this and that and then more and more and more. It's evident in the teen who sees a box of chocolates and doesn't have just one or two. If left unchecked, thirty years down the road these are the adults who go on spending sprees when they can't afford it or who down a quart of vodka in a single sitting. The bottom line for Jupiter's shadow side is that more is definitely better.

The shadow side is also at work in the individual who believes his truth is the only truth, amen.

People who have a prominent Jupiter influence in their charts often take their gifts and talents for granted. One of the best ways to avoid the shadow side of Jupiter, in fact, is to be grateful for these gifts and talents and to use them in a positive, uplifting way.

A Closer Look

The sign of your natal Jupiter indicates your *creative style*. Do you *feel* your way through your creativity? Are you an idea person? A doer? Or do you specialize in making the abstract tangible? A person with a Jupiter in Aries, for instance, is apt to have a creative style that involves pioneering, action, doing. A person with a Jupiter in Cancer is apt to have a creative style that is more intuitive and emotional and that involves traditional values in some ways.

The Jupiter signs function in much the same way as the Sun signs, but according to the nature of Jupiter. Take that person with Jupiter in Aries again. She seeks creative expansion with utter courage, through risk-taking and adventure. The individual with Jupiter in Cancer may seek to expand his creativity by developing intuitively and applying that intuition to some particular field.

The house placement of Jupiter describes the *area of life* in which an individual is lucky, the types of serendipitous experiences and events that help him to expand his creative path, and the area where he, in turn, is most generous with his time and knowledge.

Before going on to the next chapter, check the sign of your Jupiter in the appendix.

20

Jupiter in the Fire Signs

♈ Aries • ♌ Leo • ♐ Sagittarius

The secret of the world is the tie between
person and event.
—*Ralph Waldo Emerson*

Some years ago I met a man who claimed to have memories from wherever he was when he was between lives. One of these memories concerned plans for his next incarnation. "I was shown several natal charts," he said. "The idea is that I was supposed to pick the one that would best serve the lessons and challenges that I needed to learn to evolve spiritually."

According to recent research in reincarnation, this man's statement may not be as outrageous as it sounds. Authors and reincarnation researchers Brian Weiss (*Many Lives, Many Masters*) and Carol Bowman (*Return from Heaven*) discuss the ways in which the soul plans its next incarnation. Neither of them mentions looking at natal horoscopes, but I like to think that one of the things the soul would plan is the sign, placement, and aspects made to Jupiter!

Jupiter is at home in the fire signs. The planet's natural dynamism finds easy expression here; optimism tends to flourish, and action is the name of the game. And faith is prevalent. As mentioned earlier, this kind of faith has little to do with organized religion. It's more of a spiritual understanding that there's a larger picture to life, and one way or another, Jupiter in a fire sign finds it.

Individuals with Jupiter in a fire sign are often generous with their time, money, and with anything else that they value. They tend to be enthusiastic people with many outside interests that invariably involve being physically active. They are rarely passive about anything.

They have big plans, big dreams, big ideals. *Big,* however, is not necessarily better, and at times it may be unrealistic unless Jupiter is balanced with planets in earth signs. When *big* is balanced and genuinely felt, these individuals can be true humanitarians.

Self-esteem is rarely an issue for people with Jupiter in a fire sign. It's as if they come into life with an appreciation for their talents and abilities. They don't need or seek approval from an outside source. Through taking risks and seeking new experiences, they make their own creative opportunities. Due to the charisma of Jupiter in a fire sign, they often attract the people and circumstances they need for their "lucky break."

Jupiter in Aries

Regardless of your Sun sign, if you have Jupiter in Aries it's likely that you take risks and seek new experiences. You're completely without fear. That word simply isn't in your vocabulary.

You're rash and impulsive. These traits serve you well in the competitive environment in which you live. *Act now, think later;* that's your motto. This attitude is also reflected in your dealings with people. When you snap at someone or lose your temper, it's usually not premeditated. But the other guy doesn't always understand that, so be sure to make amends. Better yet, bite your tongue before you speak in anger.

Your creative urge is strong and well developed and probably isn't limited to just one area. Over the course of your lifetime, you may be involved in several creative areas. However, a word of caution is in order. If your creativity is also your career, you do best working independently. You and bosses don't get along. You don't take orders well. Thanks to your independence, you may be branded as the rebel in the office. You're smarter to put all that independence and powerful will into your own endeavors, where you call the shots.

Intuitively, you're good at picking up on future trends and sensing the direction that's best for you. Your impulsiveness, though, can some-times work against you in this sense. You may be humming along on a path that's leading you directly into the future you want; then you'll suddenly change your mind and head in some entirely new direction.

Other people tend to see you as a dynamo, a tornado of relentless energy, an innovator, an individualist. They perceive your creative style as aggressive, fearless, filled with risk. Their perceptions are all true, but you don't have time to mull them over. You're too busy doing, act-ing, creating. This dynamic combination of traits usually attracts the people and circumstances that further your creative endeavors.

One of the best examples of Jupiter in Aries is Salvador Dali. In him we see the genius of artistic innovation and a kind of fearless show-manship. In Helen Keller, we see raw courage and a creativity that re-fused to be silenced despite severe handicaps. In Lily Tomlin, we see a unique brand of comedy.

When a Jupiter in Aries is combined with a Sun in Aries, the level of creative energy leaves the rest of us choking on dust. These individuals can achieve more in a single day than most people accomplish in a year. The drawback to this combination, though, is that these people don't know when to quit. They go until they drop—or lose interest.

You get into trouble when you allow other people to divert you from your creative path. This may happen when you're younger and parents or other authority figures try to squelch your enthusiasm and creative drive. If this suffocation of your creativity continues into adulthood, a point will come where you blow—and it won't be pretty. You risk be-coming so selfish after that point that you go your own way just because it's *your* way, and your obligations to other people go straight out the window.

Best to give your creative energy expression *now*, for all the right rea-sons, rather than later, for all the wrong reasons.

Jupiter in Leo

This is one of the most creative placements for Jupiter. You have a natural flair for drama, need to be recognized and applauded for your talents, and must feel pride in your creative endeavors. That most of all—*pride*. And to feel pride, whatever you produce has to express the breadth and depth of your creative vision.

You enjoy the spectacular, the grand, the epic. If your creative vision is developed sufficiently, creating the spectacular won't be a problem. A great example of this epic kind of thinking is Richard Wilhelm, whose interpretation of the *I Ching* made this Chinese divination system accessible to Westerners. Understanding the *I Ching* became his life's work. If your vision is limited by inexperience, you'll have to rely on your considerable intuition and the expertise of other people to help you create something that lives up to your vision.

Other people see you as a bold, dramatic individual whose creativity—whatever form it takes—is one of the driving forces of your life. You tend to think of yourself in the same way. You are usually quick to recognize and appreciate the generosity of others when they help you out in any capacity, but especially when that help involves your creativity. You don't forget friends or the kindness of strangers.

Jupiter in Leo often lends itself to creative success. Part of the reason is that you are compassionate and warm, which attracts people who can open doors for you. You also aren't afraid to take creative risks. These risks aren't impulsive, as they can be with Jupiter in Aries. They spring from some deep inner source of strength and confidence and involve the breadth of your creative vision. George Lucas fills the bill on this score. His *Star Wars* movies are so vast in scope and creative vision that they approach myth. Lucas, in fact, says that it wasn't until he read Joseph Campbell's works that he understood what he was trying to do in his movies. He brought this same breadth and scope to the Indiana Jones movies as well.

F. Scott Fitzgerald, with a Jupiter in Leo, took creative risks in his novels. Ironically, he died believing that he had failed as a novelist and writer, yet today his works are considered literary masterpieces.

Genuine altruism and humanitarian concerns can accompany this placement of Jupiter. Liz Taylor, with her humanitarian fund-raising for AIDS research, is a good example. Here, fame is channeled to raise consciousness about a particular issue or cause.

You don't have to be a celebrity, of course, to be involved in altruistic or humanitarian causes. Vivian, a psychiatric nurse, is an animal rights activist who lives what she believes. As the saying goes, she walks the talk. One day on the way to work she saw a skinny, neglected dog chained up outside a house. A man was beating it. She pressed charges against the man for animal abuse and got the dog to a vet. The chain was so deeply embedded in the dog's neck that it took several surgeries to get it out. She subsequently adopted the dog, testified against the man in court, and he was fined and did jail time. To Vivian, animals aren't simply companions. They are spiritual beings.

On the shadow side, Jupiter in Leo can lead to the same excesses as the Sun in Leo. There can be an overbearing quality to these people, an extravagance that approaches the distasteful, and unbridled egotism. The shadow expression of Jupiter in Leo can easily undermine their trust in a higher power and drive away the very people who could help them achieve their creative potential. The good news about the shadow side is that once it's recognized for what it is and you work on reining it in, it tends to lose its punch.

Jupiter in Sagittarius

This is the sign that Jupiter rules, so it's happy here. The planet's energies work smoothly and efficiently. You're an idealist whose moral and spiritual base was established early in life. You're aware of a higher dimension in the universe, and much of your inner life is spent studying and trying to understand the mysteries of that higher order.

Your creativity is viewed by others as being almost larger than life. People are attracted to the breadth of your creative vision, to the certainty that you bring to your creative work. You aren't going to argue with them, of course, but at times the way other people see you may place you under inordinate pressure to live up to their expectations. This can lead to creative blocks.

When your intuition is functioning at its highest capacity, you're a visionary, capable of dipping into the collective unconscious for whatever you need creatively. Writer Herman Hesse, who is discussed at some length in chapter 9, is a prime example of this vision. You are tolerant of beliefs that differ from your own, and your broad-minded approach to life and living attracts the people and situations that open doors on your creative path.

Generally, individuals with Jupiter in Sagittarius are the true positive thinkers of the zodiac, the ones who see the glass as half full rather than half empty. Dale Carnegie, who started the Carnegie courses in public speaking, is a good example of how this quality can be manifest. However, the placement itself doesn't guarantee a sunny and optimistic disposition. Vincent van Gogh, for instance, spent much of his life in a depressed state of mind. In his case, Jupiter's placement in Sag exacerbated his mental condition but also expanded his creative output.

Like Jupiter in Leo, you may be uncomfortable at times with the emotional part of your life. You don't have a problem embracing humanity, but you may have a problem embracing your significant other.

Travel may be a powerful force in your life, especially travel in foreign countries. It gives you the opportunity to explore the spiritual and mythological dimensions of other cultures. It also makes you feel free, an important component to this placement. Freedom is, of course, an individual thing, but with Jupiter in Sagittarius, there's a real need to feel free to pursue experiences on your own terms.

When you're younger, you may express this need for freedom in an unorthodox way that the people around you don't understand. They don't have to understand it, but you do. You must always be aware of your true motives for doing anything. This awareness will keep you from promising more than you can deliver. It will keep you honest.

Yes, there's a shadow side to this placement. These individuals can be hypocritical and arrogant. They can be so certain that their truth is the real and only truth that they feel obligated to let the rest of the world know about it. They can also go blithely on their way, living their lives the way they want without regard for the people around them. This type of attitude and behavior is usually supported by other indicators in the chart.

When Jupiter in Sagittarius is coupled with a Sun in Sagittarius, many of the traits—both positive and negative—are magnified.

A Word About Houses

When Jupiter in a fire sign falls into the first, fifth, or ninth house, the houses ruled by fire, its attributes are amplified. A fire Jupiter in the first, for instance, indicates enormous creative energy and the kind of deep inner faith that can move mountains.

A fire Jupiter in the fifth suggests that creativity is a dynamic force in the person's life. This person is a doer, someone who acts on his creative convictions.

A fire Jupiter in the ninth indicates that the individual has some sort of deep spiritual or philosophical bent in life that influences her creativity. This spirituality or philosophy infuses creativity with a depth and scope of vision.

21

Jupiter in the Earth Signs

♉ Taurus • ♍ Virgo • ♑ Capricorn

Whenever the human imagination
gets going, it has to work
in the field that myths have already
covered. And it renders them in new ways. . . .
—*Joseph Campbell*

Stability and reliability are hallmarks of Jupiter in the earth signs.
These people take their responsibilities seriously and tend to be
practical realists who use what they have to achieve their creative
dreams. No one group of signs works quite as hard.

Unlike people with Jupiter in the fire signs, these individuals generally aren't born with self-confidence. It seems to be something they
have to earn through their own achievements. Their creative urge is
strong and is usually channeled into something practical or appealing
to the senses. Their strongest creative urges are often linked to the
rhythms of nature, in which they find solace and delight.

These folks usually aren't impulsive and don't take unnecessary risks
like Jupiter in the fire signs. They like to have a plan, a strategy, a direction. Some of them can be quite goal-oriented. Their creative opportunities come to them through people and circumstances that are
attracted to their responsible, practical attitude. They aren't lured by
schemes; they get things done. They're the doers.

Not surprisingly, the spiritual dimension of their lives demands
pragmatism. Even when these people are drawn to mysticism, the oc-

cult, and metaphysics in general, they're looking for a deeper order and for tangible answers to questions that ultimately may not have answers.

On the shadow side of things? Look for gross materialism and unbridled ambition.

Jupiter in Taurus

There are many expressions of the energy inherent in Jupiter in Taurus. At its highest expression, it produces a Gandhi, an Audrey Hepburn, a Picasso. At its worst, its final expression results in a Howard Hughes, hidden and isolated at the end of his life.

Your creative rhythms may be intimately linked to nature and her rhythms. You benefit from physical activity outdoors as opposed, for instance, to physical activity in a gym. Music, art, and aesthetically pleasing surroundings feed your creative urges.

You're a consistent worker, particularly when you're working at something you love. Like the Sun in Taurus, you're in for the long haul and possess the patience and perseverance to go whatever distance is needed. Through your reliable productivity and your need for tangible, practical results, you attract the people who open doors for you and the opportunities to fulfill your creative potential. Other people see your creativity as a stable, grounded force in your life, a model of endurance.

Your spiritual beliefs can take two forms—the route of traditional organized religion or a more mystical path, as in the case of Gandhi. On either path, however, you're seeking what is tangible and practical. Author and mystic Jane Roberts, whose Sun, Moon, and Jupiter were all in Taurus, spent twenty years of her life channeling Seth, a "personality essence no longer focused in physical existence." What makes her books startlingly different from other channeled material is that they unfold in the context of Roberts's daily life. They are grounded through examples of how Roberts and her husband used the material to improve their lives.

Bob Dylan also has Jupiter in Taurus. In his music, he writes from what he knows and experiences, what he feels and what he thinks. As a result, his music has formed a backdrop to some of the most turbulent times in history. John Lennon, perhaps the driving force behind the Beatles, also had a Jupiter in Taurus.

You live very much in the present, and your senses are highly attuned to your environment. Due to your enjoyment of aesthetic surroundings, you tend to be self-indulgent at times. This is most obvious when you see something you love but can't afford and buy it anyway. This same indulgence is lavished on your loved ones. When this indulgence is turned toward your creativity, you may take on too much and begin to feel burdened.

On the shadow side of things, there can be a tendency toward materialism, and the natural need for security with this placement can collapse into an accumulation of possessions, stinginess toward others, and a focus primarily on the self. In other words, selfishness and greed may be the result. Or isolation. Howard Hughes is an interesting example in this regard. In the earlier part of his life, he used his vision to build an empire. By the end of his life, that empire had trapped him.

The best advice for this placement is to use your natural talents and creative gifts to the best of your ability and then get out of the way and let the universe do the rest.

Jupiter in Virgo

Your innate kindness and willingness to help other people tend to open doors for you just when you need a break. People are attracted to your commitment to the task at hand, whatever it is. You move very much at your own pace creatively and pay close attention to details in anything you take on. These characteristics are the hallmarks of a true craftsman.

Astrologically speaking, Jupiter is in detriment in Virgo, which means it supposedly isn't happy here, that its expansive nature runs up against Virgo's orientation toward details. I've found the reverse to be true, that Jupiter's expansiveness keeps Virgo from becoming obsessed with details. If anything, people with this placement focus on the *perfection* of their craft. Frank Herbert, author of the best-selling *Dune* series, had Jupiter in Virgo. He used his penchant for details to create a world so rich and vast that to read any of the *Dune* books is to be transported to that world.

You're a natural student, with a deep need to learn whatever is necessary to further your creative ideals. Your perceptions are largely analytical, yet beneath that left-brain analysis lies a vision of *what might be*. This vision rises from learning to trust yourself—*your* perceptions, *your* hunches, *your* instincts. It may take time to do this because Virgo, by its very nature, tends toward self-criticism. Once you realize that self-criticism is a waste of time and energy, that self-exploration is far more productive, you give voice to your creative urges and do it with impeccable integrity.

A reformist tendency exists with Jupiter in Virgo that can function in one of several ways. At one end of the spectrum, it can be expressed as criticism of other people or of certain worldviews, but that's all it amounts to—empty criticism. At the more positive end, it can find expression in working to *change* what you don't like. Amelia Earhart, who sought to empower other women through her achievements, was a perfect expression of this tendency.

There's a kind of spiritual humility in you that leaves you open to guidance from your higher self, your soul, whatever you want to call it. When you learn to use this guidance in your creative life, the personal payoff can be substantial. You suddenly understand that your creative ideal is worth all the time and energy you put into it. Author Alex Haley, known for his book *Roots,* exemplifies this characteristic. Haley received only a modest advance for the book, but it influenced the entire nation's perceptions about its history of slavery.

Sylvia Plath also had Jupiter in Virgo. This gave her the ability to write with stark precision and astonishing detail about her breakdowns and suicide attempts. Granted, her expression of Jupiter in Virgo wasn't the most uplifting, but there were other factors in her chart (and apparently in her life) that led to such deep depression.

Back to the shadow. It's there, lurking in the wings of your life, ready to be petty and nitpicky and critical of everyone around you. It's easy to get lost in that world at times, to find fault rather than to appreciate, to write off self-improvement as an impossible task, to simply focus on what's going on right now in your life. To avoid getting mired in the shadow of this placement, your best bet is to find and maintain a vision of your creative goals and strive to achieve them.

Jupiter in Capricorn

You have a deep need to achieve, to leave your mark on the world. And your chances of doing it are excellent. You're the prime example of the work ethic—a hard worker, disciplined, great organizational skills. You're practical and efficient and able to put other people's ideas into action almost as easily as your own.

Jupiter is considered to be in its "fall" in Capricorn, which means it isn't especially happy here. In theory, the expansiveness of Jupiter chafes at the restrictions that Capricorn attempts to place on it. But given some of the achievers who have this placement, it can't be all that bad: Walt Disney, Dustin Hoffman, Carlos Castaneda, Paul Newman, Margaret Thatcher, Jack Nicholson, and Meryl Streep. In each instance, these individuals exemplify a steady climb toward creative achievement.

In fact, the tension between Jupiter and Capricorn may be precisely why the combination works so well in terms of creative achievement. It's as if the inner dynamics of the pairing compel you to go the extra mile, work the extra hour.

Your natural caution discourages taking risks. You aren't about to climb Mount Everest just for the fun of it, unless you have a lot of Aries in your chart. But you may invest money in business strategies or entrepreneurial ventures that interest you or put money into your own creative endeavors.

A certain skepticism rides in tandem with Jupiter in Capricorn. You aren't one to accept easy or facile answers. This is evident in the books by Carlos Castaneda, especially when Don Juan expects Castaneda to do or accept something that is invisible to him. Part of the resistance here is because you hate looking like a fool. Dignity is important to you—dignity in the way you comport yourself, in what you create, in how other people see you. Once you get over this and are convinced that what you're doing is correct, you go with the flow.

Blessed with stamina and physical vitality, you also have seemingly endless resourcefulness. If something creative doesn't work the first time, you either take it in a different direction or start over. Daunting tasks don't bother you, but the threat of failure does. You're willing to do what must be done and insist on doing it correctly.

Before you commit to something, you strive to understand the risks that might be involved. There's that caution again. Even when you realize that every risk can't be anticipated or seen before it's right in front of you—and sometimes not even then—you still try to play the odds. When Castaneda took that legendary leap into the void, was he worrying the entire way down whether he would land on both feet? Or whether he would land at all? When Disney was sketching Mickey Mouse, was he calculating the risks of starting a theme park? Probably not. I like to think that both men were caught up in the magic of *creating*.

And really, that's the bottom line for this placement of Jupiter. At some point you have to dispense with the caution, the skepticism, the utter seriousness of it all. At some point you must approach your creativity with a sense of *play*. Have *fun* with it. Be with it *now*.

A Word About Houses

When an earth sign Jupiter falls in the second, sixth, or tenth houses, the houses ruled by earth, the practicality of the sign is amplified. An earth sign Jupiter in the second house might be expressed as an individual with the Midas touch or one for whom money is everything. It might find expression as someone who hordes their possessions or someone whose collections are valuable in some way.

An earth sign Jupiter in the sixth house is sure to expand a person's work ethics. He may take on so much responsibility related to work that his life becomes all work and no play. Or he may find his creative niche through the way he earns his daily bread. Always take the simplest meanings of the sign and the house and combine them.

In the tenth house, an earth sign Jupiter is a whopper. Success is never farther away than what this person can imagine. It may take hard work to attain what she wants, it may take a deep understanding of how manifestation of desires functions. But one way or another, an earth Jupiter in the tenth achieves what she came here to do.

22

Jupiter in the Air Signs

♊ Gemini • ♎ Libra • ♒ Aquarius

> The most incomprehensible
> thing about the universe
> is that it is comprehensible.
> —*Albert Einstein*

Intellectual curiosity marks these individuals and makes them uniquely equipped as communicators. They enjoy exploring new ideas and social relationships. Their mentally adventurous natures attract situations and people that are able to help them fulfill their creative dreams.

Where fire signs take physical risks, air signs take intellectual risks. They're able to link seemingly disparate ideas with nothing more than the barest common thread and to pull together convincing arguments that support their position. Their powers of observation are usually keen, often uncanny, and always fascinating. A common lament about these people: *Where'd he get that, anyway?*

Of the three signs, Aquarius is the most adventurous intellectually; Gemini is the most adventurous in communication; and Libra, the most adventurous socially. Just as air sign Suns live much of their lives in their heads, so do these individuals. As a result, they can be out of touch with their emotions when it comes to intimate relationships and may be out of touch with their physical bodies.

Their ability and need to continually learn and expand their intellectual horizons form the core of their creative passions.

Jupiter in Gemini

Give you a book, a paper and pen, or a group of people whose interests are like yours, and you're in paradise. You're a lifelong student, eager to learn about whatever seizes your interest. Your intellectual curiosity knows no limits. So what if one day you're studying shamanism in the Amazon and the next day you're tackling the mating habits of butterflies or spiritual growth. It's all fascinating to you and provides the necessary fodder for the expansion of your perceptions.

Your communication skills, curiosity, and the reservoir of information you carry around in your head attract the people who can open doors on your creative path and attract situations that aid in the expression of that creativity. Your mind tends to be analytical and logical, and that comes across in your communication skills. You can take the smallest fact and expand it like a universe until it includes an entire cosmology of supporting facts.

Your creative style usually has a certain edginess to it, a kind of nervous energy that comes across in your communication skills. Barbra Streisand, for instance, is known primarily for her singing and acting abilities. But she has never been timid about speaking out, and when she speaks out about politics, she exemplifies the communication skills of Jupiter in Gemini.

Your respect for ideas makes you as good a listener as you are a communicator. In fact, some of your best creative endeavors may spring from ideas you've heard from other people. The risk here is that with all the emphasis on the rational mind, you may neglect your own emotional and spiritual development. Some of our deepest creative urges are born in our emotions, so it's wise for you to pay attention to what you feel.

You know the adage "Necessity is the mother of invention." It certainly fits the ingenuity of Jupiter in Gemini. Both Thomas Edison and Alexander Graham Bell had this Jupiter placement. Because Gemini is a dual sign (the twins), people with this placement often have more than one career. Jacqueline Onassis was a photographer, a first lady, and a book editor. Carole King isn't just a singer but a songwriter as well. The album for which she is best known, *Tapestry*, has sold more than fifteen million copies worldwide. Clint Eastwood has worn a number of different hats—actor, director, and mayor of Carmel.

On the downside, there can be emotional insensitivity or outright indifference to other people's moods. This tends to occur when these individuals are young and don't know better. But I've seen it in adults also—the insensitive bloke who cracks jokes at a funeral or who makes other people the brunt of his jokes. In individuals who are aware of this tendency in themselves, however, it often becomes an area they target for self-improvement.

Jupiter in Libra

You enjoy beauty in all its myriad forms. Just the sight or sound of something beautiful is enough to soothe your soul and get your creative adrenaline pumping. And your creativity can manifest itself in many ways.

Jupiter in Libra is common among musical people—Linda Ronstadt, Madonna, Mozart, George Gershwin, Johann Sebastian Bach, Judy Garland, and her daughter Liza Minnelli. Even when music isn't your primary focus, it plays an important role in your life. It might be a hobby, or it may be that you simply like listening to music whenever you can.

Intimate relationships are important to you. You're a romantic at heart, one of those people who enjoys the courting, the seduction, the roses and long walks on a beach at dusk. This romanticism plays an important role in your creativity, too, perhaps through a partner or significant other or even a close friend who provides a supportive role or inspiration. Psychologist Carl Jung, with his Jupiter in Libra, had two partners like this in his life—his wife, Emma, and his mistress, Toni Wolff.

Your balanced and objective nature, coupled with your ability to see the many sides of a single issue, attracts people who open doors on your creative path and situations in which your creativity can find expression. Your creative endeavors usually reflect your balanced perceptions.

Jupiter's influence in this sign expands your artistic talents, your ease in social situations, and your natural diplomacy. On a less positive note, it can also exaggerate your indecisiveness. Because you're able to see the many sides of an issue, you often have trouble making up your mind about which creative direction is best for you.

While Jupiter in Gemini tackles several creative endeavors at once, you just stop, glancing to the right, the left, in front of you, behind you, unable to commit to a particular path. After all, if you follow path A, you might be missing an opportunity on path B. But if you take path B, who knows what you might be missing on path C? Jupiter in Libra can take this line of thinking to the level of the absurd. It's best remedied by making a commitment, then following that path without regret, without looking back.

Your tolerance for other people's worldviews brings individuals into your life whose views and spiritual beliefs differ from your own, thus expanding your social contacts, your network of acquaintances, and your creative fodder.

The shadow sign of this placement usually shows itself in intimate relationships. At times you may find yourself taking your loved ones for granted. They are simply there, in your life, and you love them and all, but . . . you're busy, you've got things to do, deadlines to meet, a screenplay to finish. If you do this long enough, you may lose your support system, and then your creative life won't be worth a plugged nickel. Then you'll realize how difficult it is for you to create when you feel empty, when the house is silent.

Jupiter in Aquarius

An inventive intellect coupled with humanitarian ideals and unconventional beliefs: how's that sound for an introduction? But even these words don't quite capture the unique quality of this combination.

Your rebellious streak probably comes primarily from Uranus, which rules Aquarius, and Jupiter's expansiveness merely feeds it. Whatever the cause, the unconventional and the eccentric attract you and help to make you the individualist you are.

There's a genuine visionary quality to this combination, an ability that at times approaches clairvoyance or precognition. You're able to tap into cutting-edge trends, and the most direct way of doing this is through your creativity. Writer Jess Stearn did this with his book *The*

Search for a Soul: Taylor Caldwell's Psychic Lives, which portrayed the past lives of a best-selling author. Albert Einstein did it when he tackled his relativity theory.

Your independence may be construed by other people as extreme at times, but to you it's just business as usual. For the most part, you're bored by convention. And yet parts of your life are very conventional. You may live in a conventional neighborhood, for instance, or have a conventional marriage or intimate relationship. But always somewhere in your life is a pocket of rebellion.

Your creative style is seen as individualistic, eccentric, even visionary at times. Your ability to think in new ways is what attracts the people who can help you along your creative path, and your humanitarian ideals attract the situations and opportunities that allow your creativity to flourish. As you gain maturity, your social consciousness is likely to expand even more, and this, too, is reflected in your creative endeavors.

Thanks to the Uranian influence in this combination, your creativity may gravitate toward science or invention. If you write, your work will contain cutting-edge concepts and worldviews. If you're musically inclined, your ear will be unique. In whatever area your creativity is expressed, it will be different from what other people do.

Your emotional detachment is never intended to be personal, even though other people may interpret it that way at times. It's simply that Jupiter in any air sign always expresses itself that way to some degree. The problem is that unless people understand this about you, they may distance themselves in a relationship. This is why it's so important for you to communicate openly with the people you love.

Your spirituality is tightly interwoven with concepts. If the concept feels intuitively right, then you explore it. If it doesn't, you probably don't waste time on it. In some way, your spiritual beliefs are an intimate part of your creativity.

A Word About Houses

When an air sign Jupiter falls into the houses ruled by air—the third, seventh, or eleventh—communication skills are amplified, according to the nature of the house.

An air sign Jupiter in the third house, for example, heightens the ability to communicate ideas, according to the nature of the sign. A Jupiter in Aquarius in the third house might be expressed as a facility with scientific ideas, humanitarian ideals, or cutting-edge social trends.

Jupiter in an air sign in the seventh house heightens communication surrounding intimate relationships and the arts and music in general.

Jupiter in an air sign in the eleventh house heightens communication skills in group endeavors and around issues that involve society in general. Always combine the simplest description of the house with Jupiter's sign.

23

Jupiter in the Water Signs

♋ Cancer • ♏ Scorpio • ♓ Pisces

> It has been said that each individual's
> life boils down to a single
> question. Your life is the living of that
> question, the search for its answer
> and personal significance.
> —*Laura Day*

Intuition, emotional sensitivity, and a belief in some sort of higher power characterize people with Jupiter in a water sign. Their imaginations are well developed and allow them to understand the whole picture of whatever they tackle creatively.

Their emotional sensitivity can work against them if they take things too personally, which they often do. One of their biggest challenges is to develop inner strength so they are less emotionally dependent on others. Yet these same deep emotions give their creative endeavors a passionate intensity that can be lacking with other Jupiter placements.

These individuals are often introverted, with rich inner lives. As youngsters they may have imaginary playmates or see and hear things that the adults in their lives do not. If they're taught that their imaginary playmates or the things they see and hear are silly or not valid, the ability atrophies. If this part of their inner lives is nurtured and encouraged, however, then as adults they possess a powerful tool for navigating the realm of their creativity.

Compassion is also a hallmark of this placement, and it's one of the qualities that attracts people who can help these individuals with their creative endeavors. Their compassion also attracts situations and experiences that aid them in the expression of their creativity.

On the shadow side, these individuals can live so intensely within themselves that the outer world passes them by. The remedy? It starts by reaching out and touching someone, just like the ad for the phone company says.

Jupiter in Cancer

Jupiter is said to be "exalted" in the sign of Cancer. That means the planet is happy here.

You're emotionally sensitive, and sometimes that emotional sensitivity is so extreme that you feel what other people feel, almost as if you're inside their skins. This can be tremendously beneficial to your creativity because it opens up emotional worlds that you might not have access to otherwise.

Because Cancer is ruled by the Moon, which ties us into collective emotions, Jupiter in Cancer often gives you an inside scoop on the public pulse. Author Toni Morrison, musicians Paul McCartney and George Harrison, and actor Harrison Ford exemplify how Jupiter in Cancer functions where the public is concerned. These people also illustrate another facet of Jupiter in Cancer—a penchant for privacy.

You have a genuine feel for the traditions and culture of the past in general and for your own past in particular. A certain nostalgia goes along with this placement—for your early childhood days, your family, perhaps even for the values you held as a child.

You have a strong need for emotional security and understand this same need in other people.

If you were raised in a loving family that made you feel emotionally secure, then the need shouldn't be a problem in your life. If you were raised feeling emotionally starved, however, then as an adult you may look for someone to depend on or cling to relationships and situations that no longer serve a purpose in your life. In either case, pouring this emotional need into a creative outlet can be more therapeutic than sessions with a shrink.

When friends and loved ones are in need of love and compassion, you're there to offer it. In fact, this is one of the ways you attract people who can open doors on your creative path. It doesn't mean you should help others just because you think they might be helpful to you. That will backfire. The help you extend must be genuinely felt. When you live from your heart, you attract the situations and circumstances that help your creativity to flourish.

The community in which you live and the larger community of which you're a part are vitally important to you. You have a need to belong—within your family, your school, your neighborhood, your work arena, your country. Few things can disturb you more deeply than the feeling of being a stranger in a strange land.

The shadow side of this placement involves the issue of emotional security mentioned earlier. It helps to examine your deepest beliefs about yourself. If you cling to beliefs that have outlived their usefulness, you may internalize the energy, which can create health problems.

The real beauty of this placement is that intuitively you already know everything that's written here. You are aware of the inner mechanisms of your own being. Intuitively, nothing escapes you.

Jupiter in Scorpio

Any planet in Scorpio takes on the tone of the sign, and Jupiter in Scorpio is no exception. You're emotionally intense and deeply intuitive. Creatively, you are driven, often obsessive, and you're unapologetic about it. Although it's important to you to succeed at whatever you do, your drive comes from something deeper—a need to order your inner world, to understand your compulsions, your fears, your spiritual yearnings.

You seek emotionally intense experiences, yet you're frightened of being emotionally vulnerable. As a result, you build elaborate defenses around your emotions and are secretive about many things even when there's no need to be. On the down side, this secrecy can stifle your intuition and spiritual searching. But when you create out of this secretive place, you rid yourself of your demons and are often as astonished at what you find as other people are. Author Stephen King is a master at tapping into our deepest fears because he is writing from that very deep place where his own fears live.

You have a need to connect with larger ideals and causes. Actress Susan Sarandon seems to satisfy this need, to some extent, in the roles she plays. In *Dead Man Walking,* for which she won an Oscar, she makes a powerful statement about the death penalty. In *Thelma and Louise,* she makes a powerful statement about the close bonds between women and the right to self-determination. She is also active in raising consciousness about AIDS.

You're no stranger to large concepts and epic themes in your creativity. Author Jules Verne took on nothing less than the ocean in *Twenty Thousand Leagues under the Sea.* Jack London wrote passionately about the big questions and wove these ideas into his adventure stories, pitting his characters against the wild unpredictability of nature. Director Steven Spielberg has taken on some of the largest epics and archetypal themes—alien-human contact, World War II, giant killer sharks, love that survives death.

All these traits combine to attract people who can be helpful to you in the expression of your creativity. You're acutely aware of synchronicities in your creative life that seem to signal whether you're on the right or wrong path, and when you heed these signals, you rarely falter.

Sexuality is another aspect of Jupiter in Scorpio. It can manifest as a deep need to understand the role of sexuality in life, as an experimentation with your own sexuality, or as an expression of the emotions that surround sexuality. In one way or another, sexual issues play an intimate role in who you are and may play a part in your creative expression as well.

When Jupiter in Scorpio functions at its optimum, nothing is too large to tackle creatively. When its functioning is based on fear, paranoia, and secrecy, your resources begin to run dry, your energy wears down, your opportunities shrivel, and you ultimately become embittered, cynical, and in some instances vengeful. It's a risky place to find yourself. If you're aware of it, however, you can easily escape this place because you're so adept at reviving and healing yourself. In fact, the healing ability that comes with this placement can also extend to other people in dire need. Albert Schweitzer is one of the best examples of how Jupiter in Scorpio can be manifest in healing.

Control is always a big issue for Scorpio, and with Jupiter in Scorpio you may try to control things over which you have no control. This shadow side of the placement usually shows up in the area of life represented by the house into which Jupiter falls. If control issues are prevalent in your life, it's to your benefit to deal with them now. Otherwise you may attract situations and people that somehow force you to confront the issue.

Jupiter in Pisces

As co-ruler of Pisces, Jupiter is considered to be "dignified" here. That means it's happy! But how happy can that possibly be? It depends on you.

This combination produces idealism. You see what is imperfect, and you despair because it doesn't fit your ideal of what it should be. Instead of despairing, however, work to change it. Incorporate it somehow into your creativity.

Your imagination is unlimited and is one of your most powerful creative resources. J. R. R. Tolkien's idea for his *Lord of the Rings* trilogy arose from telling his youngest daughter stories at night. *Once there lived a hobbit. . . .* From that single sentence, he created the world of Middle Earth. *What you can imagine, you can create.* Post that someplace where you'll see it often.

Some people with this placement must come up against a challenge or controversy to fulfill the enormous potential of Jupiter in Pisces. Without this external trigger, it's as if they're immobilized by inertia. Charles Darwin is one of the best examples. He had to come up against his father and be stripped of his financial base before he was able to head out on his own and realize his potential.

When the vision that comes with this placement is fully developed, it might rightly be called clairvoyance. Leonardo da Vinci is a good case in point. Some of the things he conceived were so far beyond the era in which he lived that it's as if he saw into the future, much as Nostradamus did.

Compassion is another hallmark of Jupiter in Pisces. You can readily identify with other people's pain, and the most natural thing in the

world is for you to reach out to comfort them. Your ability to do this often attracts the people and situations that can be most helpful in the
expression of your creativity. Your compassion actually extends to all
creatures, and it isn't uncommon for people with this placement to
work with animals in some capacity.

Your spiritual values and interests may be reflected in your creative
endeavors. You instinctively understand that the spiritual dimension of
your life is what grounds you, and in low times it's also what gets you
through the day.

On the shadow side, there's a tendency for escapism, just as there is
with the Sun and Moon in Pisces. The trick to navigating this successfully is to channel the need for escape into your creativity. When you
begin to feel this shadow creeping up on you, get away from whatever
you're doing for a while. Head out into the country. Sit in a warm field
and smell the flowers. Have a picnic. Get down to the business of creating, and be grateful for all that you have.

A Word About Houses

When a water sign Jupiter falls into one of the houses ruled by water—the fourth, eighth, and twelfth—the intuitive and imaginative
qualities are enhanced.

A water sign Jupiter in the fourth house, for example, suggests that
your creativity was supported and nurtured in your childhood and that
your intuition is a powerful creative force in your life.

A water sign Jupiter in the eighth house suggests intuitive expansion
through shared resources and metaphysics. It may also indicate a long life.

A water sign Jupiter in the twelfth house indicates that your creativity is a conduit to the deeper parts of yourself. It can also indicate a
peaceful death.

24

Jupiter in the Houses

Creativity consists in going out to find the thing
that society hasn't found yet.
—*Joseph Campbell*

The house in which your Jupiter falls yields a wealth of information about the specific area of your life where you seek to expand and grow creatively. It describes the area where you require freedom for creative exploration, where you tend to be lucky, and where you experience frequent synchronicities. In this house, you experience self-confidence, take risks, prosper, and seek the larger picture. It's where you are most likely to be broad-minded, optimistic, and feel the need to connect with a higher spiritual power.

The significance of the houses is discussed in chapter 4, but just to refresh your memory, the four angles (Ascendant, IC, Descendant, and MC) are the most important points in a horoscope. Jupiter found on any of these angles is especially significant and something you won't be able to tell with any certainty without a natal horoscope. The angular houses—first, fourth, seventh, and tenth—are considered to be the most important, so if Jupiter is found in any of these houses, it's particularly significant.

Regardless of your rising sign or the signs on the cusps of your houses, each house is *associated* with a particular sign, element, and planet. The first house, for example, is the natural house of Aries, so it's ruled by Mars and is considered to be a fire house. The second house is the natural home of Taurus, so it's ruled by Taurus and is considered to be an earth house, and so on around the horoscope.

This means that if you have Jupiter in Cancer in the fourth house, it's an excellent position for that combination because the fourth house is Cancer's natural home. Jupiter in Cancer in this house functions smoothly. Or, for instance, if you have Jupiter in Scorpio in the eighth house, Scorpio's natural home, Jupiter also functions smoothly. By the same token, if Jupiter in Sagittarius falls in the ninth house, which is Sagittarius's natural home, the placement is especially powerful.

Since you calculated your approximate rising sign at the end of Part One and have looked up the sign of your natal Jupiter, place Jupiter in its appropriate house.

Once you know the house placement of your Jupiter, combine that meaning with the meaning of the sign and you should have a fairly accurate picture of Jupiter's influence in your life. Although brief meanings are provided for each of the houses in this section, you might want to glance through the longer descriptions in chapter 5.

Jupiter in the First House

This house symbolizes the self—our identities, our early lives, our general health. In terms of creativity, it represents how we use the talents with which we're born.

You have seemingly inexhaustible energy and a generally upbeat temperament. You tend to see the glass as half full rather than half empty, so that even during bad times you manage to find something positive in the experience. This trait is important in terms of your creative work. If your creativity is also how you earn your living, this placement helps soften disappointments and enables you to turn them to your advantage.

Your creativity is fed by a broad spectrum of experiences, and these experiences, in turn, bolster your self-confidence and enthusiasm for life. People are attracted to this enthusiasm and to your generous and fun-loving spirit. Whenever you need something that furthers your creativity or someone who can help you advance along that path, the thing or individual appears as if by magic. It's called "manifestation," and when you become proficient at it, you can achieve just about anything you truly desire.

Travel may be especially important to you personally and to your creativity. It feeds your creative passions and is part of that burning need you have for many types of experiences. It may also figure into your creative endeavors in some way.

This house placement tends to be future-oriented, so you may have a deep awareness about emerging trends that you express creatively. Or your creative endeavors may create controversy by breaking new ground. Actress Shirley MacLaine, whose Jupiter in Libra falls in the first house, created considerable controversy when she published *Out on a Limb,* a personal story about the spiritual odyssey that took her into the heart of what was considered the weird and the strange: mystical experiences, past-life regression, UFOs, alternative healing techniques, and divination.

In the book, we traveled with MacLaine to the Andes in Peru, to Hawaii, and to various power centers in the United States. We met acupuncturists, psychics, past-life therapists, nontraditional healers. We sampled meditation, certain types of body massage, dream therapy. We were *there.* The book gave MacLaine a whole new voice.

MacLaine subsequently went on to win an Oscar and continues to act and to write spiritual books. She also has a Web site that deals with New Age topics (www.shirleymaclaine.com) and has an Internet radio show. Through her continually expanding goals—*big* goals—and her broad vision, she continues to live out the energy of Jupiter in Libra and its placement in the first house of her chart.

The closer Jupiter is to the Ascendant, the greater the planet's expression in your life. Jacques Cousteau, whose Jupiter in Libra made a nearly exact conjunction with his Libra Ascendant, is one of the best examples. He not only brought the ocean into our living rooms during his underwater explorations, he also co-invented the Aqua-Lung and a one-man sub that extended the ability of divers to go deep underwater. Astrologer Stephen Arroyo, in his wonderful book *Exploring Jupiter: The Astrological Key to Progress, Prosperity, and Potential,* talks at length about Cousteau's chart. One remark is especially telling: "Cousteau never abandoned his optimistic Jupeterian expectation that the seemingly 'impossible' can become reality."

With Jupiter in the first, nothing is impossible.

Jupiter in the Second House

The good news is that Bill Gates's Jupiter in Leo is in this house. This alone should tell you what can happen with Jupiter here. But wealth isn't the only expression of Jupiter in the second.

The second house describes your personal values and the value you place on your creative expression. With Jupiter here, money is certainly important to you, but usually as a means to an end rather than an end in itself. Foreign travel, philosophical and spiritual issues, education, and all the other areas that Jupiter symbolizes may figure prominently in what you value. If travel is vital to your creativity, then money is important to you so that you *can* travel.

You're generally confident and optimistic about your ability to earn money doing what you love. In fact, once you start doing what you love, the money nearly always follows. Charles Lindbergh, with Jupiter in Capricorn in the second house, is a good example.

Many opportunities for earning money come to you, and you have a deep belief that money will always be there when you need it. The risk with this belief is that it can become distorted. You may spend, spend, spend, spend, overextending yourself, then be surprised when the money you need doesn't come in. Remember: Jupiter also means excess.

An expansion of personal values and the application of those values is one of the meanings of Jupiter in the second. Charles Darwin and Abe Lincoln are two notable examples. The expansion for Darwin happened when he signed up for a trip on the HMS *Beagle,* which led to his theories of natural selection. Lincoln recognized that slavery was wrong and acted on it.

When Jupiter has company in the second house, the other planets color its expression. One man I know has Jupiter, Venus, and the Moon in the second house. Making money is his creative and professional focus in life, and at any one time he has four or five deals going on that require his attention. He works twelve to fourteen hours a day, sleeps about four hours a night, and continually experiences abrupt changes in his finances. The Moon suggests the ups and down in his finances, Venus indicates his love for what he's doing, and Jupiter, of course, indicates that he's lucky with money and finding opportunities for making it. This man, like many people with Jupiter in the second, is intuitively tuned in to moneymaking opportunities. The downside of so many planets in the second is that he's a workaholic.

Quite often this placement indicates a tendency toward grandiosity—the biggest house on the block, the most expensive car, the loudest boom box, the coolest pets, the fastest and most sophisticated computer. All this is in keeping with the expansiveness and excess of Jupiter. The trick is to apply this expansiveness to your creative endeavors. Create with broad themes, with vision and insight. Nobel Prize winner Toni Morrison, with her Jupiter in the second, exemplifies this. When Morrison accepted a position as the first black woman writer to hold a named chair at an Ivy League university, she said, "I take teaching as seriously as I do my writing." Now *that* statement really fits a Jupiter in the second.

Jupiter in the Third House

Communication, siblings and relatives, neighbors: in short, the third house is about your day-to-day life. With Jupiter here, it's likely that your creativity is or will become a force in your daily life.

You're intensely curious about everything and are continually expanding your storehouse of knowledge. Facts fascinate you, and it doesn't much matter where they come from: books, travel, other people, movies, or simply your own observations.

Your curiosity leads you into many different areas and allows you to create your own opportunities. It attracts people who are helpful to you and your creative expression. Some of these people may be within your family and community—siblings, neighbors, relatives. You enjoy learning for the sake of learning and somehow manage to channel your knowledge into your creative endeavors.

This is an excellent placement for teachers, writers, and social and political commentators. Marilyn Ferguson captured an emerging social trend in *The Aquarian Conspiracy.* There's a certain irony about this title because her Jupiter is in visionary Aquarius. Margaret Mitchell, with a Jupiter in Sagittarius, created an epic about the Civil War and infused her characters with such realism and life that Scarlett and Rhett are a permanent part of the American literary landscape. Even though it was the only novel she ever wrote, it won the Pulitzer Prize. Although Barbra Streisand is best known as a singer and actress, she is an outspoken supporter of liberal political causes and candidates.

You may have a passion for foreign travel. Even when you're not traveling, you may be planning a trip or reading about foreign countries and cultures. Everything you learn in this area goes into that extensive database in your head and somehow figures into your creative endeavors. Ernest Hemingway, with his Jupiter in Scorpio in the third, covered the Spanish Civil War as a reporter, lived in Europe and Cuba, and hunted big game in Africa. All of these foreign experiences found their way into his writing.

With Jupiter in this house, it's important to have concrete creative goals. Otherwise you're a walking encyclopedia with no clearly defined creative direction. It's important for you to retreat every so often from the busy external world and allow all the information you've accumulated to be processed. You can unplug from your daily life and go on vacation or just find a space where the phones are off and you won't be bothered. The point is to let all this information flow through you so that your creative well is filled up. Then, when you return from this retreat, you'll be ready to create.

Jupiter in the Fourth House

The basement of the chart. It symbolizes everything beneath the surface, the psychological stuff we can't see that was seeded in early childhood. It also describes the last twenty years of life.

This placement usually indicates a positive early childhood that had a profound influence on who you are as an adult and on your spiritual beliefs. You undoubtedly have an abundance of self-confidence and radiate a certain charisma that attracts people who can be tremendously helpful to your creative endeavors.

Despite the personal privacy inherent to this placement, you are sociable and enjoy the company of other people. You are generous by nature, a reflection of the inner security you have enjoyed since you were very young. You're deeply intuitive, sensitive, and deeply attuned to your home and personal environment. If your Jupiter is in a water sign and placed in the fourth, then it's likely you are also psychic. If your Jupiter is in Cancer and is placed here, consider yourself way ahead of the game. Your intuition is one of your finest creative tools.

With Jupiter here, you have the ability to tap into the collective unconscious through your creative work. Filmmaker George Lucas, with his Jupiter in Leo in the fourth, certainly exemplifies the ability to do this. Lucas also illustrates another facet of Jupiter in the fourth: large real estate holdings. His Skywalker Ranch in northern California covers some 2,000 acres and is the headquarters for his production company.

You may have old-fashioned values or a nostalgia for the past, for simpler times, and that emotion may work its way into your creative life. Some of Woody Allen's best films are those that have this patina of simpler times. I've noticed this tendency in kids who are barely old enough to have a past, much less feel nostalgia for simpler times. My daughter, who is nearly twelve and has Jupiter in Cancer in the fourth, speaks nostalgically of the "other neighborhood" where she spent the first ten years of her life. That neighborhood is already idealized in her mind. A friend of hers who has the same Jupiter placement already speaks eloquently about right and wrong; for her, there are no in-betweens.

When Jupiter has company in the fourth, its qualities work cooperatively with the energy of those planets and generally become even more powerful. Chase, a young man of eighteen, has Jupiter, the Sun, Venus, Pluto, and Saturn all in the fourth house, in Libra and Scorpio. That's five out of ten planets. His creative passion is music, and he possesses a tremendous ambition to achieve his dream of becoming a musician. To walk into his home is to walk into a place that resounds with drums and electric guitars. He and a friend are about to cut their first CD.

As with Jupiter in the third house, you occasionally need some time by yourself to recoup your energy. These solitary periods provide excellent opportunities for discovering how to use your intuitive and psychic abilities to achieve your creative goals.

Jupiter in the Fifth House

The fifth house—symbol of creative expression, pleasure, gambling and speculation, your first-born child—is a great place for expansive Jupiter. In terms of creativity, it means that whatever you do creatively is a source of great pleasure for you. You evolve and grow through your creativity, seek to broaden your philosophical and spiritual beliefs through your creative endeavors, and find your greatest joy through what you create. Chances are you are also incredibly prolific in whatever you do creatively.

Psychic Edgar Cayce, with his Jupiter in hard-working Capricorn, is a perfect example of someone who grew and evolved spiritually through his Jupiter in the fifth. A lot of the material that came through Cayce when he was in trance conflicted with his personal religious beliefs. When he first began receiving information on his own past lives, for instance, Cayce was so disturbed by it that he and his wife prayed for guidance. He eventually incorporated reincarnation into his religious beliefs, thus broadening his spiritual and philosophical foundations.

You have a strong desire to become known for your creativity, regardless of what form it takes. This can include a desire for fame, but even more it's a desire to make an impact on the external world. You want to be remembered for your creative contributions. And with perseverance and continued passion for your creative work, you have a good shot at succeeding.

Author and mystic Jane Roberts, with a Jupiter in Taurus in the fifth, became both famous and influential by channeling the Seth material. "The Seth books present an alternate map of reality with a new diagram of the psyche," wrote Deepak Chopra. "I would like to see the Seth books as required reading for anyone on their spiritual pathway," wrote medical intuitive and author Louise Hay. From Marianne Williamson: "Seth was one of my first metaphysical teachers. He remains a constant source of knowledge and inspiration in my life." Roberts certainly lived out the potential of her Jupiter in Taurus in the fifth house.

When Jupiter is combined with other planets, the creative thrust is a dominant theme in the individual's life. Roberts's Jupiter was conjunct (at 3 degrees) her Taurus Sun. This combination kept Roberts focused on her creative life, made her enormously stubborn, and probably also kept her grounded in the real world. She also had her Mercury in Gemini in this house, certainly a configuration that explains a medium and a writer.

Anais Nin, whose voluminous diaries ultimately brought her literary fame, had her Jupiter in Pisces conjunct her Piscean Sun (at 2 degrees) in the fifth house. This pairing of planets in mystical Pisces certainly explains the intuitive introversion of her writing.

What it all amounts to with Jupiter in the fifth is this: Your creativity is a major force in your life. You get the breaks you need, attract the people who can help you, and possess the intuitive guidance to achieve what you desire. But if you lose your sense of play in the process, if your pleasure in your creative work is suppressed or stifled, then this wonderful Jupiter placement becomes just another element in your chart.

Jupiter in the Sixth House

Health, work, and service are the traditional meanings of this house. Sounds pretty boring, doesn't it? But suppose we look at this house as creative skills. How do you develop expertise in your creative endeavors? What kind of skills do you nurture? How do you perfect those skills?

In the perfection of your creative skills, your output is likely to be prodigious. Actress Meryl Streep, with her Jupiter in Capricorn in the sixth, has starred in nearly fifty films since 1977. Jack Nicholson, who also has Jupiter in Capricorn in the sixth, has been in more than sixty films since the late fifties. Part of Jupiter's expression in this house seems to be that by producing more, your skills are honed and your creative techniques are perfected.

The surest way to stifle your creative urges is to work at something that you find boring and routine. If your creativity isn't how you make your living, then it's important that you set aside time each day to do your creative work. This creative time becomes even more important if you're in a job that you dislike. It will help keep you focused on your creative goals, and the more focused you are, the easier it will be to achieve them.

Foreign countries and cultures may figure into your creative life. It's possible that you could work in a foreign country. You may be one of those people whose creativity is loosened up in a foreign culture because the unfamiliarity triggers new ways of perceiving and stirs up new emotions.

My friend Vicki, who has Jupiter in Capricorn in the sixth, has never been out of the country. She has worked at the same library job for nearly twenty years. "I don't fit that description," she said when I read her this entry.

I argued that even though the foreign travel part of this equation hadn't found expression in her life yet, it might. P.S.: She's about to make her first trip overseas. And her Jupiter has found expression in other ways. She's an accomplished astrologer, an authority on feng shui, and deeply intuitive. None of these interests are reflected in the way she earns her living, but all constitute a part of her daily life.

Musician Carlos Santana, born in Mexico, found fame in the United States, his adopted country, where his Latino music has a broad appeal. He won a Grammy for *Supernatural,* an album that combines Latino rhythms with an undercurrent of mysticism.

Walt Disney, with Jupiter in Capricorn in the sixth, carried the expansive part of this equation to the nth degree. He didn't just create cute cartoon characters; he ultimately created an entire empire that continues to branch out and to expand to other countries.

You need the freedom to explore the dimensions of your creative craft, and you definitely need the freedom to perform your daily work routine in your own way. This placement for Jupiter chafes at restrictions and demands from a boss breathing down your neck. If that happens to be your situation, the universe may be telling you it's time to get out of that job and take a leap of faith, that your creative skills are strong enough to do what you love.

Jupiter in the Seventh House

You're attracted to people from other cultures whose backgrounds are vastly different from your own. These individuals expand your worldview and your spiritual beliefs by introducing you to new concepts and creative ideas.

Since the seventh house concerns one-to-one relationships, it's important that the people with whom you become intimately involved support your creative endeavors and give you the freedom you need to explore your creativity. In fact, if your significant other doesn't give you this freedom, the relationship may not last. It may take you a long time to commit to a single relationship simply because you have such a deep need to experience many different kinds of relationships.

Your self-confidence and abundant optimism attract the individuals who help you somehow in your creative endeavors. These individuals may be dazzled by how well you work with small groups, inspiring others to reach for their dreams and achieve their potential.

Writer Gertrude Stein, with a Jupiter in Libra in the seventh house, shows many of the attributes of this planetary placement. Born in Pittsburg, she was educated at Radcliffe, where she developed a special relationship with one of her professors, William James, the first of many famous people with whom she had close friendships. After graduation from Radcliffe, Stein decided on a career in medicine and enrolled at Johns Hopkins. She subsequently studied medicine in Europe but abandoned the whole idea when wanderlust seized her.

In 1904 Stein moved to Paris with her brother, Leo, into the apartment she would live in for nearly forty years, 27 Rue de Fleurus. Leo and Gertrude collected art (the Libra influence) by artists like Cézanne, Picasso, Renoir, and Gauguin, all of them struggling artists at the time. Pretty soon their apartment became known as the Salon. As Stein herself said, "Paris was the place that suited those of us that were to create twentieth century art and literature. . . ." Their Saturday night dinner parties became legendary and were frequented by numerous artists, writers, and critics. In 1906 Stein met Alice B. Toklas at one of the dinner parties, and four years later, Toklas moved in with Stein. They were companions for the next thirty-nine years.

Although Stein wrote a great deal during those Paris years, her work wasn't well received. That changed in 1933 with the publication of *The Autobiography of Alice B. Toklas,* when Stein was fifty-nine years old. Its publication drew her back to the United States after an absence of thirty years, for a promotional tour. Here she renewed old friendships and made new ones, a list that reads like a Who's Who of the early twentieth century: Hemingway, the Fitzgeralds, Thornton Wilder, Sherwood Anderson, and Charlie Chaplin.

What's especially interesting about how Stein lived this Jupiter placement to its fullest potential is her optimism. During a bleak period when she and Alice barely escaped incarceration in a concentration camp, they had no money and had to sell some of the paintings in their vast collection. Stein often walked miles just to buy a loaf of bread. About this period she said, "Alice knows how to make everything be something, we get along fine."

The closer Jupiter falls to the seventh house cusp, or Descendant, the more powerful its influence, not only on the seventh house but on the sixth as well.

Jupiter in the Eighth House

Astrological wisdom says that houses seven through twelve are more social and outward directed because they lie above the horizon, or Ascendant. Even so, the eighth house remains an intensely private house, a place that symbolizes everything that is secretive, mysterious, and taboo. Even when Jupiter falls in the eighth, the individual is likely to be secretive.

You need time alone to explore the hidden underside of life. Taboo subjects interest you and are invariably woven throughout your creative endeavors. These taboos may involve sexuality, past lives, death and dying, whatever society doesn't like to discuss in polite conversation. At times your exploration of these areas takes on a kind of investigative fervor; you simply have to get to the bottom of the mystery, whatever it is. The deeper force of the mystery is what seizes and holds your attention and focus.

It's important that you have the freedom to investigate these deeper mysteries. Even if your family, friends, or significant other doesn't approve of your interests and investigations, you pursue them anyway. You have to. It's as if you are compelled to do so.

Harry Houdini had an eighth house Jupiter in Virgo. In addition to his meticulous magical feats, he spent much of his life debunking fraudulent mediums and psychics. Yet he was obsessed with a fundamental question: Does the soul survive death? This is definitely an eighth house question. So he and his wife, Beatrice, agreed that whoever died first would attempt to communicate somehow to the other. They created an elaborate and detailed code (Jupiter in Virgo) that they felt would show whether the communication was genuine. Houdini had a similar agreement with his mother.

Two years after Houdini's death, in 1928, medium Arthur Ford claimed during a séance that Houdini's mother was present. Ford's spirit guide, an entity named Fletcher, proclaimed that Houdini and his mother had decided upon the word *forgive* for their code. When Houdini's widow heard this, she concurred that it was correct.

In a subsequent séance, Fletcher announced that Houdini himself was in attendance and was ready to send his wife the ten-word message they had agreed upon. The message, Houdini said, was to be taken to Beatrice, and he wanted her to follow the plan they had discussed before he had died. The message read: *Rosabelle . . . answer . . . tell . . . pray-answer . . . look . . . tell . . . answer-answer . . . tell.*

When Beatrice heard the message, she requested a Ford séance in her home. Fletcher asked if the message she'd been given was correct, and she said that it was. Using the elaborate and detailed code that Houdini and his wife had concocted, the phrase broke down to a single word: *believe.*

You may be fascinated by mythology and legends or by occult and other esoteric traditions. If so, these interests will find expression in your creative projects. Your spiritual beliefs are probably radically different from the mainstream and may also influence your creative choices. Madame Blavatsky, who started the esoteric Theosophy movement, had Jupiter in the eighth house. So did Carl Jung. Neither of them held conventional spiritual beliefs. Of the two, Jung's search for the meaning of the soul was the more extensive, cutting across cultures and times to investigate folklore, mythology, symbols, dreams, and the dark underside of the human psyche.

Jung also expressed another facet of Jupiter in the eighth—foreign travel that has a deeper purpose. When you travel to foreign countries, you're doing research, investigating the way other cultures differ or are similar to your own. In Jung's case, he was always looking for the common thread that tied together the world's mythologies and religions.

One trait I've found to be prevalent for Jupiter in the eighth is clarity of personal vision. From the time you were quite young, you may have had a sense of higher purpose in everything you did, even if you didn't understand at the time exactly what this higher purpose was. Or you may have had dreams, feelings, or even psychic experiences that seemed to be pointing you in a particular direction. The meanings of these kinds of experiences tend to unfold over time and are usually easier to understand if you allow your intuition to guide you.

Your intuition, in fact, is apt to be quite well developed, particularly if Jupiter is in a water sign or in its own sign of Sagittarius. It's to your benefit to nurture and develop the ability, especially as it applies to your creativity.

Jupiter in the Ninth House

This house represents your philosophy, your worldview, the set of beliefs with which you identify. It's the place where you search for the larger meaning of life and how you fit into that bigger picture. It's probable that your creativity will express this worldview in some way.

Jupiter functions best in this house because the ninth is the planet's natural home. This doesn't mean that your creativity blossoms naturally or effortlessly, however. To a great extent the success of Jupiter's energy depends on the degree of development of the higher mind, the extent to which you have defined your personal and spiritual beliefs, and how disciplined you are in living with those beliefs.

It's likely that you have a terrific sense of humor and that your basic nature is optimistic. You have a broad outlook on life in general and are usually capable of keeping the big picture in mind even when you're right in the middle of it. Your creative life may be involved somehow with foreign countries or cultures, or you may live for a while in a foreign country.

Jupiter in the ninth house can indicate work in the publishing industry, which is ruled by this house. This fulfills Jupiter's penchant for worldviews.

You aren't the critical type who nitpicks people or situations to death. Your attitude is to live and let live, but you expect the same freedom from others. It isn't unusual to see this placement of Jupiter in the charts of people who work in the law, medicine, colleges and universities, or in the publishing industry, since Jupiter rules all of the above. It's also found in the charts of people whose creative vision encompasses some sort of philosophy or higher order of things.

Science fiction writer Frank Herbert, author of the *Dune* books, has Jupiter in Virgo here. It fits like the proverbial glove. These epic masterpieces not only take place on another planet (as foreign as foreign gets), but Herbert also created a mystical philosophy and worldview that center around the mysterious spice.

Another expression of Jupiter here is identification with a specific cause that is incorporated into your worldview and thus into your creative life. Actress Susan Sarandon, with her Jupiter in Scorpio in the ninth, is an outspoken supporter of AIDS research and human rights. One way or another, you promote what you believe through your creative endeavors.

The closer Jupiter sits to the Midheaven, the greater its influence on both the ninth and tenth houses.

Jupiter in the Tenth House

Career, profession, your public self, reputation, authority: these are the traditional meanings of the tenth house. In terms of creativity, Jupiter here indicates that your creative endeavors are likely to come before the public in some way. It doesn't necessarily guarantee fame, but it gives you a good shot at it.

Your creative reputation and status are important to you. It isn't enough that you achieve your goals; you want to be recognized and ap-

278 ❊ CREATIVE STARS

plauded for those achievements. The risk is that your achievements and recognition may go to your head. Then recognition turns to envy or, worse, to contempt.

Actor Harrison Ford is a great example of how Jupiter's energy in the tenth house finds expression when it functions at its best. Ford didn't get his first big break in the movies until he was in his early thirties, when he landed a secondary role in *American Graffiti*. It was his first collaboration with George Lucas. Even after this break, he was still making a living as a carpenter when he landed his first major role in 1977, as Hans Solo in *Star Wars*. The movie was the first ever to gross $10 million in its first weekend. It went on to gross $300 million in its first year, another record for that time. By the time *Return of the Jedi* rolled around in 1983, Ford's reputation as an action hero and romantic lead was a done deal.

He was nominated for an Oscar in 1985 for the movie *Witness* and is probably the most bankable actor in Hollywood—with good reason. To date his films have earned more than $3 billion, with seven of them among the twenty-nine biggest moneymakers. Yet Ford somehow seems to maintain a humility about his success and is especially guarded about his personal life.

Your tenth house Jupiter is a creative blessing. If you treat it as such, it will never fail you.

Jupiter in the Eleventh House

Hopes and dreams: that's the traditional meaning of this house. It also symbolizes friends—the groups you hang with as opposed to very close friends—and your fundamental ideals. It's a future-oriented house, so with Jupiter here, you've got a head start on tomorrow.

People of like mind who form a mutual support group describes one expression of Jupiter in the eleventh. Theater groups. Writers' groups. Humanitarian groups. Animal rights groups. Whatever your creative interest, there is probably a network of individuals who share the same creative goals, and you gravitate toward the group that you need. This group helps you achieve a sense of security about your creative dreams and in some ways helps you achieve your goals.

Your strong idealism is one of the guiding lights in your life and may play a pivotal role in your creativity. Author Kurt Vonnegut, with his Jupiter in Scorpio in the eleventh house, illustrates this kind of idealism through his biting social critiques. Each of his fourteen novels explores the role of human decency in a world of chaos and suffering.

Slaughterhouse Five, which grew out of Vonnegut's firsthand experience of the firebombing of Dresden during World War II, is probably his most famous novel. The main character, Billy Pilgrim, has the ability to become unstuck in time. The narrative has no chronological order—it follows Billy's movements back and forth through time. There are no dramatic confrontations, no heroes and villains. Yet the novel works because of Vonnegut's idealism and his belief that despite the enormous forces that control our lives, we must never lose our humanity.

When other planets occupy the eleventh house as well, they provide clues about the types of ideals you may hold or the types of group activities to which you're drawn. Jupiter and Mercury in the eleventh, for example, indicate group activities concerned with communication. Mars in the eleventh suggests team sports. Neptune in the eleventh may indicate a theater group.

The one risk with this placement is that you may enjoy social activities so much you don't get much creative work done.

Jupiter in the Twelfth House

When I first began studying astrology, the twelfth house always struck me as a depressing movie: secret enemies, troubles, escapism, addictions, the psychic garbage pail of the zodiac. But if we look at the twelfth house as symbolic of the personal unconscious, it isn't quite as daunting.

With Jupiter in the twelfth, your creativity begins at the deepest levels in your psyche. If you have disowned power at any point in your life, then your creativity helps to give that disowned part of you a voice. Your innate kindness toward other people attracts individuals who are helpful to you in your creative endeavors. At times complete strangers are helpful to you.

The twelfth house is the natural home for Pisces, so it shouldn't come as any surprise that you may have profound spiritual experiences and beliefs. These spiritual beliefs and rich inner experiences add a deeper layer to your creativity. Since the twelfth also symbolizes confinement, you may at times feel an internal confinement, as if you can't quite escape the pressure of your own thoughts and feelings. Your spiritual beliefs are helpful in this regard and provide a basis for understanding the feelings you may have.

You have a wonderful imagination that enables you to probe deeply into the mysteries of life. Mythology, folklore, fairy tales, and even magic may play a role in your creativity. If Jupiter is the only planet in your twelfth house and it isn't close to the Ascendant, then the limelight probably doesn't interest you very much. If Jupiter is on the Ascendant, however, or your Sun shares this house with Jupiter, then the energy of the house changes significantly. Magician David Copperfield is a prime example. Copperfield, with Jupiter and the Sun in Virgo, is known for his extravagant magic shows. Forget the guy on the stage with a hat full of disappearing rabbits; Copperfield's shows are massive productions with magic of staggering proportions.

This is the guy who flew over the Grand Canyon, vanished the Statue of Liberty and the Orient Express, escaped from Niagara Falls and Alcatraz, and walked through the Great Wall of China. On a recent special, he entered a tornado of fire that reached 2,000 degrees Fahrenheit. Even Copperfield's Web site (www.copperfield.com) is an extravaganza for the senses.

The Virgo part of the equation makes him a detail-oriented perfectionist, so that every trick he performs, every illusion, is flawless. Whether he's flying or levitating a guest or teleporting someone to Hawaii, the audience suspends its disbelief. His creativity and imagination, like yours, are born in that twelfth house.

25

Aspects and Other Details

The invitation of something not yet explored can
call forth our most creative, inquisitive,
desirous nature.
—*Paul H. Ray and Sherry Ruth Anderson*

Aspects

An aspect is nothing more than a geometric angle between planets
that links their energies. The ease or difficulty with which that energy flows depends on the type of aspect it is. Astrologers used to divide
aspects into two simple groups—good and bad—but these categories
were misleading. Nothing in a chart is good or bad. All aspects serve a
purpose, all have a function. It's just that some feel more comfortable
than others.

In terms of creativity, aspects describe the ease or difficulty with
which we tap into our creativity and express it.

Most astrologers use five major aspects: the conjunction (0 degrees
of separation), the opposition (180 degrees of separation), the square
(90 degrees), the trine (120 degrees), and the sextile (60 degrees). Before reading through these descriptions, you may want to glance
through chart 7 in chapter 4, which provides brief descriptions of what
the planets symbolize. Refer to the chart below for a synopsis of what
the aspects mean.

CHART 9 • Aspects

ASPECT	SYMBOL	SEPARATION	MEANING
Conjunction	☌	0 degrees	Fusion of qualities
Sextile	✶	60 degrees	Stimulation
Square	□	90 degrees	Resistance
Trine	△	120 degrees	Ease
Opposition	☍	180 degrees	Tension

CONJUNCTION: FUSION

Look at the chart for writer Anais Nin on pages 284 and 285. She has two planets in her fifth house—the Sun in Pisces (☉02♓03) and Jupiter in Pisces (♃00♓22). They are close together, separated by just 2 degrees. They are considered to be conjunct because they are within the 3- to 5-degree orb that most astrologers allow.

With a conjunction, the energies of the planets involved are *fused*. They are like Siamese twins joined at the hip. What activates one must activate the other. The wider the separation between the planets, the less powerful the fusion. In Nin's chart, this conjunction in Pisces in the fifth house gave her enormous creative drive and a deeply intuitive approach to her creative endeavors. A conjunction between the Sun and Jupiter is the creative equivalent of adrenaline.

OPPOSITION: TENSION

Two planets that are 180 degrees apart are in opposition. If your Sun is in Gemini and you have Jupiter in Sagittarius and no more than 5 degrees separates them, then they are in opposition to each other, about 180 degrees apart. At one time astrologers considered oppositions to be bad, or unlucky, but while it's true they aren't the most comfortable aspects to deal with, the way they play out in your life depends on how you handle them. The trick is to find a compromise between the two opposing needs.

The key word for this aspect is *tension*. Lots of it. Sometimes the tension, which is often an internal pressure, seems unbearable. You may feel as if you'd like to crawl out of your skin. In the above example, that Gemini Sun and that Jupiter in Sagittarius are never going to see eye to eye. About the only things they have in common are curiosity and the gift of gab. They're like siblings who have to be together because they're in the same family but really don't like each other's company. They are opposite sides of a coin.

The secret to successful navigation of any opposition is compromise, a balancing act in which you capitalize on what the opposing signs have in common. Once that compromise is reached, an opposition adds depth and richness to creative endeavors.

SQUARE: RESISTANCE

This 90-degree angle is another aspect that astrologers used to think of as bad. Granted, this aspect is challenging. In many ways it's more challenging than an opposition, because the two signs or planets have absolutely nothing in common. Put them in the same room at the same time and they immediately begin to argue, each one vying for control, domination, conquest. Forget compromise, and don't even whisper the word *reconciliation*. It just isn't going to happen.

The secret to successfully navigating a square is to evolve and grow in whatever areas you feel resistance or friction.

TRINE: EASE

This 120-degree angle used to be referred to as a good aspect. The energy among planets that are in trine to each other flows smoothly, seamlessly. Trines feel good. Sometimes they feel so good that we pour ourselves a margarita and head for a hammock in the warm sun. If there are too many trines in a chart, we may head for that hammock every day. Things are *too* easy.

Take a Jupiter in Scorpio and a Sun in Cancer. Both are in water signs. Scorpio expands and broadens his creative experience by delving into and exploring what is secretive, hidden, perhaps esoteric. Cancer allows him to do this intuitively, in a way that may not make sense to a bystander but that makes perfect sense to him. These two agree on vir-

Anais Nin

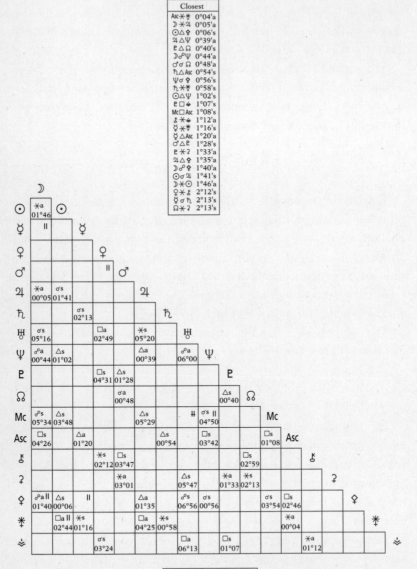

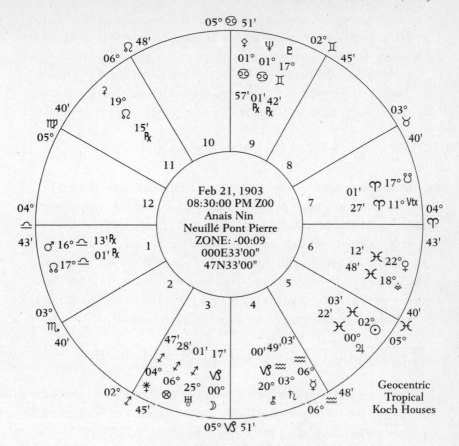

Geocentric
Tropical
Koch Houses

Feb 21, 1903
08:30:00 PM Z00
Anais Nin
Neuillé Pont Pierre
ZONE: -00:09
000E33'00"
47N33'00"

Saturday Feb 21, 1903
The 52nd day of the year
08:30:00 PM Z00 -00:09
LMT: 20:23:12
UT: 20:21:00
UT-LMT: -00:02:12
ST: 06h25m30s
RAMC: 096°22'
Local Apparent Time: 20:09:18
Equation of Time: 13m54s
Planetary Hour: Saturn (♄)
3rd Hour of Saturn-Night
Sunrise (approx.): 07:09 Z00
Sunset (approx.): 17:33 Z00
Moon in 4th Quarter
☉/☽ Angle: 298°14'
☽'s Motion: +11°50'33"

Pl	Geo Lon	R
☽	00° ♑ 16' 54"	
☉	02° ♓ 02' 36"	
☿	06° ♒ 02' 32"	
♀	22° ♓ 12' 26"	
♂	16° ♎ 13' 21"	R
♃	00° ♓ 21' 32"	
♄	03° ♒ 49' 02"	
♅	25° ♐ 01' 04"	
♆	01° ♋ 00' 39"	R
♇	17° ♊ 41' 36"	R
☊	17° ♎ 01' 07"	R
Mc	05° ♋ 51' 02"	
Asc	04° ♎ 42' 42"	
Vtx	11° ♈ 27' 23"	
Eq	06° ♒ 56' 29"	
⊗	06° ♐ 28' 25"	
⚷	20° ♑ 00' 00"	
?	19° ♌ 14' 31"	R
♀	01° ♋ 56' 37"	
✳	04° ♐ 46' 38"	
♣	18° ♓ 48' 28"	

tually everything. No conflict, no arguments. The potential for creative growth is practically infinite. With this aspect, the power of free will can bring the creative growth to fruition.

In Nin's chart, Jupiter (♃) in Pisces in the fifth house forms a trine to her Neptune (♆) in Cancer up there in the ninth house. Jupiter gave her a creative imagination, and Neptune gave her a profound intuitive ability.

SEXTILE: STIMULATION

This 60-degree angle also used to be referred to as good aspect. Like the trine, it feels good, but in a different way. Forget the hammock and the margarita; a lively exchange of ideas with friends is in order.

In Nin's chart, there's a sextile between her Jupiter (♃) in Pisces in the fifth house and her Moon (☽) in Capricorn (♑) in the third house. The sextile is very nearly exact—separated by a mere 5 minutes. Her Jupiter in Pisces is imaginative, a dreamer; her Capricorn Moon, however, makes those creative imaginings concrete, tangible.

Contacts between Jupiter and the Sun

The *conjunction* is probably the most powerful contact, because the energies of the two planets are fused. This is the creative equivalent of a shot of adrenaline. It's a powerhouse of energy regardless of which house it's in and always confers optimism and enthusiasm. Anaïs Nin and musician Paul McCartney have this combination.

With an *opposition,* the internal pressure to find balance and compromise is extreme. There may be a tendency to waste energy on excesses of all kinds. These individuals think a lot of themselves and don't hesitate to let people know it. The creative challenge here is discipline. Make a plan, create goals, and stick to them. Madame Helena Blavatsky, Johann Sebastian Bach, and actor Michael Caine exemplify this aspect.

With Blavatsky, the compromise between the opposing needs of her Sun and Jupiter was found in creating a worldview that at its peak had more than half a million followers. She became a *leader.* Bach found his balance in music. For Caine, balance lies in the ability to disappear under the skin of the character he is playing.

The *square* is a great motivator for creativity. The resistance and friction so desperately need expression that if they aren't channeled in a constructive fashion, they implode. The greatest asset these individuals have is intuition. It leads them wherever they need to go to grow and evolve.

Filmmaker George Lucas, actress Jodie Foster, actor Jack Nicholson, writer and past-life researcher Carol Bowman, and Zelda Fitzgerald demonstrate this aspect. In Zelda's case, the square probably contributed to her mental condition. She couldn't grow and evolve in the external world but managed to do so once she was institutionalized.

The *trine* offers great potential for creative growth, but to maximize its potential, it may need squares and oppositions to set things off. Bill Moyers is a good example of how a trine between the Sun and Jupiter can capture the big picture and impact the lives of millions of people. But he also has Jupiter square Mercury, so he has a great need to express what he learns and knows, and Jupiter opposes the Moon, which demands that he satisfy an emotional hunger for truth. Michael J. Fox also has this trine, and so did Jimi Hendrix.

The *sextile* between Jupiter and the Sun forms a creative support system. They applaud each other's efforts. Stephen King's Virgo Sun gives us details—the taste of the summer air in Derry, Maine, the heart-pounding fear a character experiences when confronting the unknown. His Jupiter in Scorpio scares the wits out of us. Madonna also has a sextile between her Sun and her Jupiter. It gives us . . . well, Madonna, a complete original.

The Other Planets

The irony of a book like this is that creativity can't be pigeonholed. It's impossible to say with any certainty that because your Sun and Jupiter are conjunct in the fifth house or at the Midheaven or in the second house, you are a creative person. Or that you will be a famous creative person. Or that you will be a rich and famous creative person. All that can be said with any certainty is that particular propensities exist, but that the rest of the chart has to be taken into account as well.

A chart should be read like a story or a novel. Who are the main characters? What motivates them? How do they think? What do they feel? What are their worldviews; their spiritual beliefs; their attitudes regarding work, their professions, money, family, relationships, children, health? Even if all these elements aren't written into the story, the writer has to know about them because these details spell *potential*.

In addition to the sign, house placement, and aspects between the ten planets, astrologers also look at the following:

* the phase of the Moon

* the signs on and aspects made to the four angles—the cusps of the first, fourth, seventh, and tenth house

* the signs, house placement, and aspects made to the nodes of the Moon

* the placement of and aspects made to the rulers of each house

* the distribution of planets in the elements and modalities

* the overall shape of the chart

* which planets are retrograde

* the distribution of planets beneath and above the Ascendant and to the left or right of the MC/IC axis

* whether house cusps or planets lie in late degrees (28 to 30 degrees)

* aspect patterns (see section below)

* repetition of themes

A chart has many layers, and as each layer is stripped away, the deeper potential in the horoscope is revealed. In addition to the list above, I also use the sign, house placement, and aspects made to the part of fortune ([⊗]), which is a lucky element in a chart, where your "pot of gold" lies, and to the Vertex ([Vtx]), a point that involves fated or destined encounters. I also use Chiron (a planetary body first sighted in 1977) and four of the asteroids—Juno, Vesta, Pallas Athene, and Ceres. Other astrologers use other points and factors in a chart to glean additional information. There are also numerous minor aspects that can be used.

Noted astrologer Robert Hand, for instance, is a major proponent of midpoints—the points midway between any two planets. Bernadette Brady uses fixed stars, and her book by the same name is one of the best ever written on the subject. Astrologer Marc Edmund Jones brought Sabian symbols to the attention of the astrological community—a symbolic representation of each of the 360 degrees in a horoscope. In other words, there are numerous techniques and schools of thought that can be brought to an interpretation of a chart.

When you begin reading charts, it's best to keep things simple, using just the major planets and aspects and house interpretations. In the section below, I've provided brief descriptions of other points and aspects that you may want to use.

Other Celestial Bodies

CHIRON ⚷

Astrologer Barbara Hand Clow wrote one of the definitive books on Chiron (titled *Chiron*) and considers it to be a major player in the overall scheme of things in astrology. She makes a convincing case for Chiron as the ruler of Virgo and the sixth house.

Astrologer Gail Fairfield, writing in *Choice-Centered Astrology*, says, "Chiron's function is to define the highest of ideals and to manifest them in reality. It is able to imagine perfection and to envision the practical applications of its imaginings." It solves problems, fixes what's wrong, and attempts to heal. In terms of creativity, Chiron's sign describes the energy you bring to your creative endeavors, how you attempt to make something whole. Its house placement describes the area of life in which this happens.

CERES ⚳

This asteroid represents the universal mother. By sign, it symbolizes how you nurture your creativity. By house, it describes the area of life in which that creativity may be expressed. Stephen King's Ceres, for example, lies in his tenth house in Taurus. This suggests that the nurturing of his creativity is a relentless but grounded process (Taurus) that finds expression in public life (tenth house).

In mythology, Ceres was separated from her daughter, Persephone, when Persephone was abducted to the underworld. Sometimes this theme of separation can be seen in a horoscope. King's Ceres in the tenth house, in its most simplistic terms, may indicate his separation from his father (tenth house) when he was a toddler.

PALLAS ATHENE ⚲

Astrologer Demetra George calls Pallas "the warrior queen" and equates her with creative intelligence. By sign, Pallas describes the kind of perception that is brought to creative endeavors. By house, it describes the kind of creative expression that may be manifested.

Stephen King has Pallas Athene in Pisces in the eighth house. This suggests that King is exceptionally intuitive and uses it creatively in exploring (and writing about) the more mysterious aspects of life.

VESTA ⚶

Demetra George calls Vesta "the eternal flame." This asteroid symbolizes commitment to a particular creative path, even if that path necessitates sacrifice of some kind to attain the goal. By sign, it describes the kind of energy used to attain that goal, and by house, it describes the context in which that dedication occurs. Deep faith in one's creative abilities also accompanies this placement.

King's Vesta in Cancer is in the twelfth house. This indicates a need to nurture his relationship with his family, which provides him with the stability he needs to work in isolation.

JUNO ⚵

Demetra George calls this asteroid "the divine consort." Juno describes relationships with other people and the role those relationships play in our lives. In terms of creativity, Juno's sign indicates how you create meaningful and equal relationships that support your creative endeavors. By house, it indicates the areas in which strong relationships are important to you.

King's Juno in Sagittarius is in the fifth house. This indicates that the most important relationships in his life are those that support his creativity and broaden his worldview. His spouse plays a tremendously supportive role in his creative work.

The Moon and Its Phases

The Moon symbolizes our intuition, our emotions, our ability to nurture and be nurtured, our experience of the parent who nurtured us. In creative terms, the sign of the Moon describes the way you nurture your creativity and the emotional needs that surround your creative endeavors. The house placement indicates the area of life where creative expression may be manifested most strongly.

Look at Anais Nin's chart. Her Capricorn Moon in the third house (☽00♑17) suggests that she had an emotional need to communicate (third house) her creativity. Even though her diaries started out as a way of working through the labyrinth of her inner world, she had an emotional need to be recognized and applauded for her work (Capricorn). Since the third house symbolizes, among other things, written communication, Nin's life followed the potential of the Moon's placement.

Every month, the Moon goes through eight distinct phases: new moon (0 to 45 degrees ahead of the Sun); waxing crescent moon (45 to 90 degrees ahead of the Sun); first quarter moon (90 to 135 degrees ahead of the Sun); gibbous moon (135 to 180 degrees ahead of the Sun); full moon (opposite or 135 degrees behind the Sun); disseminating moon (135 to 90 degrees behind the Sun); last quarter moon (45 to 90 degrees behind the Sun); and balsamic moon (0 to 45 degrees behind the Sun). Each of us is born under a particular phase, and it influences our creative thrust and expression.

NEW MOON. Moon and Sun are conjunct or nearly so. These people are creative innovators. They have the ability to spot the next trend and tend to be very intuitive. Examples: Carlos Santana, Toni Morrison, Edgar Allan Poe, Jimi Hendrix, Paul Cézanne, Carol Bowman.

WAXING CRESCENT MOON. Here, the Moon and Sun are one or two signs apart. These individuals search for new creative horizons and fresh approaches to everything they undertake. They are builders. Examples: J. R. R. Tolkien, Stephen King, Clint Eastwood, Madame Blavatsky, Jacques Cousteau.

FIRST QUARTER MOON. Moon and Sun form a 90-degree angle. These people possess an inner creative impetus. They take creative risks and may go against established norms to usher in a new paradigm of beliefs. Examples: Shirley MacLaine, Gloria Steinem, Susan Sarandon.

GIBBOUS MOON. The Moon and Sun are now four or five signs apart. At four signs the Moon and Sun form a trine; at five signs the harmony begins to unravel. These people seek to perfect their creativity. Introspection is the key to their creative process. Examples: Bill Gates, David Copperfield, Ralph Nader.

FULL MOON. The Moon and Sun are now in opposition. For these people, creativity is expressed through a polarization of opposites. Conscious awareness plays a vital role in attainment of goals. Examples: Warren Beatty, Michael Crichton, Gertrude Stein.

DISSEMINATING MOON. The Moon is now waning and is about four signs behind the sun. The creative thrust for these people lies in spreading the word, disseminating information and knowledge. Examples: Albert Einstein, Helen Keller.

LAST QUARTER MOON. Creativity for these individuals involves the release of beliefs that are outmoded and no longer serve any purpose. As the old stuff is released, new creative energy enters into the picture. Examples: Carl Jung, Mick Jagger, Charles Lindbergh, Steven Spielberg, Bill Moyers.

BALSAMIC MOON. People born under this phase are creatively intuitive, visionary. They may have a sense of destiny. Examples: Frank Herbert, Johann Sebastian Bach, Beethoven, Bob Dylan, Rod Serling, Charles Darwin.

The Part of Fortune (⊗)

This is one of more than thirty Arabic parts that are vestiges of medieval times when Arabian astrology worked its way into Western astrology. The Part of Fortune is considered to be a fortunate point in a horoscope, one that denotes ease, success, and harmony.

The sign indicates the energy we bring to the creative process, and the house placement describes the area of life where creative expression can manifest itself most easily if we don't compromise our ideals. In Anaïs Nin's chart, her Part of Fortune in Sagittarius falls in the third house. It suggests that Nin was always seeking the common thread to her experiences, the larger picture, and this was evident in her writing.

King's Part of Fortune falls in his tenth house, indicating that his career and profession are his pot of gold. Who can argue with that?

The Vertex (Vtx)

I first became aware of the importance of the Vertex when an astrologer compared my chart and that of my daughter and informed me that she was my appointment with destiny and would alter my ambitions and dreams. The reason? My Vertex in Virgo is in the eleventh house (dreams and ambitions) and is conjunct my daughter's Virgo Sun.

In creative terms, the sign of the Vertex suggests destined encounters with individuals for whom that sign is prominent. The house placement describes the area in which this individual is likely to be most helpful to you. Nin's Vertex in Aries in the seventh house suggests that she had destined encounters with Aries individuals who were helpful to her creativity in intimate and business relationships.

Interpretations

To get a feel for interpretation, take a look at Nin's chart again. Locate Jupiter (♃) on the left side of the aspectarian and follow it over one square, to the spot where it coincides with the Moon at the top of the aspectarian. The symbol in that square is the sextile: ✱. We know that a sextile means stimulation, that the Moon has to do with emotions and intuition. How would you interpret a sextile between Nin's Jupiter and Moon?

One possible interpretation is that the source of her creativity was emotional. She was *driven* to create—not because ambition was paramount in her life but because she *needed to express what she felt.*

Now take a look at King's chart. Locate Jupiter in the aspectarian and follow it over to the point where it connects with the square just under Mars (♂). The symbol in that square—△—is a trine. We know that a trine means ease and that Mars represents energy. How would you interpret this aspect?

One possible interpretation is that King pours enormous amounts of energy into his creative life. Simple, right?

By keeping your interpretations simple, they're easier to learn. And once you learn them, it's then less daunting to add additional planets and points to your interpretations.

Contact the author at: trmacgregor@worldnet.att.net

APPENDIX

Jupiter Ephemeris

Find your date of birth and locate the sign of your natal Jupiter. The abbreviation *Ju* stands for Jupiter, and the Sun signs are abbreviated as follows: Ar=Aries; Ta=Taurus; Ge=Gemini; Ca=Cancer; Le=Leo; Vi=Virgo; Li=Libra; Sc=Scorpio; Sa=Sagittarius; Cap=Capricorn; Aq=Aquarius; Pi=Pisces.

The dates provided in the ephemeris are the day that Jupiter *entered* a particular sign. So if your birth date is June 7, 1947, look for that date in the 1920–1949 column. That date falls between 9-25-1946, when Jupiter entered Scorpio, and 10-23-1947, when Jupiter entered Sagittarius. So your Jupiter falls in Scorpio.

1900–1919

01-01-1900 Sa	03-08-1905 Ta
01-19-1901 Cap	07-21-1905 Ge
02-07-1902 Aq	12-05-1905 Ta
02-20-1903 Pi	03-10-1906 Ge
03-01-1904 Ar	07-30-1906 Ca
08-08-1904 Ta	08-19-1907 Le
09-01-1904 Ar	09-12-1908 Vi

1900–1919 (*continued*)

10-12-1909 Li

11-12-1910 Sc

12-10-1911 Sa

01-03-1913 Cap

01-22-1914 Aq

02-04-1915 Pi

02-12-1916 Ar

06-26-1916 Ta

10-27-1916 Ar

02-13-1917 Ta

06-30-1917 Ge

07-13-1918 Ca

08-02-1919 Le

1920–1949

08-27-1920 Vi

09-26-1921 Li

10-27-1922 Sc

11-25-1923 Sa

12-18-1924 Cap

01-06-1926 Aq

01-18-1927 Pi

06-06-1927 Ar

09-11-1927 Pi

01-23-1928 Ar

06-04-1928 Ta

06-13-1929 Ge

06-27-1930 Ca

07-17-1931 Le

08-11-1932 Vi

09-10-1933 Li

10-11-1934 Sc

11-09-1935 Sa

12-02-1936 Cap

12-20-1937 Aq

05-14-1938 Pi

07-30-1938 Aq

12-30-1938 Pi

05-12-1939 Ar

10-30-1939 Pi

12-21-1939 Ar

05-16-1940 Ta

05-27-1941 Ge

06-10-1942 Ca

07-01-1943 Le

07-26-1944 Vi

08-25-1945 Li

09-25-1946 Sc

10-24-1947 Sa

11-15-1948 Cap

04-13-1949 Aq

06-28-1949 Cap

12-01-1949 Aq

1950–1979

04-15-1950 Pi

09-15-1950 Aq

12-02-1950 Pi

04-22-1951 Ar

04-29-1952 Ta

05-10-1953 Ge

05-23-1954 Ca

06-13-1955 Le

11-17-1955 Vi

01-18-1956 Le

1950–1979 (*continued*)

07-08-1956 Vi	06-16-1968 Vi
12-13-1956 Li	11-16-1968 Li
02-20-1957 Vi	03-31-1969 Vi
08-07-1957 Li	07-16-1969 Li
01-14-1958 Sc	12-17-1969 Sc
03-21-1958 Li	04-30-1970 Li
09-07-1958 Sc	08-15-1970 Sc
02-11-1959 Sa	01-14-1971 Sa
04-25-1959 Sc	06-05-1971 Sc
10-06-1959 Sa	09-12-1971 Sa
03-02-1960 Cap	02-07-1972 Cap
06-10-1960 Sa	07-25-1972 Sag
10-26-1960 Cap	09-26-1972 Cap
03-15-1961 Aq	02-23-1973 Aq
08-12-1961 Cap	03-07-1974 Pi
11-04-1961 Aq	03-18-1975 Ar
03-26-1962 Pi	03-26-1976 Ta
04-04-1963 Ar	08-22-1976 Ge
04-12-1964 Ta	10-17-1976 Ta
04-23-1965 Ge	04-03-1977 Ge
09-21-1965 Ca	08 21-1977 Ca
11-17-1965 Ge	12-31-1977 Ge
05-06-1966 Ca	04-12-1978 Ca
09-28-1966 Le	09-05-1978 Le
01-16-1967 Ca	02-28-1979 Le
05-23-1967 Le	04-20-1979 Le
10-19-1967 Vi	09-29-1979 Vi
02-27-1968 Le	

1980–2020

10-27-1980 Li	02-21-1986 Pi
11-27-1981 Sc	03-03-1987 Ar
12-26-1982 Sa	03-09-1988 Ta
01-20-1984 Cap	07-21-1988 Ge
02-07-1985 Aq	12-01-1988 Ta

1980–2020 (*continued*)

03-11-1989 Ge	09-24-2004 Li
07-31-1989 Ca	10-25-2005 Sc
08-18-1990 Le	11-23-2006 Sa
09-12-1991 Vi	12-18-2007 Cap
10-11-1992 Li	01-05-2009 Aq
11-09-1993 Sc	01-17-2010 Pi
12-09-1994 Sa	06-06-2010 Ar
01-03-1996 Cap	09-08-2010 Pi
01-21-1997 Aq	01-22-2011 Ar
02-04-1998 Pi	06-04-2011 Ta
02-12-1999 Ar	06-11-2012 Ge
06-28-1999 Ta	06-25-2013 Ca
10-22-1999 Ar	07-16-2014 Le
02-15-2000 Ta	08-11-2015 Vi
06-30-2000 Ge	09-09-2016 Li
07-12-2001 Ca	10-10-2017 Sc
08-01-2002 Le	11-08-2018 Sa
08-27-2003 Vi	12-02-2019 Cap

INDEX

5/18
T 23
L -1

12/17